Ant Covered Chocolates

A Year of Serendipity in the Serengeti

a memoir by

Vicki Vance Stanton

Vicki Vance Stanton
Tucson, Arizona USA
AntCoveredChocolates@icloud.com

Prepared for publication by Ghost River Images
Tucson, Arizona USA

ISBN 979-8-9920563-0-3

LCCN: 2024924752

I dedicate this book
in loving memory of my sister
Valerie Vance
who made it all possible

Preface

On this, the 50th anniversary of my arrival in Nairobi, Kenya, I sit down to write my memoir of a serendipitous year. Over the years, I have shared some of the experiences through slide shows for family and friends and in my sons' grade school classrooms. In the early 2000s I digitized all the slides for my sister Valerie. In 2017 I created a printed photo album from them and gave a book to each of my sons so that one day my grandchildren might glimpse into my past. For me, it is far easier to tell a story through photographs, but they tell only part of the story. Last year I completed the task of digitizing the journal I kept. I was amazed at how much I had forgotten and would laugh out loud at many of the entries. I don't recollect some of the people who are mentioned, primarily because I do not have a photo of them. Though their faces may be lost to me, each and every person contributed in his or her way to a year I will never forget. This memoir is a companion to the *Serendipity in the Serengeti* photo album. I invite you to come along with me on a safari through the year of 1973 in Tanzania and Kenya. *Karibu!*

Vicki Vance Stanton
January 7, 2023

Table of Contents

Prologue

The wheels of the Olympic Airlines airplane lifted off the tarmac. Now what?

I had just spent four months backpacking through Europe on $5 a day, traveling by train with a Eurail Pass and staying in hostels with my college friend Mary Sue Hickcox. We had parted New Year's Eve in Bologna, Italy. Mary Sue was headed back to the States and I was headed for Tanzania via Athens, Greece and Nairobi, Kenya. My week in Athens had been spent sightseeing, meeting some U.S. sailors who invited me to tour the U.S.S. Forrestal, one of the largest aircraft carriers in the world, and booking my 45-day round-trip excursion to Nairobi. There was only one flight a week and it left at 11:15 p.m. on Saturday night.

My sister Valerie had been hired to be the catering manager at a game lodge in Tanzania. In October of 1971, she and a college friend had taken a three-week safari to East Africa. Ron Johnson, the manager of Seronera Tented Safari Camp had learned that she was in restaurant management. He told her that with her experience, she could easily get a job with all the new game lodges opening up. She replied that she wasn't interested because she loved her job. Valerie was the first female assistant manager at Lawry's The Prime Rib in Beverly Hills, California. Two months later, when Ron was hired to open up a new game lodge, Fort Ikoma, he wrote Valerie in California and offered her the job as Food and Beverage Manager. When offered the adventure of a lifetime, my smart sister jumped at the opportunity. Now that she had been in Tanzania almost a year, our parents planned a trip to visit her. Since I figured I would never be closer, I decided to join them. My flight would arrive in Nairobi the same day as theirs, Sunday, January 7, 1973.

On Saturday, January 6th, I arrived at the in-town airport terminal in Athens at 9:00 p.m. to check in for my 11:15 p.m. flight. Upon presenting my ticket and passport to the agent, he glanced over the documents and then inquired as to my visa. Visa! I didn't have a visa! A visa for what? "Why," he said, "you need a visa to enter Kenya." Now, I learn at 9:00 on a Saturday night that I need a visa before boarding the one flight a week to East Africa! Why hadn't the travel agency where I purchased the ticket taken care of this? Four months in Europe and 18 countries and I hadn't needed one visa. I never even thought to inquire as to needing a visa. What to do?!? I started to cry.

As I sat down to ponder my fate, a kind gentleman sitting next to me asked me if something was wrong. Wrong? I poured out my miserable situation to him. He said to me, "Why don't you call the American Embassy and see if they can help you." Call the Embassy on a Saturday night? Sure, why not. He helped me place the call on the pay phone in the terminal. Who would be at the Embassy at this hour? The phone rang and rang. Finally, someone answered it. It was a night security guard who was American and spoke English. I explained my predicament.

2

Apparently, the desperation in my voice prompted him to suggest that I call the Assistant Consulate. He gave me her home phone number and wished me good luck.

Trembling, I dropped more coins into the phone and placed the call. Luckily, someone answered. I asked for Miss Campbell and he said just a minute. I could hear glasses tinkling in the background and lots of chatter. Apparently, she was having a party. As soon as she said hello, I just knew everything was going to be all right; she sounded just like Valerie. I again explained the situation. She instructed me to get on the shuttle to the airport terminal and plead with the ticket agent there. Just as luck would have it, she had been assigned to the U.S. Embassy in Nairobi at one time. She knew of instances when people had flown to Kenya without a visa and said that I should have no hassle getting a visa at the Nairobi airport. My only chance was to go out to the airport and use the contact names my sister had given me. She wished me good luck and rang off.

Soon the passengers were called to board the shuttle bus. Pleading with my big blue eyes, the in-town agent reluctantly let me board. Off we went. At the airport I hastened to the ticket agent. When he realized who I was, he said he had told the in-town agent not to send me out. I politely demanded to speak to the person in charge. I poured out my tale of woe and dropped Miss Campbell's name and the names Valerie had sent me. One was the general manager of the Nairobi Hilton Hotel and the other was the manager of the Pan Am Airline office in Nairobi. I bemoaned the fact that I knew nothing of the need for a visa to Kenya and that the Athens travel agency had said nothing either. I implored with him that my parents and sister were meeting me there tomorrow and then we were driving to Tanzania. "Oh, help me, help me!" He explained that if I were an "undesirable alien" in Kenya, Olympic Airlines would have to pay for my return trip. I explained that I already had a round-trip ticket and I wasn't an undesirable alien. I pleaded with him that if he didn't let me go, I would have to wait a whole week before another flight left and then I would miss the trip planned with my parents. Oh, what to do, what to do? He must have taken pity on me, because as my flight was announced, he gave me my boarding pass and said that if Kenya wouldn't let me in, I would be the responsibility of the two people whose names I had given him.

I boarded the plane and stashed my gear overhead. As I buckled my seatbelt, a huge smile spread across my face. I was on the plane that would take me to Nairobi. Soon, we were taxiing down the runway. As the wheels lifted off and we flew into the clear night sky with a million stars twinkling, panic gripped me. Oh my God, now what? What if Kenya won't let me enter? Oh well, at least it would be an adventure. Little did I know just what an adventure I would be having.

Jambo

O ne time zone and six hours later, the Olympic Airlines airplane landed at the Nairobi Airport at 6 a.m. local time, Sunday January 7, 1973. Close to the equator as we were, daylight and nighttime are each about 12 hours long, and so we landed as the last vestiges of night were giving way to the first light of day. I was in no hurry to get off the plane. I felt it would be best to be the last one to go through Immigration considering my circumstances. I took my time descending the stairs to the tarmac. Ah! How wonderful the air smelled. It reminded me of the desert air of my Arizona home which I had been away from for four months now. This incredible feeling of being home swept through me. From the moment my feet hit the ground, I knew I belonged here.

Midway between the airplane and the terminal was a little kiosk. The Immigration official was checking passports there. He greeted me with, *"Jambo, passport please."* I handed him my passport. He flipped through it, then flipped through it again. Finally, he said, "Where is your visa?" I told him I didn't have one. He looked at me kind of funny and then said, "That will be 22/50 shillings, please," while he handed me a form to fill out. I quickly did so and then handed him four American dollars to which he returned change in Kenyan currency. He stamped my passport and I was now officially here.

As I entered the terminal through the baggage claim area, many friendly Kenyan skycaps greeted me with *"Jambo"* which I knew to mean "hello." The other words they called out I didn't understand except for one, "Missouri." Thinking that a tour from Missouri had just arrived, I answered, "Arizona." They smiled, nodded and repeated their greeting including the word "Missouri." Later that day when I had learned some Swahili, I realized that they had been saying, *"Jambo"* (hello), *"Habari yako"* (how are you), and *"Mzuri"* (good).

I located my backpack at baggage claim and proceeded through the doors to the public terminal. Valerie was nowhere to be seen. She had written that reservations had been made at the Nairobi Hilton. After exchanging traveler's checks for Kenyan currency, I located a hotel minibus and set off for the big city. The drive to the hotel was beautiful. Bougainvillea, Jacaranda trees, Acacias and other tropical foliage were a feast for the eyes. Sashaying through the streets and around round-abouts amid buses, lorries, Land Rovers, minibuses and compact cars, we eventually arrived at the Hilton. I disembarked and headed in to register. All the men were wearing safari suits or safari shirts. The African women working at the hotel wore uniforms made from the colorful, patterned African fabric with headdresses to match. After the seriousness of Europe's workforce, the gaiety of Kenya's people appealed to me greatly.

Sure enough, a room was registered in my name. I was shown to my room and felt that I had stepped into a palace. After four months of youth hostels, pensioni, and the occasional stay in an apartment of an acquaintance, to be in a room with a comfortable bed and an adjoining bathroom was deluxe indeed. I savored the shower which actually had water pressure. Clean and tired, I headed for the bed and promptly fell asleep.

Something woke me from my slumber. What is it? Oh, there it goes again. Wait a minute. I know that sound. It's a telephone ringing. Why is it ringing? I pick up the receiver. "Hello." A voice on the other end starts talking to me. I don't understand a word he is saying. Who is this man with an unfamiliar accent? He seems to know my name, but says "Wicki" instead of "Vicki." His name is Shakir, he says, but when I first hear it I can't make heads or tails of it. He mentions "Walerie Wance" a lot and says that he is a friend of hers. He informs me that he will meet me in the lobby and take me to lunch.

I quickly get up and dress. My curiosity is aroused now. Shaking off any lingering sleepiness, I head downstairs. Four men, Asians, approach me. Shakir introduces himself, his cousin Mamudt, and their friends Ferdie and Aires. He recognizes me immediately because he says I look so much like my sister Walerie. Shakir explains that he is the booking agent for Fort Ikoma Lodge where Valerie works. The rains have come, the river is up and Valerie cannot cross it to come to Nairobi. She contacted Shakir in Arusha to meet me and our parents in Nairobi and arrange for our travel to Fort Ikoma.

The four men and I squeeze into a compact car and fall into the dizzy traffic. We go to the New Continental Hotel for drinks. I am so hungry. They order me something I don't recognize, but it certainly hits the spot. I learn that their ancestors are from Goa, a former Portuguese colony, but now a country within India and part of Indian rule. They have lived all their lives in East Africa and consider it home. When Kenya and India were both a part of the British Empire, the Indians were brought to British East Africa to build the railroad. When the railroad was completed, most of them stayed. Thus, a large population of Asians, as they are called, now resides in East Africa.

Shakir drops off his friends and he and I head to the airport to meet Mom and Dad's plane. They arrive. We see them through the large windows separating baggage claim and Customs from the waiting crowd. It's so good to see them! It's been four months! Dad can't find the claim checks. He checks his pockets. He's sure Mom has them. "No," she says. Finally, Dad finds them. They haven't changed a bit! At last we are together. I introduce them to Shakir and explain the situation about why Valerie is not here. We head to the Hilton. Shakir helps Mom and Dad register and then says he will meet us back here to take us to dinner in the hotel dining room.

We head up to our rooms. Like a child at Christmas, I can't wait to see the camera they have picked up for me in Tokyo. It's an Asahi Pentax single lens reflex camera with a 50mm lens. I had asked them to buy me one while in the

Orient since Mary Sue had borrowed her brother's camera for our European travels. Mom and Dad found such a good deal that they bought the identical camera for Valerie as well.

After Mom and Dad rested, we readied ourselves for dinner. I wore the caftan that I had purchased in Athens from a street vendor. My wardrobe was rather meager. Dad was tired and ordered room service. Mother and I joined Shakir, Mamudt and his girlfriend for dinner.

The next morning I needed to head back out to the airport to get a cholera shot. Then, it was time to hit the shops and buy some clothes. The small shops, called *dukas*, were within walking distance of our hotel. It reminded us of shopping in Nogales, Sonora, Mexico. Mom and I bought the typical tourist safari outfit: slacks, a short-sleeved safari shirt, a long-sleeved safari jacket, and shoes, which I called "boonie" boots. They reminded me of the buckskin, tied shoes that Dad always wore. Music blared from one of the *dukas*. Soon, a familiar song filled the air. It was Linda Ronstadt singing *Blue Bayou*. Small world, Tucsonans hearing a Tucsonan singing halfway around the world.

Then it was off to Nairobi National Park "within a lion's roar of Nairobi" with Mom. The park is a combination zoo and a 44-square mile park that one must drive around. Our driver, Mbinda, knows Valerie. We saw giraffe, Thomson's gazelle, Grant's gazelle, wildebeest which are called gnu, eland, warthog, ostrich and other birds, bushbuck, and a cheetah eating a kill. The cheetah was not the least bit perturbed by the many vehicles surrounding him and everyone taking pictures. Nairobi also has a museum and a snake park, but we did not visit them.

That evening, Shakir and Ferdie took Dad, Mother and me to the New Stanley Hotel for dinner. I had Nile perch. It is the largest freshwater fish in the world, weighing 400 to 500 pounds, and is found only in the Nile River and Lake Rudolf (Turkana). It was very tasty. We had live entertainment during dinner which was very good and then, afterwards, Shakir, Ferdi and I went to Club 1900 for more dancing and drinks. It was a late night. I'm not used to this night life.

Off to Tanzania

M other and I did some more shopping Tuesday morning and then for lunch we were treated to an ethnic dish – *ugali* stew. It is chunks of lamb in a sauce and served with maize, a corn version of mashed potatoes.

At 3:30 we left for Arusha with our driver and Shakir in a very comfortable Mercedes-Benz sedan with excellent shock absorbers. Arusha is approximately 175 miles south of Nairobi and it is a good road all the way. It's a beautiful drive with lush greenery and desert-like areas. On the Kenyan side of the border we enjoyed a relaxing tea in a very charming hotel and viewed some giraffes. The Maasai tribe is settled in this area between Nairobi and Arusha. The young men are cow herders. The women have shaved heads. All wear ornate native beaded jewelry. Their earlobes are pierced and then stretched using tubes, creating very large holes. They all have big smiles and beautiful white teeth.

At the Tanzanian border we obtained our visas which were 22/50 Tanzania shillings each (about $3.25). We spent the night at Hotel Tanzanite, about 10 miles south of Arusha. It is a cabin-type setup. Mosquito nets are available in the rooms but they are not needed until about March. We had a very good view of Mount Kilimanjaro at about

6:30 p.m.   Usually the snow-covered top is obscured by clouds.

Next morning we took it easy. I fiddled around with my new Asahi Pentax camera. There also was a small zoo with this lodge and it had a very nice swimming pool. It is run by Mr. and Mrs. von Nagy, a Swiss couple who are friends with Valerie. Our accommodations were comped which was very nice. That afternoon we took a drive through Arusha National Park. The park features Ngurdoto Crater and Momella Lake. It also offers an excellent view of Mount Meru which is not as high as Mount Kilimanjaro, but much more difficult to climb. We saw Colobus monkeys with black and white faces and long, full white tails, waterbuck, flamingo, baboons with lots of character, elephants with babies. We stopped to watch the elephants – truly the king of the jungle – but they seemed to become concerned about us possibly endangering their young, so with the possibility of them charging us, our driver Gerald said, "We go now!" We also saw Cape buffalo, rhinoceros, hippos, warthogs, giraffes, guinea fowl, and dik dik. The dik dik is a miniature antelope when full grown and the smallest in the antelope family. We also saw a blue monkey which has a baboon face.

That evening we had dinner with Shakir and his girlfriend Beryl. She is from England and teaches at the Greek school.

I was able to get a good picture of Mount Kilimanjaro from Hotel Tanzanite. We have a new driver now for the same comfortable Mercedes sedan. Thomas Joseph will take us to meet Valerie. Our first destination is Tarangire Tented Safari Camp. Though we will be sleeping in tents, our accommodations are very deluxe.

Each tent has twin beds, bedside tables, a dressing table, mirror, and a private loo and shower behind it in an enclosed canvassed area. Water will be brought to the room by buckets and put into the 5-gallon canvas bag that is the shower. Each porch has two canvas chairs and a table. There is electricity day and night. The camp is on a crest overlooking a valley that reminds me of the Garden of Eden. When I think of prehistoric animals, I picture the land that they roam to look like the valley below. From camp we saw giraffe, impala, and rhino. The vegetation is primarily savanna. Acacia trees and fan palms dot the landscape. The acacias are thorny trees that provide sustenance for giraffes. The landscape is beautiful and green. It is a hot and humid day, 90°F in the shade. Lots of flies and tsetse flies, but no worry because this is not an infected area. The tsetse fly carries sleeping sickness. There is no preventative inoculation for sleeping sickness, but there is a cure for it. We drove through Tarangire National Park. Saw ostriches, baboons, lots of impala, warthogs, rhino, elephants, giraffes, vultures, crested crane, various other birds, jackal, and saw the ears of a lioness but the rest of her was hidden by the grass. The animals roam free while we are the ones in the cage, in hopes of spotting the Big 5: elephant, rhinoceros, Cape buffalo, lion, leopard.

Fantastic cocktail hour on the terrace from where we could watch the impala at the waterhole and rhino lumbering about below. There is a fire pit on the terrace that is lit at night for the guests to sit around and enjoy and not be bothered by the few bugs remaining after sunset. After I was back in my tent, I showered in the moonlight. How nice to be able to look up and see the stars and crescent moon. The air was cool and perfect for sleeping. No bugs either.

On Friday we drove to Lake Manyara National Park, approximately 50 km from Tarangire, and spent a good part of the day in this beautiful park. The foliage is quite dense, lush and green with a few open spaces here and there, especially by the lake. The lake is home for hippo, flamingo, storks and many other birds. Saw elephant, impala, zebra, baboon, hippo, and Cape buffalo, warthogs, giraffe, and the tall majestic crested crane bird. We saw one lion with two lionesses lying right beside the road. Lake Manyara Park is famous for having the lions that climb the acacia trees to rest and recuperate after eating a huge meal. Unfortunately, we didn't see any lions in trees, though we looked for them. The park also claims a hot spring, tall palms, mahogany trees, and baobab trees with trunks at least 5 feet in diameter.

In a designated area, we ate our picnic lunch that had been packed for us by Tarangire Safari Camp. Each of us had a box filled with fried chicken pieces, a roll, cheese, fruit and a piece of cake for dessert. We are definitely not going hungry! Afterwards, we stopped by Lake Manyara Lodge. It reminded me of a motel with a pool, but with a picturesque view of the valley and lake below.

Upon leaving Lake Manyara, we continued up the escarpment of the Great Rift Valley toward Ngorongoro Crater at an elevation of 7,500 feet. Along the way we saw a disabled green tractor on the road shoulder. Thomas Joseph said that it had been there for a year. It was a brand new Chinese tractor that broke down when first used and no spare parts to fix it were available. It was still there when I left a year later, more rusted, though. Our first glimpse of the Crater was from a scenic vantage point along the rim. Thomas Joseph took a photo of Mom, Dad and me. Over the years, as I look at other people's safari photos, they all seem to have a photo taken at this very spot. We stopped in at the Wildlife Lodge to have a look. It is very elegant and new looking with lots of rock work and beams. It boasts a beautiful view of the Crater. We are staying at Ngorongoro Crater Lodge. This is an older lodge and is owned by the same group of people who own Fort Ikoma Lodge where Valerie works. Ngorongoro Crater Lodge has a very rustic atmosphere with its cabins and a cozy fireplace in the bar and dining room. I had a zebra steak for dinner. It was very tasty and reminded me of a steak grilled over mesquite wood.

The next morning was our trip down into Ngorongoro Crater. We must go by Land Rover or a 4-wheel drive vehicle. It's a very steep descent 2000 feet down to the floor. The crater itself is 10 miles by 10 miles across and is the largest inactive volcanic caldera in the world. The foliage is very lush on the slopes of the crater, but the actual floor of crater is all grass with several lakes and only

15

a few oases of trees. Supposedly a great migration is going on now, which is very apparent with the many different kinds of birds here from Europe and Asia. There were also plenty of indigenous birds – flamingos, storks and ostriches. Lake Magadi is a salt lake abundant with flamingos that get their red leg color from the carotenoids in the food they eat, such as algae and brine shrimp. And in the fresh water lake we saw plenty of hippos. The plains were abundant with wildebeest (also called *gnu*), zebra, hyena, jackal, rhinos with the ever-present tick bird on their backs, Thomson's and Grant's gazelles, elephants, and a whole pride of lions including grandpa. If it weren't for the ears twitching, we might never have spotted one lion hidden by the tall grass. Our picnic lunch (boxes from the Lodge) was by a Maasai village in the Crater. Photos of the Maasai are not allowed because the government feels they will not tend to their cattle if they start posing for photographs. Several colorfully dressed Maasai came to where we were eating lunch though, hoping to have their picture taken for a shilling. Quite incongruent to see these people carrying on life as their ancestors have for centuries, but sporting a Johnson & Johnson Band-Aid. After another hour or so of animal viewing, we headed back up to NCL to shower and dress for dinner. After dinner we were delightedly surprised to see Shakir, Beryl, his friends Azghar and Mac arrive on the scene. Mom, Dad and I joined them for after dinner drinks along with Justus, the manager of the Lodge. Azghar is quite a character. He went on for half an hour about how I should exploit my beauty.

The next day was Sunday. We had arrived a week ago and Valerie still hasn't been able to meet up with us. Today is the day! Shakir had let us know last night that she was going to be able to get to Seronera. The Grumeti River was down and she would be able to cross it.

Leaving the rim of Ngorongoro Crater and descending to the plains below, one is afforded a beautiful sweeping vista of the vastness of the Serengeti Plains. To this day, whenever I recall seeing that initial sighting, it still takes my breath away. Yet, nestled between the lushness of Ngorongoro Crater and the grassy plains of the Serengeti is a dry gulch area called Olduvai Gorge. Olduvai is a Maasai word meaning "the place of the wild sisal." If one did not know the significance of this place, one would most likely drive on by. However, it is where the remains of the oldest known man were found by Dr. Louis Leakey. Actually, his wife Mary made the initial discovery in July 1959. Dr. Leakey had spent 28 years in this area before uncovering the remains of the Zinjanthropus Man. In the same area, the jawbone and hand bone of the Homo habilius man were found by their son Jonathan Leakey. A guide led Mother and me down into the ravine where the discoveries were made. Quite astounding to be standing where the first human species lived. Several miles away was an area where primitive stone-age tools had been uncovered. As we drove over to see, we spotted our first cheetah.

17

The entrance to the famous Serengeti National Park is marked by a simple sign. We stopped to have a photo taken before finding a beautiful lone Acacia tree under which we ate our box lunches. Then, on to Seronera, the administrative center for the 5700 square mile park. Thomas Joseph drove us to Seronera Tented Safari Camp where Valerie was waiting for us. How joyful was our reunion! The last time we had been together was Christmas 1971 when Valerie came to Tucson.

It was fitting that we should meet Valerie at this very spot because it is where Valerie met Ron Johnson. He had been the manager of the tented camp at the time when she and her college friend Linda Holt had stayed here on their Unitours safari in October 1971. In a conversation, Ron learned that Valerie was in restaurant management. The tented camp was owned by the same people who owned Ngorongoro Crater Lodge and soon would open Fort Ikoma Lodge. A few months later, Ron was named the manager of Fort Ikoma and wrote Valerie to offer her the job of Food and Beverage Manager. When she came to Tucson for Christmas, she shared this news with the family. She said that she didn't want to be sitting on her rocker in old age and regret that she had not taken the job. So, in February of 1972 she took off for Tanzania and...here we are!

We bid a fond *kwaheri* (goodby) to our driver Thomas Joseph. Then Valerie introduced us to Babu, the manager. I never knew his first name because he went by Babu, his surname. He and his wife Shushila were Asian, or what I would think of as Indian. We learned that Seronera

Tented Safari Camp would be closing in a few months. A new lodge, Seronera Wildlife Lodge, had been built and would be opening soon. Fortunately, we had the opportunity to stay here before it was history.

Mother, Dad, Valerie and I sat in canvas chairs on the porch of one of our tents to catch up Valerie on what we have been doing the past week. At the same time, we were entertained by the hyrax running around the property. They are small squirrel-like creatures with the distinction of being the closest living relative to the elephant, of all creatures!

Tomorrow dawned and we would finally arrive at our destination, Fort Ikoma. Babu had arranged for one of the camp's Land Rovers and a driver to take us game viewing around Seronera before driving us to Fort Ikoma. It was a beautiful sunny day, but previous rains had left patches of black cotton mud. Soon, we came across a minibus of tourists stuck in the gooey muck. Our driver tied a rope to the tow hitch and the other end to the front bumper of the minibus and successfully pulled the vehicle out. The park is huge so we kept our game viewing around the Seronera area. After lunch at Seronera Tented Safari Camp we thanked Babu for his kind hospitality and bid *kwaheri* to him and Shushila. It would take us an hour to drive to Fort Ikoma, or longer, when you have to wait for a giraffe to move out of the road, or follow two very skinny lions walking down the middle of the road. Down by the Seronera River we spotted the famous 3-legged crocodile and then stopped by the Retima Hippo Pool to watch the hippos as their heads bobbed up and down in the water. The hippo's eyes, ears and nostrils are located at the top of its head, staying just above water level. Who would guess that about one and half tons of hippo is under water?

The road was so bad in places. We came across a Musoma city bus stuck in black cotton mud. It must have happened a few days earlier because no passengers were around. It must have been traveling from the Arusha area en route to Musoma, located on Lake Victoria, because this is the only way to go. We exited the park through Ikoma Gate and continued on for half an hour until the turnoff. In the distance, up on a hill, I spied the towers of Fort Ikoma. But first we must cross the infamous Grumeti River. The rains had ceased and the water level had finally lowered enough to reveal the concrete drift to ford the river. The road wended up the east side and I could see a semi-circle of thatched-roof round buildings that Valerie called *rondavels*. There were 30 of these guest rooms. On around we went and then drove up the driveway to a parking area and a large planter area in front of the commanding entrance. There was a majestic Euphorbia succulent in the middle of the planter with vibrant red canna lilies planted all around it.

We got out of the Land Rover and surveyed the area. To the west were six tents on each side of a walkway. To the east was the walkway leading to the portico between towers with narrow slit windows from which hung a sign that read: Fort Ikoma Lodge. We are here...finally!

Fort Ikoma Lodge

Fort Ikoma Lodge was built among the ruins and two remaining towers of a pre-WWI German East Africa fort built in 1905. When the Germans were defeated in World War I, the territory became part of British East Africa and was named Tanganyika. Tanganyika achieved independence in 1961. In 1964, it united with the island of Zanzibar and was renamed the United Republic of Tanzania.

Fort Ikoma lay derelict until a group of investors, including two Americans, bought the property and developed it for the ever-growing tourism trade in East Africa. Valerie started working at Fort Ikoma Lodge, or FIL, or the Fort, or the Lodge, as we would refer to it, soon after it opened. She had now been here almost a year.

One of the two original towers anchored the north end of the west wing. The current offices, reception area and gift shop were renovated from the ruins of this former administrative post. The other original tower anchored the southeast corner of the dining room and kitchen. A third tower was built at the southwest corner to match the originals and housed the bar. Two smaller towers were built on the west wing to create the entrance under which we walked into the courtyard. A large Acacia tree graced the area. Inside the stone planter were two tortoises chomping on leaves, while two crested cranes strutted by as if they owned the place.

We checked in at the Reception Area and received our room keys. To the east of the courtyard we walked by some old ruins and down a gravel path to our *rondavels* 9 and 10. The guest rooms are round stone buildings with conical roofs covered in thatch. Two *rondavels* to a plot. Each room has twin beds, a seating area and full bath with hot water. A large picture window looks out onto a small patio with seating and the Serengeti plains beyond. Valerie and I will share a room. She doesn't have a place of her own yet and so she sleeps wherever there is a room available. Right now, with the rains and few guests, she sleeps in a *rondavel*. When they are full, she sleeps in one of the tents. When they are full, she sleeps in a bunkbed in her office which is upstairs in one of the entrance towers.

Valerie continued giving us the tour. There are 30 *rondavels* that can bed 60 guests. On the west side of the property are 12 tents that can be used for overflow or for the guest wanting a more authentic experience. Each tent has two beds and an attached canvas-walled bathroom with a chemical toilet, a wash basin with a pitcher of water, and a gravity shower supplied by solar-heated water in a 5-gallon canvas bag with a pull rope. When the lodge was at full capacity, it could handle 84 guests. Staff quarters were down at the bottom of the hill and we did not tour it, but had driven by on our way up the hill. Drivers would stay down there. Tour guides and pilots would stay up on the hill. When the Lodge was full, it didn't mean that there were 84 people as some guests had single room occupancy, it just meant that every room was booked.

Valerie took us into the dining room, bar and kitchen to meet the staff. This is her domain. She is in charge of staffing, ordering the food, liquor and supplies, planning the menus and making sure that all runs smoothly. It's not an easy job because all supplies come from long distances, either Arusha which is eight hours away by truck, or Musoma which is three hours away by truck. No last minute shopping out here! Other challenges include training the staff. Can't take anything for granted. She said that with her wait staff she had to teach them that it is improper to pick their nose or scratch their privates in public. As she explained, these young men had no prior restaurant experience, let alone even having dined in a restaurant. Fort Ikoma is pretty remote so all the staff lives on property in the staff quarters. They would work seven days a week for several months, then take a month or two off and go home to their family village. They came from different tribes: Ikoma, Chaga, Arusha, Luo, Kikuyu and Maasai come to mind. There are many smaller tribes, too. Unlike Kenya, Tanzania does not have a dominant tribe.

Our first evening, we dined with Skip Leavitt, the manager and one of the American investors, and Mario Guerra, the electrician who came from Arusha to work on the generators. Originally from Italy, Mario came to East Africa as a Prisoner of War in WWII, and he stayed after the war. Mario had made lasagna noodles with his pasta machine and we enjoyed his homemade lasagna for dinner. Later that evening, it rained.

We took life easy the next day. Skip got a lift to Seronera with some tourists who were departing. It would be the last that we would see him for five days. It was a rainy day and the river was getting higher, making crossing impossible.

We showered and dressed for dinner. I wore the kaftan that I had bought in Athens from a street vendor. I had very few clothes. No worries. Valerie and I wore the same size and we would share clothing from here on out. Valerie filled us in on the past year of her life. When she arrived in February 1972, Ron had his fiancée by the name of Victoria Fowler visiting. Vikki had met Ron on a previous safari. She was from the Los Angeles area. Her grandfather developed Southern Comfort liquor and the headquarters were at Sunset and Barrington, an area Valerie knew well because it was two blocks from her apartment on Sunset Boulevard in Brentwood, California. Valerie and Vikki soon became fast friends.

Valerie had difficulties getting her work permit, even though she had the job before she came. The country makes an ex-pat (expatriate, a foreigner; someone who is not a citizen of the country) jump through a lot of hoops to get the proper documentation. In other words, it's not until enough money has been passed under the table, so to speak, that the final papers get stamped for approval. At one point, the government worker told Valerie that she could not stay at Fort Ikoma until she got her papers because she wasn't eligible to work yet. So, Ron had her go stay at Seronera Tented Safari Camp while the paperwork was being handled. Well, it turned out that David Babu was the new Chief Park Warden of the Serengeti National Park and Dr. Tumaini Mcharo was the new Director of the Serengeti Research Institute located in Seronera. They had much to learn about the Park and invited Valerie to join them on their excursions. What a fabulous opportunity that was for her! Then Ron left. Actually, he did what she called "the midnight flit." It's where someone is at dinner, then gone without a trace before breakfast. Rumors surfaced that it had been discovered that he was actually a South African. In 1973, apartheid was still the government policy in South Africa and Tanzania did not recognize the country. Another rumor was that he was exchanging currency on the black market. The Tanzanian shilling was worthless outside the country, and there wasn't much to buy inside the country either. Kenya, Tanzania and Uganda were part of the East African Community (EAC). Tourists typically flew into Nairobi, Kenya to begin their safari through the three countries and would exchange their hard currency (American dollar, British pound, German mark, French franc, etc.) for Kenyan shillings. In Tanzania and Uganda the tourist would have to exchange hard currency for Tanzania shillings. (Kenya was getting most of the hard currency and not sharing it equitably with the other two countries. This would later become a big problem. Also to note, at this time no one was traveling to Uganda because the murderous dictator Idi Amin was in power. In fact, thousands of citizens, especially Asians, had already fled the country.) At the time I was there the exchange rate for $1.00 was 7 shillings, be they Tanzanian or Kenyan (written TSh 7/= or KSh 7/=). However, you could not spend Tanzanian shillings in Kenya or Kenyan shillings in Tanzania. Whatever his reasons, one day Ron was gone for good. And Valerie did know that he was planning to marry Vikki and live in the States. Skip was one of the two Americans who, along with the two other investors who I never met, owned Ngorongoro Crater Lodge, Seronera Tented Safari Camp and Fort Ikoma. As an owner/manager, Skip left NCL where he had been and came to manage Fort Ikoma. If it weren't for Skip and a few other people, I would never have been able to stay as long as I did.

Wednesday was another rainy day. There weren't many guests booked at the lodge, fortunately. In fact, the three guests who took off that morning for a game run in the Serengeti were unable to cross the Grumeti River in the afternoon. Not sure whatever happened to them after that, but I am guessing that they continued on with their itinerary and that their luggage eventually caught up with them. It doesn't rain all day long, just off and on, but the river flows westward ending at Lake Victoria. Folks around here liked to think that the Grumeti was the head water of the Nile River. A joke, of course. Valerie said that she and Ron would get into arguments about the term the "river is up" versus the "river is down." For Valerie, up and down referred to the level of water. For Ron, when the river was "up," that meant that the water was upstream and you could cross the river. When the river was "down," it meant that all the water was at the present site and so the water level was too high to cross. It made her crazy.

Mom, Dad, Valerie and I sat out on the terrace during the patches of sunlight and looked out onto the plains stretching all the way to the Park boundaries. Dad brought up his desire to own a dude ranch in the States and we discussed the idea. Down below, out of view but within earshot, we could hear the Grumeti River raging.

Adjacent to the Park boundary nearest Fort Ikoma was a hunting block. Jurgen Josch was a German professional hunter who had a tented camp within a quarter of a mile of Fort Ikoma. His clients would come for a minimum of a week, and longer if they were after big game. The arrangement was that Jurgen and clients would hunt game to supply meat for the Fort and in turn, the clients had pool and bar tab privileges, and use of the airstrip at Fort Ikoma.

On Thursday, the 18th, two of Jurgen's clients, French hunters, were flying out. Though it wasn't raining, the airstrip was very soggy. Mid-morning, the turboprop twin-engine Cessna 406B buzzed the Fort, alerting us of its arrival. That was the method since there was no other way to communicate. The pilot would fly low over the central area and someone would jump into a Land Rover and drive down to the airstrip. In this case, the four of us plus some others piled into Mario's unbelievably old Austin Gypsy truck, circa 1939, and he drove us down to the airstrip. Soon, Jurgen arrived with his clients. The pilot has to first buzz the field to chase away any animals grazing on it. On this day, the pilot buzzed numerous times to check the sogginess of the field. He would let his wheels touch ground, but kept his speed up to see how much water was displaced. He wouldn't land if he didn't think he would be able to take off after loading up two passengers and all their gear. Also, Fort Ikoma is at 4500 feet elevation so that has to be factored in as well. After the tenth buzz, the pilot landed to a round of applause. The pilot didn't want the plane to sit on the wet ground too long so he hurriedly got the gear and clients loaded onto the plane and took off without incident.

The only way to communicate with the outside world from Fort Ikoma was by two-way radio. Shakir ran the booking office in Arusha and he, or someone in his office, would contact the Receptionist daily with updates. Isaack Mushi was the assistant manager and handled reservations. We called him by his last name, Mushi. His wife Dionisia ran the gift shop. They were of the Chaga tribe near Moshi, about an hour south of Arusha. He had gotten a call that day that a plane would be arriving in the afternoon to drop off some guests. Mother and Dad had decided that if they were going to fly half way around the world to visit Valerie, they might as well make an "around the world" trip of it. It was time for them to return to Nairobi and continue on with their journey. Since the pilot would be flying back to Nairobi with an empty plane, he agreed to take Mother and Dad with them. It was sad to say goodby, but we were all so grateful for the time we had together. They departed for Nairobi in a Cessna 182, the same kind of plane that Dad used to fly when he co-owned Whitaker Pools. *Kwaheri! Safari njema!*

The tap water went off about noon. Another problem to deal with. Thank goodness for the swimming pool that is full. Buckets of water were taken to the kitchen where it would be boiled and used for cooking and drinking. Buckets of water were taken to the few *rondavels* with guests, and us, to be used for washing and filling the toilet tank. Meanwhile, with Skip gone, Mushi set off to figure out what the problem was.

I helped Mario make tagliatelli with his pasta machine. He first made the dough by making a well with the flour, then cracking the eggs into the center. Using his fingers, he would mix the egg up, maybe with a little water, don't quite remember, then slowly start incorporating the flour into the liquid until he had it all combined. He would knead the dough a little, then break it into balls that he would flatten and then roll through his pasta machine to desired thickness and then through the cutters to make long noodles about half an inch wide. Because they were fresh, the noodles cooked up really quickly. There was only a small group of us for dinner that evening, Mario, Grant, a German couple and us and so we all ate together and enjoyed Mario's pasta. Grant was a young American working on a project somewhere in the area and had stopped by the Fort for a few days. The Fort is in the crossroads of any traveling between Lake Victoria and

Arusha so people always stop, and sometimes they stay awhile.

We still had no water the next day. It turns out that the water pump is on the other side of the river and so Mushi had someone throw the key with instructions to someone on the other side. Even though the pump got turned on this morning, still no water in the tap. Obviously, the main water pipe that crosses the river has been busted by the raging river and all our water is going downstream.

And another day with no water. We went swimming since we couldn't bathe. Actually, we aren't faring too badly because we do have plenty of food, except for meat. To drink we have soda pop, beer and wine. And, we have a beautiful view!

The generators are working and we have electricity when we need it. I don't recall if there were two or three generators, but their main purpose was to keep the refrigerators working. The stoves used gas. Power for the rest of the lodge was on for an hour or so in the morning and then three hours in the evening. Lights out at 10:00. The generators generally ran about 10 or 12 hours a day. Other than the inconvenience of no water, we were able to enjoy the good life. The German couple left after a lovely lunch by the pool, leaving me as the only one here without a job. The rains certainly are no good for business, but do allow one to have a relaxing time. This is supposed to be the dry season so these rains are a surprise to everyone. But today there is no rain and the river is going down. This is good news.

Another sunny day dawned and another day by the pool. The river is now passable and some guests are arriving. Still no water, though. Skip returned in the afternoon, after his one day foray turned into five days. It was good to see him. Mushi then left for somewhere to find a water engineer. He should be back in three days or so. Now Valerie and I are hoping for rain so that we can wash our hair in the rainwater!

And another day of swimming. What else is there to do? Valerie and I made a fabulous pizza for lunch. Augustino is the baker and we would pinch some of his bread dough, roll it out, open a tin of tomatoes to spread out over the dough and then add all sorts of vegetables and goodies, then cover with cheese. Mario had shown us what to do. Oh, and I'm sure we sprinkled olive oil over all of it, too. Mushi returned late with a water pipe crew!

Jurgen's girlfriend Caroline came up to the Fort the next day with three French hunters to go swimming. We had a great time around the pool. There always seems to be something to do even though we are miles and miles from anywhere else. And then at 6:00 in the evening, presto, we had water! Hallelujah! It's been five and half days without water, but we haven't suffered much precisely because we didn't have a lodge full of guests.

Thursday, January 25th. Today is my birthday. Just a few months ago, who would have thought that I would be celebrating in the Serengeti? I am thrilled and delighted! Patrick Duncan, a researcher at the Serengeti Research Institute (SRI), is studying topi. He had set up camp across

31

the river. Valerie and I went down to visit him and learned that he actually studies their scat. That is, their droppings. He gave us quite a lesson. By studying an animal's scat, one can learn what the animal eats, how it is digested and how it may impact the environment. The Serengeti plains can support many different species of animals because each species eats a different plant. We may just see grass, but it turns out that the zebra, wildebeest, topi, *kongoni*, Thomson's and Grant's gazelles, impala, Cape buffalo, waterbuck, etc. are eating different types of grass, each to their own. Valerie and I were getting zinged by tsetse flies at his camp, especially with his samples of dung all around. He had a can of Black Flag bug spray which we sprayed on our arms and legs, while saying, "If we ever get cancer, we'll know from where." That memory haunts me.

Except for my peeling skin from all of that swimming and grass itchies all over my feet, I was feeling very good on my 23rd birthday. Patrick joined us for dinner along with Mario. Skip made spaghetti with garlic and oil at table side and with a lot of fanfare. We had wine to drink. I learned that an Italian monk came to the Dodoma area of Tanzania to plant vineyards because the climate in that region was advantageous for grape growing. He taught the local natives how to care for the vines. After he left, someone had the bright idea to add manure to the beds. Now all the wine from that region tastes like fertilizer. I was surprised with a birthday fruitcake for dessert and the singing of Happy Birthday by everyone in the dining room. It turns out that an American guest from Connecticut was also celebrating his birthday. I even got a birthday gift, a beautiful black and white beaded necklace made by the Maasai.

It was a week after my birthday and Mario had been at the Fort for several weeks now. Not sure why because most of his later work-related visits just lasted a few days. Maybe the rains had something to do with it, or he had nothing pressing in Arusha which is where he lived. Anyway, he was heading back to Arusha. Skip needed to go to Dar es Salaam so he hitched a ride as far as Arusha with Mario in "Carolina," the name Mario had given to his old Austin Gypsy. While Skip had Mario occupied with something else, Valerie and I pinched his pasta machine. Two days later we got frantic note from Skip saying that Mario was very upset about his missing pasta machine and to please get it to Arusha as soon as possible. It really was a pretty mean joke on our part, especially in light of all the great meals Mario had prepared for us with it while here. Fortunately, it wasn't too difficult to find someone heading that way and so the pasta machine was on its way back to Mario.

Before Skip left, he asked me to stay on. He saw no reason for me to leave at the six-week date of my return ticket to Athens from Nairobi. Valerie heartily agreed and I saw no reason to go back home, I was having too good of a time. Skip also had an ulterior motive. He needed someone to oversee the gift shop the hour before dinner and during breakfast while Dionisia would be on vacation in a few weeks.

The next day a Lindblad Wing Safari tour group arrived at Fort Ikoma for a two-night stay. This was the ultimate way to travel in those days. They arrived on a Trislander airplane, with an engine on each wing and one above the tail. The plane looks like a bunch of scrap metal sheets nailed together, but apparently it is very comfortable. It has been modified to carry 12 persons which includes the pilot, the courier and 10 clients. Jerry Rilling, a fellow American, was the courier. Valerie and I came to rely on Jerry as our traveling encyclopedia. He was very well educated about African flora and fauna. Jerry suffered polio as a child, but his crutches never impeded his adventurous lifestyle.

Jerry gave us a very detailed description of a termite hill which gave us an entirely new respect for these insects. The termite hills look like mounds of dirt but actually are made from digested cellulose. Above the ground one sees the mound with a "chimney" on top. Underneath the ground is more of the termite home. Inside the outer wall is a circle of latticework. Inside this is a chamber and inside that chamber is the Queen's chamber. On the surface there are several terrain level openings which are not easily detected by the eye. There is also a tunnel that goes from the bottom of the latticework down into the ground 150 to 200 feet to a waterbed. Worker termites will travel down to get one drop of water and bring it back up to the chamber to maintain optimal humidity. Here's a recap of his fascinating description of the termite hill:

1. Termites live in the chamber and number about 20 million.
2. The humidity inside the chamber must remain as constant as possible at about 80 to 90%. Workers bring drops of water into the chamber to maintain humidity. If ever a chamber becomes too hot they will carry water to a terrain level opening. Air coming into the latticework structure at this point will cool over water, circulate around the chamber, cooling inside, and hot air will be sent up the chimney, much the way an evaporative cooling system works. Latticework helps to maintain temperature and humidity balance.
3. Queen termite is impregnated by King who lives in her chamber. She lays about 3000 eggs per day for the next 12 to 15 years. She is about 3 inches long and white. There are secondary and tertiary queens which take over for Queen after she dies and their reigns are 5 to 7 years and 3 to 4 years, respectively. The Queen has a scent which becomes weaker when she is about to die. If a foreign king and queen enter the mound at this time, they will be able to move in as the foreign queen also has a queen scent.
4. Queen lays haploid and diploid eggs. Haploid eggs develop into the workers and diploid eggs develop into reproducing termites. The Queen probably lays 90 to 95% haploid and 5 to 10% diploid. It is not known how she decides what type of an egg to lay, but a certain ratio is maintained.
5. At certain times of the year, when weather conditions are just so, usually before a storm, all the reproductive termites fly from the colony, mate with the opposite sex, and then the male and female nest under a rock until the female produces workers to start building their own hill. The male and female are the king and queen of this colony.
6. The outside of the hill is composed of almost solid cellulose. It is started out as a miniature of the large hills which stand 3

to 6 feet high, and is constantly expanded until full size. Full size depends on type of termite and locale.

7. Termites cannot digest wood, but are host to a protozoan parasite which digests the wood (cellulose) for them. The termite digests the cellulose, secretes it, digests it, secretes it, and then uses this secretion to build the walls. Therefore, the walls are primarily compressed cellulose, with a little bit of saliva and dirt mixed in, resulting in very strong walls. The Queen's chamber is composed of the same combination and is very rigid and smooth on the inside, rough on the outside.

8. Each hill has a lifespan of about 25 years, or until the tertiary queen stops reproducing.

9. The reproducing termites are at least twice the size of the workers.

10. Termites avoid light, come out only at night.

11. Ants behave similarly. Each worker ant must bring food back for the Queen, drops the food off, walks around the Queen, eats some of her secretion, picks up an egg and carries it to the nursery. Ants have scouts who look for food, then send a message to workers to come and fetch.

The Night of the *Wezi*

W hile Skip was gone, Valerie and I stayed in his room 11. We had dinner with a tour guide and guest from Chicago. It was a late evening and we didn't get back to the room until just before 1:00 a.m. Lights went out soon after. (The generator governing the lights stayed on later when guests were still in the dining room.) I was in the bathroom when Valerie heard somebody running on the terrace past the room a few minutes later. The person was running fast and sounded as though he was barefoot. She quickly locked the door! A little before 2:00 a.m. we heard a knock on the door of the adjacent room 12 after hearing some movement outside. We almost jumped out of our skins! Then we heard someone whisper, "Miss Valerie." We realized someone was in trouble. Valerie opened the door and asked, "Is someone calling Valerie?" Then Dionisia, holding her daughter Judy who was 18 months old, and the young *ayah* (nanny) came running into our room. They were on the verge of hysteria, but Dionisia was calm enough to say, "It's Mushi, I think he's dead, they've taken him away, they may have killed him." We closed the door and locked it and got them settled down. Dionisia then recounted the whole story, never once resorting to Swahili.

Just after the lights went out, the old *askari* (night watchman) came to Mushi's house saying that eight policeman and government officials had just arrived and wanted beds. As the rooms were full, Mushi told the *askari* to give them tents. About five minutes later they heard the *askari* crying outside. "I'm dying, I'm dying, let me in! Bwana Mushi, help me!" Apparently, the eight men had beaten the *mzee* (the old and honored one) and had pulled him along the ground by a rope around his neck. He managed to get back to Mushi's house and the *wezi* (thieves) followed him. They beat in the door and three of the *wezi* entered. One had a pistol and one had a Maasai *panga* (machete). While they were beating in the door, Mushi, naked and barefoot, jumped out the window. The *wezi* had surrounded the house. They threw rocks at him and tried to follow him. Mushi ran through the bush, past the swimming pool and dining room terrace, and then through the *shamba* (garden), passing by the *rondavels*. Valerie and I had heard someone tear across the terrace of room 11 and realized then that it had been Mushi.

Meanwhile, back at the house. When the *wezi* entered, there were only Dionisia, the *ayah* holding Judy, and a friend of Dionisia's. Dionisia stepped forward when they came in and demanded the key to the safe. She said, "Take anything, take my soul, my belongings, anything but don't hurt the others. We do not have the key to the safe. The manager has it and he is in Dar es Salaam." One of the *wezi* was saying to the one with the gun, "Shoot the baby, shoot her." With that, Dionisia jumped out the window and hid in the grass. She took off her white nightdress so she wouldn't be seen and left it in the grass. After a while, she heard nothing and so crept back to the house. No one was there. She quietly called for the *ayah* and Judy and found them in the outhouse. The *wezi* had threatened to kill Judy, but the smart thinking *ayah* said that Judy was her baby and they had just arrived yesterday from Arusha and knew nothing about any key. She told Dionisia that they had taken the other girl with them. Then Dionisia, the *ayah* and Judy, frightened as they were, snuck through the bush alongside the dining room terrace to make their way to room 11.

A few minutes later the lights came on. Someone had turned on the generator about 2:00 a.m. We quickly turned off the lights in the room. We were afraid that if the *askari* was severely questioned, he might say that a Mama in room 11 might know about the key. A few minutes later we heard a Land Rover start up. Then about 10 minutes later, the Land Rover that was parked between the kitchen and first *rondavel* started up. Val said that it might be Mushi looking for Dionisia. We finally decided to make our way down the path carefully to staff quarters, about a quarter of a mile away. At 3:00 a.m. we left room 11. Without benefit of a flashlight, and just by the light of the moon, the five of us stealthily moved down the path in single file, Dionisia leading the way. Sweet Judy never once made a peep from the time this whole ordeal started.

Safely arriving at staff quarters, we found Dionisia's friend in Michael and Abasai's room. She had been kidnapped by the *wezi*. They thought she was Mushi's wife. They took her in the first Land Rover we heard take off and drove towards Sabora. They threatened to kill her and she kept saying she was not Mrs. Mushi and knew nothing about the key. At Sabora they saw other headlights and thinking someone was following them, pushed her out of the car and kept going. She then ran the 8 miles back to Fort Ikoma. Meanwhile, as we found out from the others at staff quarters, Mushi had gone immediately to the Hunters Camp after jumping out the window. He got clothes and two of the hunters, then went to staff quarters where he got Abasai and Michael, fellow Chagas, and Joseph. He sent William to turn on the generator, cleverly thinking the lights would scare away the *wezi*. It was Mushi and others who had gotten in the second Land Rover. Joseph had the keys. They were out looking for Dionisia, Judy and the other two. That is when they found the *askari* beaten up, with a rope around his neck, in Mushi's house. Apparently he had been dragged by the rope and left for dead. He had been badly shaken and hurt from the rope burn, but no lasting physical damage was done. About 4:30 a.m. Mushi and others returned. Mushi was badly skinned on the legs and had thorns in his feet, but the relief he felt for finding Dionisia and Judy safe and sound was the greatest cure. Mushi's wounds were cleaned up. Removing the two-inch long acacia thorns imbedded in his feet was painful to watch. He literally turned gray with pain. Mushi had run barefoot through the bush so as to not make a sound. Valerie and I commented on how quietly Dionisia and the *ayah*, carrying Judy, traveled the path and how conscious Valerie and I were of how loud our footsteps sounded, though we were trying to be as quiet as possible.

Afterwards, the Mushi family, the *ayah* and friend, and Valerie and I were driven back up to the Lodge. Dionisia said she never wanted to go into their house again. Who could blame her? We did check it out though. Other than breaking some furniture and making a general mess, Mushi found only two sheets and his radio missing. The five of them accepted the keys to Skip's room most graciously and Valerie and I slept in the office. We slept until 3:00 that afternoon. The *wezi* got away with what was taken from Mushi's house and that was all. They had removed the rotor cap from the one Land Rover down at the drivers' quarters because they wanted to immobilize us, but they didn't bother with the minibuses and never did see the Lodge Land Rover parked behind the kitchen. What a night!

Meeting the Robinsons and Vishnyakovs

I first met some of the Robinsons the afternoon of February 10th out on the terrace. Valerie knew Leonard Robinson and was meeting sons Ron and Larry for the first time. They had come here to meet up with another couple, Olga and Yuri Vishnyakov, whose acquaintance we also were making for the first time.

Several months earlier, Leonard and his wife Ruth had met Yuri and Olga at Fort Ikoma when both were spending the night. The Robinsons lived in the village of Busegwe, on the way to Musoma on Lake Victoria. They were an American missionary family. Leonard was president of the Seventh Day Adventist (SDA) church in Tanzania, which was sponsoring an agricultural project in association with Loma Linda University. Yuri was with UNESCO, in charge of adult education in Tanzania. The Vishnyakovs lived in Mwanza, also on Lake Victoria. Fort Ikoma was a convenient and enjoyable place to stop on their travels between their homes and Arusha. On that occasion, Ruth and Leonard were seated at a table in the dining room next to Yuri and Olga who were with their daughter Lyuba. Lyuba was regaling her parents with a story about a Catholic nun at her school. In fact she was doing an imitation of the American nun. Leonard leaned over and asked if they were Americans. They looked at Leonard incredulously and Yuri replied, "No, we are Russian."

Everyone laughed and a friendship began. In the course of their conversation later that evening, Yuri expressed an interest in going hunting and Leonard offered to take him.

And now, here they were. This was the reason for the rendezvous at Fort Ikoma. They were going to spend two nights in the bush. As the conversation progressed, Valerie and I were invited to join them. We eagerly accepted. It didn't take long for us to pack. In fact, our Asahi Pentax cameras had come with nifty bags large enough for us to pack a change of clothes, a toothbrush and the camera.

Off we piled into the Robinsons' Land Rover and Yuri and Olga followed in his United Nations station wagon. We drove to a hunting block area and set up camp. Since there were only three tents, Valerie and I would share one with Yuri and Olga. Valerie and I laughed to ourselves thinking of what our grandfathers Clark and Pop would think about this. Mind you, this was during the Cold War between the United States and the Soviet Union.

Dinner was a simple menu of tinned (the British term for canned) food. The SDAs are vegetarian, but the Robinson men ate meat when out hunting. It was so enjoyable sitting around the campfire and talking. Yuri and Olga's English was quite good so we did not have difficulty communicating. We learned that they had an older son who was living with grandparents in Moscow because the Soviet Union would not allow all the family to live abroad. They had been here for five years and Yuri hoped to have his term extended. Because Valerie and I were last minute add-ons, supplies were short. Yuri amused us by using the can opener as his utensil for eating. We found stumps of wood that served as two more chairs.

By the time we crawled into the tent that night, we too, had become good friends with Yuri and Olga. We managed to get comfortable with whatever the bedding there was. I could hear the hyenas laughing and lions roaring. I dreaded the thought of having to exit the tent to go pee in the middle of the night and, of course, I had to go in the middle of the night. I was armed with only my flashlight and quickly did my business and scuttled back into the safety of the tent. With the presence of three others in the tent, I felt quite safe and actually got some sleep, even though only canvas less than a quarter-inch thick separated us from the wilds of Africa.

The next morning we went out hunting. Ron, Larry, Valerie and I sat on the roof rack of the Robinsons' Land Rover while Leonard drove with Yuri riding shotgun and Olga in the back seat. It was great fun, like riding a bronco as we zipped through the bush. We spent the day looking for Thomson's or Grant's gazelle, or impala to eat. We saw some waterbuck with the distinctive white "target" on their hind end, but Ron told us that they don't hunt them because the oily meat tastes tainted. Yuri got an impala and Larry got a Thomson's gazelle. Back at camp, Larry skinned and butchered the animal to roast over a fire for dinner. He wanted to make a handle cover for his *panga* (Maasai knife with a broad blade) so he very meticulously removed the hide from the leg of the animal, keeping it intact. Ron helped him by carefully grasping the blade so that Larry could slide the tubular skin onto the handle. Leonard wiled away the afternoon scraping the bark off large sticks of sugar cane and cutting off chunks for us to suck on and enjoy the sweet treat.

Ron and Larry were born in the Congo and had spent the majority of their lives living in Africa. During the Congo Rebellion, around 1961, there was a 24-hour cease fire and all expatriates were ordered to leave. The Robinson family left Elizabethville and settled in Loma Linda, California. There, Leonard proceeded to have a nervous breakdown after all the torture and death he had witnessed. His doctor suggested to Ruth that she have another child so that he could see life. Eddie and Freddie were born a year apart. I would meet Ruthie, and Eddie and Freddie who were 8 and 7 at the time, a little later. Ruthie figured that if she were going to have one more child, she might as well have two so that they could be companions. The Robinson family became Valerie's and my American family in Tanzania.

The next day, Leonard left with Yuri and Olga in Yuri's UNESCO car. They needed to get back to Busegwe and Mwanza, respectfully. Ron and Larry were staying at the camp one more night and invited Valerie and me to join them. We spent the day driving around looking for game. I shot a Weatherby .257 rifle. I aimed at a Tommy (Thomson's gazelle) and missed, thankfully. A great storm was brewing in the afternoon. The sky was very dark blue in the distance and the sunlit open plains looked so vibrant.

Ron and Larry knew a lot about photography and helped me get some great time exposure photos of us sitting around the blazing fire under the stars. I have never seen so many stars! We are in the southern hemisphere and the Southern Cross is easily seen. Ron had a large square mesh rack with long legs that he positioned over the fire. On this he draped thin pieces of Tommy and impala meat to make biltong, or what we would call jerky. Over the embers, the meat would slowly dry out. Hyenas surrounded the camp during the night, eating the remains of leftover impala and Thomson's gazelle lying about. An occasional lion joined the hyenas. We could hear the low rumbling roar.

Over the course of the year that I was in Tanzania, I got to know the Robinsons very well. And they had a plane at their disposal. It was a Cessna 206 Super Sky Wagon with the Robertson stall system and a turbocharged 300 hp engine. As Mr. Robinson needed to fly all over Tanzania to oversee the churches and missionary work, the plane was of important use. Years later I learned from Ed Robinson that his dad talked two wealthy doctor friends into donating it to the church. They did and the two doctors flew the plane from Southern California to Busegwe, with no GPS! Both Mr. Robinson and Larry had their PPL (Private Pilot's License) and flew the plane. If they were ever in the area of Fort Ikoma, they would buzz our tent. With the Robertson stall system they could fly very slow. When Valerie and I would see that it was the Robinsons we could have our Carly bags packed in minutes, which is what we dubbed the bags that came with our Pentax cameras. The story goes that our dad and his cousin Carl would many times go and spend a day up at Mount Lemmon or take a day trip somewhere outside of Tucson. Carl would always take his camera and inside his camera bag he had goodies like candy bars and nuts. Dad always referred to that as his Carly Bag. Well, we didn't have candy or goodies to pack in the bag, but a toothbrush, a brush and a change of clothes fit in very nicely with our cameras. The Robinsons might say they were off to so-and-so for the day and ask, "Do you want to go with us?" It was great fun.

A week after our camping trip, Leonard and Larry buzzed the Fort and from the plane dropped us a note tied to a rock. They were on their way to Moshi and Dar es Salaam for a few days. Valerie and I had been prepared to go with them in case they were going to Arusha for the day and then coming back.

February Adventures

Gideon invited me to go hunting with him and his two clients. Gideon, of the Kikuyu tribe from Kenya, was a professional hunter who worked for Jurgen. He was quite a character and would make really big eyes. He reminded Valerie and me so much of the American comedian Flip Wilson. I was invited to have dinner at the Hunters Camp and learned quite a lot. Open and controlled hunting areas are divided into blocks. Each block is rented out for a period of one week. If hunting plains game, need only to rent block for one week. If hunting for big five other than Cape buffalo, must rent block for a period of four weeks. One week hunting safari averaged $1000. That included the cost of the professional hunter, block rental, vehicle transportation while hunting, room and board. If hunting lion or leopard, must reserve block for four weeks, even if only to be here one week for hunting. Hunting licenses would be additional and varied in price according to animal. A license to shoot topi might be $100. To hunt for a leopard, it might be $5000 and with no guarantee that you were going to get your leopard, and no refund if you didn't.

Skip returned in the Lodge's new Land Rover. It's a beauty! When tour groups arrived by air, the Lodge had to provide the vehicles and scouts for the game runs.

Skip, Valerie and I loved it when a Lindblad Wing Safari tour group flew in. We got to know the couriers quite well and would look forward to seeing them once a month. Cathy Potter was about our age, and fun. She wore a kanzu to dinner that we admired and she offered to pick us up some in Lamu and bring them next month.

Valerie gave me a primer on basic Swahili expressions and improper gestures soon after I arrived. She stressed the importance of understanding the culture. Greetings are very important and not to be rushed. It's not just a hello, but "How are you?" "How is the family?" Never delve into the purpose of the conversation prior to some pleasantry. This is a graciousness I have endeavored to extend ever since. To motion someone to come to you, it was extremely impolite to use your index finger. That would be the equivalent of giving someone the "middle finger" in our culture. Instead, use both hands, palms down and pull fingers toward you. To ask someone to "come here" the proper conjugation is *"njoo hapa."* It would be very rude to say *"kuja hapa"* which is the command given to a dog. Mr. Robinson explained that Swahili is one of the most beautiful languages with the ability to describe nuances in such rich detail. Unfortunately, I never became very proficient. I marvel at the many East Africans who speak English because that would be their third language after their tribal language and Swahili.

Fort Ikoma was busy with tourists now and I was becoming familiar with the routine. The tour group typically arrived by small aircraft, minibus or Land Rover in the later afternoon. The guests checked into their rooms, maybe took a swim before dinner, or bathed and relaxed.

It's dusty out on those roads so one typically gets out of his or her traveling clothes, showers and dresses for dinner. Guests can relax on the patio in front of the *rondavel* or come to the terrace outside the dining room which offered a beautiful view of the savanna. The bar was open and dinner was served at an appointed time. After dinner, guests usually went back to their rooms to turn in early. If guests were staying two nights, they would be up the next morning for breakfast before collecting their box lunch and heading to an awaiting vehicle for an all-day game run, then back for another evening. On departure day, the suitcases have to be packed and ready, breakfast eaten, box lunch collected and at the vehicle by 8:00 a.m. because they will have a long drive to another guest lodge, with game-viewing along the way.

Because guests typically did not stay more than two nights, Valerie had a limited dinner menu rotation. This was also due to the fact that there wasn't much variety available. The meat was wild game: zebra, topi, wildebeest, eland, buffalo burgers. Saidi was the official hunter for Fort Ikoma. I went out with him a few times. Because Muslims were on the staff, it was important that the animal be "*chinja*-ed." This meant that before the plains game that was shot took its last breath, someone would run up to it and cut the jugular with a knife to let the blood drain out. This insured that the meat was *halal* (clean). Muslims do not eat the meat of an animal that is dead before this can be done. Game also came from the Hunters Camp. Chicken and eggs could be purchased locally, meaning within 50 miles. Staples were trucked in from Arusha or Musoma. Vegetables consisted primarily of onion and garlic, potatoes and cabbage. The fruit was fabulous – mini bananas, and the most delicious papaya and mangoes I have ever eaten. That's where I first learned the technique of how to score a mango and then push up from the skin side. Orange juice came in cans and one label advertised that it was made from fresh pineapple. Fresh bread and dinner rolls were made daily by Augustino, the baker. John Wangere made delicious desserts which usually were a steamed pudding of some kind, served with a custard sauce. Coconut and marmalade were my favorites. Valerie was able to get butter and cheese, but milk was powdered. No chocolate, but could get Nestle's hot chocolate mix and cocoa powder. Coffee was an instant powder. We made quite a concoction with the Nestle's instant coffee, hot chocolate mix and powdered cream. For lunch or dinner, Valerie would type up a daily menu which consisted of the soup of the day (made from a Knorr dry soup mix), two entrees with sides and dessert. It was fun for us when Mario was there because he would go into the kitchen and cook up something special for us.

Valerie and I would be awakened each morning at 7:00 by our room steward with a *"Hodi, hodi, hodi"* and a tray with two cups, a pot of hot water, instant coffee, sugar and powdered creamer. *Hodi* is a wonderful greeting that essentially means, "Hello, anyone home?" We would answer *"Karibu"* which means "welcome, you may approach." He would set the tray on the table outside our tent so that we could enjoy our first cup of coffee of the day while getting dressed. The room servants woke the guests by knocking on their door because there were no alarm clocks in the rooms since no generators ran at night. The staff called Valerie "Mama mBoom mBoom" as a sign of respect and because she was a boss. That is why we got the morning coffee service.

Breakfast was a busy time because guests wanted sustenance before heading out for a long day of game viewing or driving to another destination. There weren't snacks so mealtime was important. There was no bottled water either so drinks were usually sodas in a bottle. Water was carried in a thermos and portioned out by the cup. And if really thirsty, a warm beer hit the spot.

After breakfast, Valerie would go into her office to do her daily paperwork. I would wander around the Fort, help Dionisia in the gift shop or watch Isaac the Tailor make uniforms for the staff on his treadle sewing machine. I loved to watch how he would make a few dashes with chalk on fabric and cut out a piece. He needed no pattern to make the black pants and colorful shirts for the dining staff and room stewards, and the white uniforms for the chef and cooks. He let me try sewing on the machine. It was difficult to master the rhythm of the treadle.

I was trying to learn Swahili and so I carried around a book with me. I need to see the word as my auditory skills are hopeless at best. Well, that proved a problem. Every staff person I would pass would ask what I was learning. I said "to count to 10 in Swahili." And then they would say that they wanted to teach me how to count to 10 in their native tongue. I think I was taught in six different languages that day.

Valerie and I would meet for lunch and then while she went back to work in her office or was doing inventory with the bartender or chef, I would go back to the room and read for a few hours. On occasion, I helped Valerie with some work-related project. When Skip was around, he had me record his records onto cassette tapes so that he could play music on his Sony portable tape recorder after the generator went off. I would set up his record player in the dining room during the quiet afternoon. After putting the record on the turntable, I would insert the cassette tape into the recorder, position the microphone, set the needle down on the record and quickly press the record button on the Sony. Then I would sit as quietly as possible and hope that no one would open a door and come in because if there was an outside noise I would have to start the process all over again.

For dinner, we usually sat with Skip when he was at the Lodge and on many occasions a tour guide would join us. The guides (or couriers as some were called) were coming through every month so it was as if an old friend stopped by. Sometimes one of Jurgen's hunters would bring clients from the camp after their dinner to have drinks in the bar and we would join them. Something was always going on. We had no television, no radio, our only means of communication to the outside world was by two-way radio, yet we never lacked for good conversation and the joy of surprise visits.

A game that Valerie and I had made up and liked to play if we were dining by ourselves, and the dining room was full, was "Can you find?" I would find someone in the crowd who looked like a cross between two people who would be familiar to both of us and tell her the names. Then she would scan the crowd to see who I had in mind. One of the best was "Edna" (who worked for Grandma and Pop) and "Jonathan Winters" (a comedian). Valerie howled when she found the person. I can't even remember if it was a man or woman I had spotted.

Gideon was due back from a Nairobi peanut butter run, or as we called it, "Peanut butter safari." We didn't much care for the Chinese peanut butter and so if someone was going to Nairobi we would ask them to bring us back Skippy's peanut butter, Cadbury chocolate bars or Crest toothpaste. We would request only one item, as we didn't want to overdo a good thing. Tanzania was a socialist country and economically dependent on Red China. There wasn't much availability in the country in the way of consumer goods. I will admit that the Chinese toothpaste and toilet paper were decent products, but most everything else was disappointing. Valerie told the story of needing drinking glasses for the dining room. She had to order them from the nationalized restaurant supply store. She kept getting replies that the glasses were not in stock. She finally got so frustrated that she made a special trip to Arusha to go to the store. When she got there, the clerk opened up his big ledger, traced his finger down the page and announced in a dispassionate voice that there were no glasses. Valerie asked if she could go look on shelves and she was told that she couldn't. So she left. She decided to walk around to the back of the building. A door was open and she walked in. No one was around so she quietly walked between the tall shelves. Up there, high on a shelf, were cases and cases of glasses. Valerie marched up to the front of the store, told the clerk to follow her and pointed to the boxes. She told him in Swahili that this is what she wanted and how many cases she needed. She followed him back to the front desk whereby he opened up the ledger and once again traced his finger down the columns. He finally found them listed under "Fragile, Handle with Care." Valerie said it was times like that when she wanted to bang her head against the wall and mutter, "Had I only known to ask for Fragile!"

Jerry Rilling was back with another group and we always enjoyed it when Jerry was here. He brought a treat for each of us, a Cadbury chocolate bar. What a pal!

Mario and Jogi arrived the next day. Jogi is a water *fundi* (expert). He is going to build a walking bridge over the Grumeti so that we won't have to resort to the drift and be stranded when the river is up. As if to welcome them, it rained really hard around dinnertime.

We had dinner with several people on a Nile Star tour. Nile Star books clients for tours and then never makes reservations for them at the lodges on the loop. It plays on the sympathy of the innkeepers and puts the clients in an awkward position because they were informed that they had confirmed reservations along the way. Then we heard a story about a leopard attacking a woman in a minibus in the Serengeti. Apparently the leopard had been chased and trapped by two minibuses. The leopard clawed at the woman's chest. The leopard was acting purely in self-defense and the poor woman was the unintentional victim.

On the 22nd, Mushi and Dionisia left for a well-deserved two-week holiday. I will mind the curio shop while Dionisia is gone.

And two days later we had a very pleasant surprise. Yuri and Olga, with their 14-year-old daughter Lyuba, arrived to spend the weekend here. Lyuba's name means "love" in Russian. Yuri said he wanted to send a cable, but didn't think it would get here before they did. What it would have said was, "The Russians are coming!" He is such a hoot! Olga gave us a beautiful hand-painted plate in the Russian folk-art style and Yuri brought a bottle of real Russian vodka. He explained to us that vodka is made out of whatever is a surplus crop. One year it might be made from potatoes, another year from corn. It's a small bottle, 0.25 liter. Yuri poured us each a shot, then regaled us with a toast to which we were to down the shot and shout "Ваше здоровье," pronounced "Vashe Zdorovje." That's the Russian version of "To Your Health." I have kept two of the bottles, wonderful souvenirs of my dear friendship with the Vishnyakovs.

On Sunday, Yuri went hunting with Gideon to get meat for the Lodge. Yuri shot two plains game and finally got his topi, taking home two of the legs. The topi is a taupe color antelope with a bluish cast to its haunches. It was my favorite hide of the plains game. We made plans to visit them in Mwanza soon.

David Babu and Obadiah Ndosi, David's deputy, plus Babu the manager at Serengeti Safari Camp, came for the afternoon. Had a great time with them. We made plans with them to go to Seronera on March 11 to have a goat roast. Ndosi came into the Gift Shop while I had it open. He asked me which necklace I liked the most. After showing him the black and white Maasai beaded choker I had been eyeing, he bought it and presented it to me. How nice of him! I had assumed he was buying it for his girlfriend and wanted my advice. The Africans are very generous people. I must learn the art of not admiring something because they are quick to give it to you if you remark about it. He also told me that he is writing a letter to Dad saying that I am employed and can't leave.

I tried taking photos of this lively group, which included the Vishnyakovs and Gideon, without a flash while we were all sitting in the bar. They turned out blurry from not holding the camera still during a slow shutter speed, but the photos capture a very special memory for me.

Met Gerard Ambrose and Margot Sheesley who came to Fort Ikoma for the night. They are running a Ker, Downey and Selby tented camp at Kirawira. It is called Grumeti Safari Camp. Margot is an American.

And on Monday, Dr. Tumaini Mcharo and Haunga came around dinnertime. This is my first introduction to

Mcharo who is head of the Serengeti Research Institute (SRI). He spent 11 years in the States obtaining his Bachelor of Science degree, Masters and PhD. I had heard so much about him that I was happy to finally meet him. He is delightful. On the other hand, Haunga was a very ingratiating chap.

And the next day...if it isn't one surprise, it's another. Larry Robinson and friends of his family from Loma Linda, Dr. and Mrs. Jesse, stopped by for lunch on the way to Seronera. They will be back through in a few days. I just looked at my visa. Oops! It expired three weeks ago!

And on the last day of February, Jogi made curry for all of us, Gideon is off to Maasai land, Joseph Nyakachara's clothes-es (as he says it) have been stolen and Gideon's ammo stolen. Major Lemu of CID (Criminal Investigation Division) was contacted to take care of the situation.

March Rolls in with a Roar

T he last couple of days have been full of crises: no petrol, no eggs, no meat, low on candles, low on gas cylinders, theft, etc. As Skip was fond of saying, "When you lose your sense of humor, it's time to get out." Are we there yet? And being that it was the first day of the month, Valerie needed to inventory the liquor in the bar and the food in the kitchen. I helped her with that. I also had to do inventory of the gift shop. It sold African souvenirs like wood carvings, fly swatters made from gnu tails, beaded jewelry, African *kitenges*, and film when it was available. The storing of the film wasn't ideal, but we had some rolls for the desperate photographer who was usually me.

Subsequent days were filled with their own dramas. The hunting expedition wasn't doing much better. It got one topi with 12 bullets. So Skip decided to go catch fish. Valerie and Jogi joined him. No fish luck either. Seems like others from staff quarters had better luck hunting within the 5-mile reserve around Fort Ikoma, if that was a gunshot Valerie and Jogi heard.

Major Lemu arrested the chairman of the Workers Committee on charge of theft of four Lodge sheets. He was *kamata*-ed (handcuffed) and put in the Musoma jail. We congratulated Skip on how he handled a camper who came up to him while we were sitting on terrace to report that his bag with two cameras, passport and $300 in traveler's checks had been stolen from his car at the staff hostel while he was eating dinner. Apparently, it happened when lights were out for half an hour due to the generator overheating. I don't recall what Skip's retort was, but do recall that it was choice! And *mingi* (many) French Canadians drove me nuts in the Gift Shop.

Things perked up on March 4th when Mrs. Robinson arrived with Eddie, Freddie and three friends. It was our first time to meet them. Later, Mr. Robinson and two others flew in for lunch. I told Mr. Robinson that my visa had expired. He said to give him my passport and he would take care of it. Thank heavens for friends like Mr. Robinson!

David Babu, Ndosi and a colleague of theirs came for lunch. Jogi, Valerie and I went on great game run with them to Sabora Plains in one of the Serengeti National Park (SNP) Land Rovers, TZ14677. Because most Land Rovers look alike, they are referred to by the license plate number and this one would be called TZed14677, Zed being the British way to say the letter Z. Saw lots of Cape buffalo, impala, gazelles, giraffe, gnu. There was a pride of nine lions that were full after a huge meal on a buffalo, and now very lethargic. Just before we spotted the lions, here came Mr. Robinson and Skip in the Cessna 206 and buzzed us, coming very low and slow and probably scaring the poor lions to death. We followed the lions and witnessed their encounter with a porcupine. To be out on a game drive in the Serengeti with the Chief and Deputy Chief Park Wardens is really a thrill.

As we were heading back to FIL, we came across four *Waikoma* women They were carrying heavy loads of firewood on their backs which caused them to stoop over and walk slowly. In Swahili, the *Wa* prefix to *Ikoma* translates as "the people" (plural) of Ikoma. We didn't get back until 7:00. I was a wee bit late in opening the gift shop. Oh well.

All *wageni* (guests) left really early. David Babu came back with Derek Bryceson (Director of Tanzania National Parks) for lunch. Great lunch, too, chicken salad in half an avocado. Serge with Jet Tours arrived. Larry Robinson with Dr. and Mrs. Jesse and Gunnar, a Swedish student on a volunteer program in Ethiopia, arrived about 8:00. They were coming back through from eastern Tanzania. We all had dinner together. It must have been full capacity with the arrival of the Robinson group because Valerie and I slept in Serge's tent and he slept in the office.

We were awakened at 5:00 a.m. the next morning by the Maasai *askari* (guard) and one other having big to-do, as to whether or not we were in the tent. Finally, one unzipped the flap, shone light in, took one look at a very displeased Valerie, and quickly turned away saying, "*wageni*." Larry and Gunnar came by about 6:00 a.m. We all went onto the terrace and watched the sunrise. Before the Robinson party left at 8:30 a.m., Larry invited me to join him on two-day business flying trip around Tanzania on the 12th and 13th. If it works out, I would be able to see parts of Tanzania I probably wouldn't see otherwise.

A Lindblad Tour arrived with a group from Muncie, Indiana. A big storm came up at 5:00 p.m. Then Ron Robinson surprised us at 8:30 p.m. He just came for the night for a visit. Gideon is back. All of us, plus Serge, had dinner together. Gideon left and we all continued to party in Skip's room.

Before Ron left the next morning, I made arrangements with Ron and Skip for Ron to mind the store while I joined Larry on his southern Tanzania business trip. Yippee! Ron left later that morning.

While Jogi is here to build the foot bridge across the Grumeti River, he is also constructing a permanent tent site for Valerie. It is located to the west of the property, beyond the guest tents. It will have a plumbed bathroom with a shower, sink and flush *choo* (toilet). First, a plinth has to be built. That is a concrete slab that will provide the foundation for the tent and bathroom. The bathroom walls will go up 7 feet high and a thatched roof will be built over the entire plinth. The back of the tent will butt up against the bathroom wall. It will be unzipped with flaps folded back to reveal the door that will lead into the bathroom.

Today, we had good ol' hamburgers on buns for lunch, not bad. It's a very foggy day and a big rainstorm lasting about 15 minutes came through at 5:00. Valerie and I have been using the office bathroom because we never know where we might be sleeping each night. If the Lodge is full, then we sleep in the bunkbeds in her office. I was taking a shower and the water wouldn't drain. Valerie asked Saulo, the plumber, to check it out. Outside the bathroom wall is a small bricked square where the pipe leading from the shower drain goes. The sides are built up a few inches, and the depression was full of water. Saulo stuck his hand in the water and quickly pulled it out. He discovered a black mamba curled up in the outside drain. Fortunately, the snake must have eaten recently because Saulo was not bitten. The black mamba is a very deadly snake. The mystery of the non-draining drain was solved. The snake was carefully removed and dealt with.

March 9th was a very fortuitous day. It was the tent-raising of Valerie's (and my) soon-to-be new home. After the hoopla we headed across the river to do some leopard sleuthing, but had no luck so we came back and then had to deal with a bat in Valerie's office. It was imperative to get it out because we would be sleeping there that night. We took a blanket off one of the beds and was able to trap it by throwing it over the bat while it was flying around the room at great speed and right over our heads. Whew! Another huge rain storm at 6:00 which created a Lake Victoria right outside the gift shop door.

It's fun having Jogi here. He is of the Sikh sect from India. They were the warriors of bygone days. While Jogi isn't a current-day warrior, he still follows the Sikh tradition of not cutting his hair, wearing a turban made from a long piece of gauzy cloth, and though he doesn't carry a sword, no doubt always has a knife on him. The customs have significance though I can't remember all, but one I do is the turban. If injured during fighting, the cloth could be used as a tourniquet. In a dust storm it can be wrapped around the face. Since there is no construction work on the weekends, Jogi would make chicken curry for dinner. What a treat to watch him cook in the kitchen. And the aroma was heavenly! He gave me the recipe, but you have to know the size of his fist to know how much *ghee* to sauté the onions in. Ghee is clarified butter with a long shelf life.

Jogi had a driver by the name of Joseph who took Jogi, Valerie and me on a game drive along the Grumeti River. The next day we did a game run out past the airstrip. All of the marabou storks followed us to the *taka taka* (garbage) dump because they recognized Jogi's truck as the one that has been bringing the *taka taka*.

Sunday evening Skip made moussaka for dinner. When the men are cooking, we dine well.

On Monday, Mr. Robinson and Larry flew in at 1:00. They were returning from a two-day trip to several missions in Tanzania. It turns out that Larry's business trip has been canceled so the trip to fly with him is a no go. However, Mr. Robinson had my passport with the visa extended to June 30. Fabulous!

The next day I went to Musoma with Skip, Valerie and Jogi while Saulo minded the store for me. It's a 3-hour drive. Skip had business to conduct. First, the Lodge rifle's registration had to be renewed and the rifle must be presented. Then we went to see the recovered Land Rover that had been stolen a few weeks earlier by poachers. It now looked like a pickup truck. The top had been hack-sawed off and seats removed so that carcasses could be piled up. And a license plate number had been painted on the rear of the vehicle. We ate lunch on an old wharf on Lake Victoria and then went shopping – real *dukas*. Great marketplace, much like Mexico. All the women look so colorful in their bright *kangas* (colorful cloth). We ran into Ron and Larry. Actually, they ran after us. They spotted Skip's Land Rover and chased us down. Skip met two *wageni*, Terry and Bruce, who needed a ride to the Serengeti, so we gave them lift to Fort Ikoma. We gave Ron and Larry a lift back to Busegwe because they had to leave a car at the mechanic in Musoma. All eight of us piled in and headed for the Robinsons' home. It was Eddie's birthday so we serenaded him with Happy Birthday and played with his neat kite and gliders before heading back to Fort Ikoma, arriving about 8:30 that night.

And the next day we thought we heard a lorry (truck) arriving, but it turned out to be Ron and Larry. What a noise Ron's Peugeot 404 makes, with the aid of three huge red cans bouncing around in the back! They were on their way from Busegwe to Mwanza. Fort Ikoma is a good three hours out of their way! Jogi made curry for dinner. Patrice DuFar, a courier for Unitours, joined us for dinner. I was so stuffed that Skip made me run around the pool. He really is a card. Afterwards we all moved out to Valerie's tent and had our very first fire in the fire pit. Neat. Valerie, Larry, Ron and I slept outside on the terrace. All the *askaris* included us in their rounds so they could sit by the fire. Some great lines that night: Valerie: "Speak up, my cookie can't hear you." "And there were my contacts, under the bed." Larry: "Yeah, right where you last put them."

65

Next morning, when asked if the tent got off the ground, Skip replied, "Indeed, it must've gone at least twice around the hill."

Ron and Larry were off early the next morning for Mwanza. They are due back at Fort Ikoma on the 16th. Mushi and Dionisia returned around dinnertime. Valerie and I made brownies. Super!

On March 16th, Valerie and I celebrated Mother's birthday with the brownies we had baked. She would approve. Ron and Larry returned late afternoon and we had a slideshow as soon as electricity came on. Larry showed us the slides he had taken on the February camping trip with the Vishnyakovs. What fun!

The next morning we all tromped down to view the progress on Jogi's bridge only to discover that all the cables from Jogi's bridge were pinched by poachers and most likely are being used for snares now. I waded down the Grumeti with Larry. Then Ron let me drive his Peugeot 404 pickup truck. It's the first time I've driven since September 3, 1972 and with steering wheel on right, no less. Every vehicle is manual drive. So was my car at home so I knew how to drive using a clutch and gear shift. Fortunately, I didn't have to worry about any other cars on the road. Ndosi arrived at 5:00. We all had a quick swim and then Valerie, Ndosi and I left for Seronera. Larry had left just before us, and Ron was staying on.

Ballooning

Mike Norton-Griffiths was a British scientist at the Seronera Research Institute, studying migration. He was also a licensed hot air balloon pilot and owned his own balloon. Mike wanted the balloon for his research. He could float over the plains virtually soundless except for the occasional blasts of butane flames to heat the air. However, Mike needed David Babu's permission to balloon over the Serengeti and David, who was the Chief Park Warden of the Serengeti National Park, had been adamant that there would be no ballooning in the Park.

Valerie and I were enamored with the idea of hot air ballooning. On a visit to the Fort, Mike had mentioned to us about David's opposition to ballooning over the Serengeti. Valerie suggested to Mike that he invite David to go ballooning with him to see for himself what it was like. She would also work on David, and she told Mike that if she got him to go, Mike would have to "take my sister and me, too!" Finally, reluctantly, David agreed to go.

On March 17th Ndosi came to pick up Valerie and me. After a quick swim, the three of us left for Seronera to have dinner at the Seronera Wildlife Lodge with David, Patrick Duncan and others. Before dinner, Ndosi gave me a beautiful beaded necklace. What a lovely surprise. I had met Ndosi on only a few occasions and so was somewhat taken aback, though this is the second necklace he has given me. After dinner we went over to Mike's for a briefing and to see his Super 8 movies on ballooning. Our final instructions were to meet back at his house at 5:45 a.m.

Ndosi had invited Valerie and me to spend the night at his house. As we were settling in for the night, we discovered that Ndosi did not have an alarm clock and we had not brought one. Ndosi had no telephone either. Sunrise isn't until 6:00 a.m. Ndosi assured me that he would wake us up in time, but I was unwilling to take that chance so I suggested that we take turns staying up all night and that I would take the first shift. None of us wanted to miss the ballooning, so it was agreed.

I settled onto the couch in the living room to read. Valerie was in the adjacent bedroom. A few minutes later, Ndosi came out and joined me on the couch. He started chatting with me, and within minutes was proposing marriage to me. Needless to say, I was startled by this completely unexpected request and was flabbergasted as to how to extricate myself from this delicate situation. Here I was, a guest in his home (thankfully with my sister on the other side of the wall), and I had only met Ndosi a few times before. I mumbled something about how flattered I was that he would want to marry me, but that we didn't know each other very well and I wasn't at a point in my life that I wanted to get married. He told me that he wanted a wife who was educated and had interests. He continued that he knew he could be very happy with me. I asked him about the women with whom he had grown up or gone to school. There in lay the problem. Ndosi had a Masters degree from a University.   There are no educational opportunities for girls in Tanzania much beyond elementary school level. With the males being afforded the opportunities to continue on with their education, a huge educational gap was developing.   Simply speaking, Ndosi did not want to marry a woman with a sixth-grade education who was content to hoe the *shamba* and tend to the chickens and goats. He wanted a wife who would be his partner in life and share his interests, who would feel comfortable traveling in the same circles, among educated people.   I really felt for him in his quandary.   This is a problem that third world countries are facing.   The educated are not content to return to the old ways. Educational gaps between the male and female populations pose serious problems.

About this time, ESP had worked its magic ways and Valerie came out to the living room. We three chatted for a little while, then Ndosi went to bed. I told Valerie what had happened and thanked her for her timing. It had been an awkward situation.   I genuinely liked Ndosi, and did not enjoy having to disappoint him by answering "no" to his marriage proposal, but I was in no position to say "yes."

Our taking turns worked.   I didn't fall asleep until 4:30 a.m. and was awakened at 5:30 a.m. We jumped into our clothes and headed over to David Babu's where we had to wake him up.   A little late, but we rendezvoused with Mike and his wife Anne at their home. Mike was heating a gas cylinder on his gas stove. A little unnerving, but necessary. I was thankful that the house didn't blow up with us in it. Propane gas is more ideal, but it is unavailable here. Therefore, butane is used, but it must first be heated. The huge cylinders are laid on top of the gas stove burners and gently heated. The cylinders are then wrapped in padded canvas to retain the heat. By caravan, we headed out to Simba Kopjes to launch the balloon. Living up to its name, a pride of 8 to 10 lions, curiosity peaked, lay about 200 yards from our launch site.

Everyone needs to help launch the balloon. Unloading the basket from the Land Rover is a team effort. It is not easy to get a comfortably secure grip and it is unwieldy. First, the four butane gas cylinders needed to be strapped into the four corners of the basket. Next, the balloon needs to be laid out flat on the ground. Its height is equivalent to a three-story building so it covers a lot of ground. Guy wires attach the balloon to the basket which is lying on its side.

Now the fun part; the flapping begins. All manpower stands at the mouth of the balloon and flaps the upper layer. It's a great touch-toes, stretch-up exercise. This allows air to get into the balloon and make it easier to fill the balloon with hot air. As we were flapping the brightly colored balloon with its patches of orange, white and purple, the lions roared in amazement. The black-maned male lion could not figure out what was going on, kept pacing back and forth, but kept his distance, thankfully.

After flapping, someone must walk inside the balloon and hold up the upper layer of the balloon with a special stick (in this case, a mop). Two other people must stand on either side of the mouth and hold it open as wide as possible. Valerie and I had the task of holding onto the crown rope. This rope is attached to the top of the balloon. Mike then started filling the balloon with hot air by using the jet burner which heats up the surrounding air. This is a delicate operation because one must be careful that the flame does not burn the balloon. If a wind kicks up, the balloon is harder to control and the material is a very thin heat-treated nylon. The fabric is very durable, but should be handled as little as possible. Load tapes that run lengthwise and crosswise are what one holds to pull and stretch the balloon. As the balloon inflates, it begins to right itself. At this point the person with the special stick (mop) exits. Valerie and I had to hold the crown rope until the balloon bounced up. Then, it is the 100 yard dash to the basket because all manpower must hold the basket on the ground until lift-off.

At this elevation (4500 feet above sea level), the balloon can carry only two passengers, one of which must be the licensed balloon pilot. At sea level it could accommodate three passengers and the pilot, but it would be a tight fit. Mike and Anne took off first. The rest of us piled into the two Land Rovers and followed them. The balloon's course is dictated by the thermals. Ballooning is done early in the morning when the thermals are still somewhat cool. As they heat up, the air becomes more unpredictable and rough. The pilot can only control altitude. A blast from the burner heats up the air in the balloon and causes it to rise. As the air cools, the balloon descends. The chase vehicles must be prepared to follow the balloon wherever it goes which makes for some interesting driving. As the balloon sails serenely ahead, we in the chase vehicles are bouncing along the plains of Africa. "Watch out for that termite hill." "Yikes, a stream, where are we going to cross?" "Low trees ahead." "Now which way is the balloon heading?"

After about 15 minutes, Mike came down for a switch of passengers. It was decided that I would be the guinea pig and go first. I had to jump out of the Land Rover and run after the basket as it bumped along the ground. I grabbed hold of the side of the wicker basket, but there is no way to get a foothold. The basket is about 4 feet long by 3 feet wide by 3½ feet high, with a butane canister in each corner and guy wires leading up to the balloon. Mike is 6'5" and stands just below the jet burner. Anne had positioned herself on top of the basket, between the angled guy wires, but could not jump out until I was in or else the basket would lift off because of the loss of weight. The thermals were still moving the balloon along, so I held onto the basket as I ran after it trying to hoist myself in, with little success. Finally, Mike reached over, grabbed me by my arms and belt loops and pulled me inside. I made a nosedive into the basket with my feet up in the air. It took me a few minutes to get my strength back, I was laughing so hard. I finally got myself back on my feet. Later, I showed two bruised knees, a bruised shin, two bruised thighs and scratched up arms as a result of my entry. There are no photographs of my entry because Valerie was laughing so hard she couldn't hold the camera still. I later learned that Anne practically did the splits trying to get off the basket, which would have been a priceless picture as well. Her heel was stuck in the wicker rim and she was hopping along on one foot while waiting for Mike to extricate the other.

However the entry, it was well worth it. Soaring over the Serengeti is an unbelievable experience. Here I was, the third person to ever have the opportunity to do it, too. We sailed at an altitude of about 5,500 feet (or 1,000 feet above the ground) at a speed of about 10 miles per hour. Mike would have to blast some hot air into the balloon once a minute. The sound would frighten the animals, but curiosity got the better of them as they watched this big orange balloon sailing in the sky. The silence between jet blasts was awe-inspiring. No man-made noises whatsoever could be heard. Nor could we really hear the sounds of the animals although they were running beneath us, yet avoiding the shadow of the balloon as if it were a bottomless hole. It was like a ballet as the thousands of plains game such as wildebeest, topi, gazelles leaped and ran in one direction. As the shadow of the balloon would encroach upon them, they would move sideways out of its way, yet the flow was unbroken, much like river water flowing along its banks.

The rest of the changeovers were just as hilarious and I was able to capture some on film. At one of them, another Land Rover approached us. It was Alan Root, a renowned wildlife cinematographer and fellow balloonist. He recognized Mike's balloon, and wanted to see if we needed any help. The chase vehicle carrying Mike's wife and her friend Linda was no longer with us so Alan offered to look for them.

David, the biggest skeptic of all who had once said, "No ballooning in the Park!" and "I will not go up in that balloon!" went twice. He loved it and agreed to rethink his position on the subject. At the final descent, the landing is achieved by dropping a rope hooked to the basket, which acts as a drag to reduce the speed and direct the basket to fall on the proper side. The balloon then follows, sometimes draping over the basket. Out popped Mike's head, but it seemed an eternity before David came crawling out from the bottom of the basket. Because we were down a vehicle, there were only five of us to fold up the balloon, pack up the equipment and load it into the back of the Land Rover. Then we squeezed into the vehicle and headed back to Seronera.

Back at the Norton-Griffiths, we found Alan Root, but still no Anne or Linda. Eventually they returned after a series of mishaps and adventures. Alan has filmed a number of National Geographic films including *Mzima Springs; Baobab;* and *Man of the Serengeti.* He is presently working on a documentary about the wildebeest migration. He has lived a life of adventure, including missing one index finger which was amputated because of a bite from a puff adder, one of the deadly snakes that live in East Africa.

March Roars On

After our fabulous balloon ride, Valerie and I headed over to Seronera Lodge to have lunch. There, we met Jogi's brother, sister-in-law and sister who were on their way to visit Jogi at Fort Ikoma. Lucky for us, we could hitch a ride with them. We were so tired that we crashed at 6:00 and slept 14 hours.

Jogi's relatives stayed for a few days. Before they headed back home to Arusha, though, Jogi took us all to search for an old gold mine that is nearby, apparently. We had no such luck finding it, but it was fun to explore anyway.

After they left, we played cards all afternoon with Ron and later Valerie and I taught Ron and Jogi how to play bridge. We drank beer, ate peanut butter and crackers and had a great time. For dinner we had the birds that Ron, Jogi and Skip had shot the day before. Skip demonstrated his "above all, the innkeeper must have dignity" by tearing away at his bird and throwing the carcass over his shoulder and onto the terrace. Great *Tom Jones* eating scene. News before we turned in was that there were troubles down at staff quarters. Some knifings and rock throwing. Another problem that Skip will have to deal with.

Jogi left in the morning, but not before he had amassed a long list of things to do for FIL in Arusha. We played cards in the morning and I took a nap after lunch.

Larry arrived at 4:00 with news that Ron had to get to Nairobi in day or two to meet up with their father. The Trislander arrived bringing Jerry Rilling and his Lindblad group, but with an uptight pilot whom Skip advised against our asking for a lift for Ron.

Mario arrived before dinner and we all went to cheer him up because his daughter and son-in-law were flying to Italy that night. They had been living in Uganda, but because of recent troubles, they were getting out of Uganda and moving to Italy. There is heavy border tension between Uganda and Tanzania. War is scheduled to break out in a day or two. Fortunately, we are far away from that border, with Lake Victoria and southwestern Kenya as buffers.

With Mario here, we had pizza for dinner. It was a very lively meal. Bernard, another tour guide and a friend of Serge's joined us. Ron hid my shoes, and had everybody under the table looking for them. What a group! And people think we get bored here!   We adjourned to Skip's room for a little party. Bernard brought his Pink Floyd tape, great sound.

Valerie and I slept in room 20 that night. In the middle of night, we were awakened by a clumping sound of movement in the grass. The curtains and windows were wide open and I soon realized the sound was made by two giraffes eating the thatched roof and various other things.

Bernard's group was leaving at 8:00 sharp in the morning. He was a stickler for punctuality. After last night's late party in Skip's room, he overslept. He came bounding into the dining room about 7:55 and plopped down at the table where Valerie and I were sitting. The waiter came over to take his order and he snapped, "A 3-minute egg, and make it fast!"

Telling time in Swahili has a unique method. Since sunrise and sunset occur about the same time every day throughout the year, being so close to the equator, the 24-hour day is divided into 12 hours of light and 12 hours of darkness. Typically, the sun rises at 6:00 a.m. and so the first hour of daylight is figured as 7:00 a.m. But in Swahili, this is considered 1:00 since it is the first hour and is spoken as "saa moja." The Western 8:00 a.m. would be saa mbili. In other words, one needs to add or subtract 6 hours to convert between Swahili and the Western way of telling time. To denote daylight, mchana is used with the preposition za and to denote nighttime, usiku is used. Saa sita za mchana would be noon and Saa sita za usiku would be midnight.

Skip saddled Larry with the task of driving part of the Lindblad group on a game run. Ron left with Jurgen and Caroline for Nairobi. Valerie's tent is coming along, the beds were moved in. Valerie and I accompanied Skip and Larry on a mission to check out the four-wheel-drive on Skip's Land Rover which has been giving him trouble. Larry said "let me show you how you can go into low range while moving." Skip replied that the book said it couldn't be done. Larry said he never read the book, then proceeded to demonstrate how it could be done. This is how four-wheel-drive works: Yellow knob is high range. When depressed, the vehicle goes into four-wheel-drive at whatever gear the motor is already in. This is quick and good for long stretches of sand or mud. Red knob is low range. When pulled toward driver, it puts car in low range four-wheel drive, giving motor two gears lower than ordinary first gear. Low range is used when going up or down steep grades and tires need traction. The succession of gears when using low range are as follows:

1 low range
2 low range
1 regular 1st gear
3 low range
2 regular 2nd gear
4 low range
3 regular 3rd gear
4 regular 4th gear

Always press the clutch when shifting into low or high range four-wheel-drive.

Afterwards, I took some photos of Fort Ikoma from the Water Tower Hill with Larry and Jerry. I wanted to use up the roll of film with the balloon ride. I put the exposed film roll in my shirt pocket while we were sitting out by the swimming pool in the later afternoon. All of a sudden, I got lifted out of my chair and thrown into the pool by a chap named John Cook and Larry. I rose out of the water cussing up a blue streak and quickly climbed onto the pool deck. I was horrified that the film of our ballon flight might have been ruined. Fortunately, it had stayed in my pocket. I took it out and dried off the film canister, praying that not much water had seeped through the narrow opening. Larry felt really bad when he realized why I was so upset and left soon after. It was a quiet, early evening. Skip gave Valerie and me his air gun in case any trouble should arise.

Fortunately, there were no troubles during the night and we had a relaxing day. We made another pizza for dinner. News came to us from travelers. We had no radio, never got a newspaper, and the Newsweek magazine came in the mail and was old news by the time it arrived 3 weeks after the issue date. We heard that the area around Kigoma had been bombed – a village on the Tanzania-Uganda border near Burundi – a nothing village. Joke is, Uganda was probably aiming for Bukoba, but since it hit this village, is now saying Rwanda is out for Uganda. Crazy Idi Amin.

The next day I sat out by the pool. Larry stopped by around lunchtime. He had a group he was taking on a game run around Seronera. It was a crazy group of people. Even Larry said they were weird. The man asked me if I was Christian. I said yes. Then he asked Valerie and she said she was my sister. Then he asked if we love Jesus.

Mario left after lunch and a little later Paul and Betty Jean Hunt arrived to spend the night. Paul is manager at Ngorongoro Wildlife Lodge. We also had a group of about 24 students from World College Afloat here. They were American. It was especially fun for Valerie to chat with the group because she had gone on the inaugural University of the Seven Seas in the fall and winter of 1963-64. One of the professors with them was Dick Sense from the University of Arizona Anthropology department.

I sat out by the pool with Paul and Betty Jean the next morning. They left after lunch. Valerie felt ill all day long, must have been the midnight swim. With a bunch of college kids here the night before, everyone partied late. I started feeling bad in the afternoon. Both of us turned in early that evening.

Gerard and Margot came for the day. They didn't have any clients at Grumeti Tented Camp and it's just about an hour's drive from there to here. We talked them into staying overnight. Skip prepared chicken tetrazzini for all of us, including JP, a courier with Travelworld, and from Mauritius. We ate dinner on the terrace of Taj West (as opposed to the one in Agra, India) with a fire blazing. The party continued, but I fell asleep on the terrace. I woke up in middle of the night to find everyone gone except for Skip. Although I was constantly being bitten by mosquitoes, I couldn't leave Skip alone on the terrace. Apparently, he thought the same about me so we both stuck it out all night, bug bites and all.

Mingi Mini Safaris

G erard and Margot invited Valerie and me to drive back
to Kirawira with them. Their camp is in the western
corridor of the Serengeti National Park and so most of the
driving is on dirt tracks. We saw a family of cheetahs along
the way. To reach the campsite, we had to cross the
Grumeti River at a drift and arrived just in time for lunch.
After a delicious meal prepared by the cook, we went
looking for crocodiles, but scared them into the water
before seeing them. Back to the camp for afternoon tea and
a chat, then off on a game run just before sunset. Currently,
there are no guests so putting us up in a tent and two more
mouths to feed is not a problem.

After breakfast we went on another game run.
Gerard is a professional hunter so we referred to him as
GWH (Great White Hunter). Later, we went down to the
hippo pool. There must have been at least twenty of them.
Hippos make a grunting, snorting sound as they come up
for air. Then it was off to the crocodile pool. The crocs were
at least 10 feet long, but hard to get a good look at them
because they slither into water at the first noise from
approachers. Gerard and I went trekking on foot for Cape
buffalo, but didn't see any, fortunately. I may be with a
GWH, but he isn't carrying a rifle on our foot safari. At
sunset we all went on a game run along the road to
Handajenga (the southwest quarter of SNP) and saw Patas

81

monkeys, a rarity for this area, eland, and some ostriches having a race. A special treat was spotting a bush baby. They are nocturnal animals and live up in trees and so are difficult to see, but if the headlights or flashlight catch their eyes, two large round yellow eyes look right back at you. We went back to the camp and had a delicious dinner that had been prepared by the cook on his outdoor "stove." The cooking is done over a fire and the ashes are built up to create a cooking surface. Even bread is baked this way. The loaf pan is put directly on the hot ashes and a *sufuria* (large metal bowl) is inverted over it. Hot ashes are then picked up with a shovel and carefully laid over the bowl to create heat from above. This "oven" cooking method may be rustic, but we had delicious fresh-baked bread at every meal and a fresh-baked dessert, too. After dinner, we enjoyed the evening sounds as we sat out by the fire.

Gerard taught us how to make elephant hair bracelets. It's a rather complicated knotting process. The hair comes from the tail of the elephant and is comparable to a thin, flexible wire. A series of twists and turns and knots create a round bracelet that can be adjusted by squeezing the knots together or pressing apart. I have no recollection of how to make the bracelet, but I own a few and marvel at their design. The four of us left after lunch for Fort Ikoma, but there was a problem with water in the petrol so it delayed our departure. We got back to the Fort at 6:00, in time for dinner.

After breakfast, Gerard, Margot and I went on *recce* (reconnaissance mission) and for target practice with the airgun at an old hunter's campsite on the other side of the river. While there, Danny McCallum, a professional hunter from Kenya and his client Fred from Fort Worth, Texas arrived to set up a camp. They came up to the Fort for lunch. We decided to have a pig roast at the Taj and sent Dan and Fred out for warthog, although they were hunting for *simba*. Meanwhile, Gerard and I played English monopoly. Dan and Fred didn't come up with a *simba* or warthog, so no pig roast.

Skip left for Nairobi to pick up his daughter Putney at boarding school the same day we left for Kirawira. They had not returned as we had expected, so Valerie, Margot, Gerard and I went down to Danny's camp for martinis and ended up staying for dinner. Margot was too much that night. She made the martinis – called them Silver Bullets. Her recipe: Pour gin into martini glass. Pour dry vermouth into cap of bottle. Waft cap over glass without pouring any vermouth into glass.

My head was hurting from all those Silver Bullets so a swim in the morning felt good. The four of us left after lunch for Kirawira again. The area is called Kirawira and Grumeti Tented Camp takes its name from the river that runs through the area. We passed by some burning grass fires and then came across a herd of buffalo with a newborn calf that could not have been more than 10 minutes old because the umbilical cord was still attached. The mother and rest of the herd had run off at the approach of our vehicle and the calf was left behind. She was quite frightened, cold, hungry and immediately came up to the car thinking it was her mother. We tried to reunite the calf with the mother, but the mother was out of sight. We figured that the mother would most probably come back when she felt there was no danger. An electrical storm was brewing and so we headed to camp. It was a weird overcast and smoky day.

Seronera Tented Safari Camp (STSC) was scheduled to close on March 31st which was today so Gerard drove Valerie and me from Kirawira to Seronera. On the drive we passed a great migration of wildebeest. We also saw a pack of wild dogs, a first for me. We did a game run around Seronera in the afternoon and saw three lions by the side of road, one leopard descending a tree into tall grass, and a mama cheetah and her five 5-month-old cubs that seem very tame. I took at least 30 pictures of the cubs frolicking around. Mama is the cheetah that we hear loves to jump on the bonnet (hood) of a vehicle, but she didn't jump on ours.

It was bittersweet to be here for the last dinner served at STSC. This is where Valerie had met Ron Johnson which ultimately resulted in her moving to Tanzania to take the job at Fort Ikoma and where Mom, Dad and I had rendezvoused with Valerie. It was fitting, therefore, for us to dine with Babu and Shushila who had successfully managed this tented camp that now was closing because of the opening of the Seronera Wildlife Lodge. George from Mwanza, his 5-year-old son Stefan and friend Johnny (also 5) were the last guests at STSC, not counting us. George is a British electrician at Mwanza's textile factory. We had heard about him from Margot. He's quite a character, a typical Lancastrian, apparently.

Close to camp this morning, we spotted the spoor of hippos. To shield themselves from the sun, they stay in the water during the day and come out at night to graze. Gerard and I went on an early morning game run. We passed through Donald Ker's Dam where 200 wildebeest had drowned a few days before while migrating northwest. The stench was terrible and the bloated bodies attracted a lot of marabou storks and vultures. Later in the morning Gerard took Valerie, me, George and the boys on another game run. We spotted two young leopards in a tree and the mama *duma* and five cubs resting under another tree.

We lunched at the new Seronera Wildlife Lodge which opened today, April 1st, for lunches only. It will open May 1st with 50 beds and three meals daily. The lodge looks very unfinished and it has a serious water problem. Lo and behold, Skip and Putney arrived at the lodge for lunch. Putney is Skip's 9-year-old daughter who is on a school break from her boarding school in Nairobi. I had heard a lot about Putt Putt and it was wonderful to finally meet her. She is a darling girl with long, straight platinum blond hair. The group of us – Skip, Putney, Valerie, Babu, David Babu, the manager Brian Payne, Gerard, George and his boys, and I – enjoyed the delicious buffet lunch that was set out. Shakir was to arrive at Seronera Tented Safari Camp this evening, but I didn't see him because I drove back to Kirawira with Gerard, with me at the wheel. It is so much fun to drive a Land Rover, especially with the steering wheel on the right and shifting with my left hand. We passed through the great wildebeest migration again. They make a lot of grunting sounds. After dinner, Margot played the guitar. Such an enjoyable few days!

Gerard, Margot and I drove to Mwanza. It's a 2½ hour drive over a very bumpy road! We visited Olga in the afternoon, whom they had met on their first visit to Fort Ikoma. Yuri was off to Dar es Salaam and Lyuba was in Musoma for a Swahili course. Later, we had drinks with some of Gerard and Margot's friends and then we all went to the Yacht Club for dinner. They then took me back to Olga's where I spent the night.

The Victoria arrived the next morning about 8:00. It is one of the largest ships on Lake Victoria and carries passengers from one port to another. We could go onboard from 10:00 to 11:30. I was able to get a photo of me, Vicki (nickname Victoria), on the Victoria on Lake Victoria! How cool is that? Gerard, Margot and I joined some of their friends at the bar onboard. In Tanzania, it's the only place where one can get Kenya beer. Then we ran errands around town. The marketplace was very colorful. A fellow, about 20 years old, was standing in the middle of the marketplace, eating from a lunchbox, wearing tattered shorts with no zipper and his privates were hanging out. Won't Skip love to hear about that! Left Mwanza at 4:00 and arrived back at Kirawira about 6:45. A neat sunset and a nice evening. We all agreed that Mwanza is boring and would much rather be in the Serengeti.

I enjoyed another day in Kirawira until it got stifling hot in the afternoon. We made it an early evening as everybody was tired.

Gerard and I drove back to Fort Ikoma after breakfast, passing through lots of burned-out areas. We even had to stomp out part of a fire so that we could get through. There is no road from Kirawira to Fort Ikoma so travel is through the bush. This route has been done enough times that tracks are visible, but I would get thoroughly lost if I were driving. These people know the trees, the layout of the land, the direction of the sun, other markers I wouldn't even notice, to find their way to wherever their destination may be. No one needs a map.

Gerard, Putney and I hung out together in the afternoon. We climbed the water tower ladder to the top and I took some photos. What a fantastic view! Climbing down was scarier for me, but we managed quite well. Putney wanted her hair trimmed so I got some scissors and managed to do a decent job. A German hunter joined us for dinner. He had shot an eland which is the largest of the plains game antelope family and is excellent eating. Valerie had the chef prepare *sarara* (boneless roast) of eland. It is the tenderloin and he stuffed it with garlic cloves before roasting. It was delicious. We usually have zebra steak which eats like a cube steak, so this was a rare treat. It was a stifling hot night. The days are very dry and windy, no air movement at night, but plenty of mosquitos so we need to use the mosquito nets. This is the weather expected in June and July. This is early April and it's supposed to be the rainy season.

Gerard left for Kirawira about 11:00. I gave Putney a swimming lesson. It was a lazy day. Skip fixed chicken tetrazzini for dinner. Gideon and Michael from the Hunters Camp joined us. Then Putney got us all to dance after dinner.

Gideon was going to Arusha so I sent a roll of black and white film to have developed. Valerie and Mushi were off to Seronera. I wrote letters and a long one to Mom and Dad. Putney and I made brownies in the afternoon. I went to sleep at 8:00 and woke up the next morning at 10:00. It's been a jam-packed few weeks!

Putney and I were sitting out by the pool when the Robinson clan arrived, minus Ron and Larry. With them were friends of theirs, other SDA missionaries, Martha Martinsen, her daughter Valerie, and a Swedish couple, Terry and Veronica Joshua. Mrs. Robinson had brought us a gallon of peanut butter. They had come for a swim and to meet Ron and Larry and four others, who had been on a camping trip, for a picnic lunch down by the Grumeti River. Putney and I joined them. After lunch, we all came back to the Fort for a swim. We had a great game of keep-away in the pool. The Robinsons left about 4:30 and took Putney with them. She, Eddie and Freddie are about the same ages and have a lot of fun together. Valerie returned at 5:00. She said Seronera was deader than a door nail and there is absolutely no water! Gerard arrived to see if we wanted to go back to the Grumeti Tented Camp. Valerie couldn't go, but I could and we left about 6:00.

It was a beautiful drive back to Kirawira in the evening twilight. Though the distance between Fort Ikoma and Grumeti Tented Camp isn't that far, it takes about an hour to drive, with lots of shifting between 1st, 2nd and 3rd gears. We passed a great number of gnu. We saw a mama hyena and two baby pups, who were the cutest little fuzzy things. At Doyles' Drift, we surprised Alan Root who was bathing. He's in this area filming a sequel on the wildebeest migration. He had shot film that morning of a crocodile snatching a wildebeest as the gnu were crossing the Grumeti. He said that five had drowned and would be stinking up the river. He showed me how his Land Rover is outfitted for his camera equipment. A case was built to fit perfectly in the back seat. Lenses and camera equipment each have their own cutout in foam for storage so that they are protected while driving over rough terrain.

We arrived at camp to find 29 campers with Penn Overland, one of those cross-country camping safaris. They travel independently with their own provisions for camping and food for meals. Word travels through the bush and they probably heard about Grumeti Tented Camp and figured it was a good area for them as well.

Gerard and I did an early morning game run to look for the lions that sounded so close to camp last night. No luck finding the lions, but lots of wildebeest in the area. And we were treated to a rare sight – a giraffe was giving birth. The mother stood about 100 yards away from us, with her legs spread out. We arrived just in time to see the baby giraffe, somewhat protected in the amniotic sac, fall head first to the ground from a height of at least six feet. In no time that baby giraffe, which probably stood six feet tall, was up on its wobbly legs while the mother licked her baby clean. We didn't want to hang around, but felt so fortunate to have witnessed the birth.

Clients were to arrive today by plane before lunch, but as of 3:30 they were not here so we enjoyed a late lunch of chicken curry and papadums, a crispy tortilla-type Indian bread. There were lots of Vervet monkeys playing around between the mess tent and the river. It was hot and stifling, but overcast. Will it rain? The clients never arrived and there was no word. Gerard, Margot and I went on a game run at 5:30 and it started to rain. We checked out the crocodile pool where Alan Root had been filming the wildebeest crossing when some crocodiles grabbed some of them several days before. We saw no traces of gnu, only a few crocs swimming in the water. On the way back to camp, we came across eight hyenas, several of them pups, who played peekaboo with us from behind a thick bush. A little farther on we came across a lioness lying by the side of the road. Gerard held her fascinated with his lion noises. He described how to imitate a lion. Pretend you are blowing through a hose that is inside a trash can. She just sat and watched us. It rained off and on through the night. I could clearly hear the lions nearby; there must have been a kill.

Alan Root came for breakfast. The film he is working on now is about migration. He says the film takes about six to eight months to shoot, spread over several years. He does the filming, writing and editing of the script and then collaborates with someone in England on music and final editing. NBC airs his documentaries in the States, with Kraft and American Gas Co. as sponsors.

The German foursome arrived by air. This was the group that was expected the day before. The pilot, Phil Riddell, was a pleasant chap. He taught us how to play "twitch," of which I have no recollection of how it is played. It rained in the late afternoon and drizzled through dinner. We sat by the fire and sang to the tunes Margot played on her guitar. *Siafu* (safari ants) were crawling all around. They really come out when it rains. It's imperative to stay away from these ants because they have a mean bite and can eat an animal to the bone if the animal can't escape.

Gerard took the Germans on a game drive in the morning and then later Phil took Gerard, Margot and me up for a quick flight when he had to check out the plane before departing that day. Fun! Phil and the Germans flew off at 3:00. We went on a game run to the croc pool – saw a couple of big ones. Fortunately, we got back to camp before it rained hard in the late afternoon.

Gerard had to drive to the bank in Mwanza on Thursday and I decided to go with him. We left at 8:00 but didn't get there till 11:00 because the road to Ndabaka Gate was so bad with pools of water from the rains. Money was supposed to have been cabled to the Mwanza Bank by the head office and it had not arrived so the trip was unnecessary. We lunched at the New Mwanza Hotel and saw his friends Hans and Bryan whom I had met on our last trip to Mwanza. Phil surprised us. He had to land at Mwanza on the way to Bukoba because of bad weather. It rained in Mwanza at noon. We did a little shopping. Before leaving town we stopped by to see Olga and Yuri and I firmed up plans for Valerie's and my visit the last weekend in April. We left Mwanza at 4:45 and had car troubles about half an hour later which delayed us another 30 minutes. We made it to Ndabaka Gate a little after 7:00. This is the western gate to the Serengeti National Park and Kirawira is located within the boundaries. Fortunately, the guard let us through. We made it back to camp a little before 9:00. The road to camp was bad because it had rained heavily in the area that day. We found June Capon and Squeaky, her 15-month-old daughter, with Margot. They had gotten stuck about 4 miles from camp and had to walk. John had used another vehicle to go back to the car to get belongings. He arrived later. John and June will be running the camp when it reopens in June. They had come to see the tented camp before it closes down for six weeks. It's been a long day for everyone.

The next day we moved the mess tent to dryer land, but meals are now served under the three huge Tamarin trees in the open air, very delightful. No rain today.

Gerard had to go to the bank in Mwanza again because he needed to pay the staff. It closes early on Saturday so we got up at 5:00 a.m. and left for Mwanza at 6:20 in the Toyota pickup with seven *watu* (staff). We got stuck in black cotton mud about 10 miles from camp.

Everybody got out and had to find something to wedge under the tire for traction. Gerard was standing by the vehicle when his helper started up the truck and Gerard got splattered with mud. Oh, how we laughed! We finally were on our way once again, after having been delayed a good hour. We made it to Mwanza Bank at 10:30 (closes at 11:00 on Saturday). As he got out of the car, Gerard asked, "How do I look?" as he brushed off dried mud from his face and shirt. The money to pay the staff still had not been cabled, but John had written a check just in case and Gerard was able to cash it. The staff went off to spend their wages and Gerard and I headed to the bar at the New Mwanza Hotel where we each had two double *Konyagis* (Tanzania gin) before lunch – yow! Hans and Bryan were there, no surprise. We did some shopping and then rendezvoused with the staff and departed Mwanza at 3:45. It is 80 miles from the center of Mwanza to Ndabaka Gate and 20 miles from the gate to camp. No car problems on way back to camp, arriving at 6:30. The *siafu* were horrible!

The next afternoon we took off for a game run and had a puncture. Had to walk back to camp, about 1 mile. Always something.

On Monday we packed up and were off to Fort Ikoma at noon with the Toyota truck full to the brim with baggage, gear and eight people. Margot will come with the Capons. We dropped off his staff at FIL staff quarters. They will make their way to their home villages for a long vacation and then return when the camp reopens.

Gerard left after breakfast for Arusha and Dar es Salaam. I certainly hope he gets everything taken care of so he can leave for the States on the 25th, a week from now, for an International Game Conservation convention in San Antonio, Texas. Gerard is a resident of Tanzania. I don't recall if he carries a British passport or a Tanzania passport, or both. Apparently, to leave the country, he must prove that he doesn't owe any taxes.

The Capons and Margot arrived about 4:30. David Babu and Mcharo flew in here for about 45 minutes. After they left, Valerie and I headed to room 10 where she has been staying, to bathe before dinner. I had the drapes open and could look east across the plains. What I saw was a stunning moon rise. The last light of the day was on the hill and the plains were blue, with the almost full moon slowly ascending over the horizon. I hollered for Valerie to get out of the bathtub to enjoy the splendor, and then I ran over to herald Skip and Putney. Valerie joined us, wrapped in a big towel, and we all sat on room 11 terrace, listened to Pink Floyd's *Atom Heart Mother* on Skip's cassette player, and soaked in the view. As the moon rose, it would disappear behind the thin wispy clouds, then reappear, as if choreographed to the music. To this day, if I hear *Atom Heart Mother*, that incredible memory comes flooding back to me.

The Capons joined us for dinner. Margot was not feeling well. Gideon arrived about 9:30 to say his clients were in Robanda drinking beer because they had gotten stuck while out hunting and had to walk to Robanda. We all hopped into Skip's Land Rover, with beers in hand, and set out after them, stopping every two minutes for a bush stop because of all the beer we had been drinking. Met them along the road. They had hitched a ride on some huge lorry. Got them back to the Fort about 10:00, fed them dinner while we danced and a few went swimming.

Recce (reconnaissance) with Capons and Margot before lunch. Went as far as Nata. They wanted to scope out some possible campsites. Babu came for lunch. Not sure what he will be doing now that STSC has closed. We had *sarara* of eland for dinner, thanks to Gideon's hunter. Cocktail party beforehand in room 10 (ours) with Margot, Capons and Skip as guests. Brought out our reserve.

Up early and off to Arusha by 7:00 with Skip, Putney and Valerie. Skip had a meeting at 3:00. We stopped at Ngorongoro Crater Lodge for coffee and Mto-wa-mbu for petrol, making it to Arusha just in time for his meeting. Skip gave Valerie the checkbook and off we went shopping for some things needed for FIL. Happy day! The mail delivery included our balloon pictures. They are fantastic! Fortunately, they weren't ruined when the roll of film went into the pool with me. The last few photos on the roll, taken around the Fort, were streaked, but they weren't the critical ones.

Shakir joined us for dinner in the Grill Room at the New Arusha Hotel where we were spending the night. Afterwards, Valerie, Shakir and I went to see the John Wayne western *Big Jake* at the cinema. He was a popular actor here, having filmed the movie *Hatari* just outside

Arusha in 1961. We met up with Azghar afterwards. Valerie had been talking about this great hamburger drive-in that whet our appetites so off we went, but they were out of hamburgers.

Good Friday was a holiday in Arusha. As we were leaving our hotel room for breakfast, we ran into David Babu and joined him and Tumaini Mcharo for breakfast. They had flown in the day before for business. What a perfect opportunity to show them the balloon pictures!

We left at 10:30 after stopping at the Arusha open market for vegetables. Made it to Ngorongoro Crater Lodge about 1:30 where we had lunch. Left at 3:30 and drove straight through to Ikoma, arriving at 8:00. Total distance is 314 km. From the Naabi Gate pyramid that marks the eastern boundary of Serengeti National Park to Ikoma Gate, it takes an hour and 45 minutes to drive with no stops.

Mr. Robinson, Larry, Eddie and Freddie were camping about 7 miles from here and so they popped in for lunch. It started raining about noon and continued on through early afternoon so they stayed until the rain stopped. Valerie and I joined Skip and his Polish friends from Nairobi for dinner which was a fabulous *sarara* of eland. Such a treat!

Gideon brought a pangolin, a member of the armadillo family, which he had found in the *porini* (the bush). He put it in the turtle tree well where we had hoped it would stay, but alas, it escaped during the night. It's Easter today, but not celebrating it in any way. A lazy morning, read *Info Please Almanac*. I didn't feel well after lunch and went to bed about 4:00. It rained in the afternoon and a beautiful rainbow appeared. I could see the entire arch except for a portion near the peak that was partially covered by clouds. The colors were the most vivid I had ever seen. Valerie, Skip and Putney had dinner at the Hunters Camp, but I wasn't feeling well and didn't join them. It feels like the flu or maybe a touch of malaria. We take a daily anti-malaria pill as a prophylactic so if I do get malaria, it should be a mild case. It was a miserable night, though.

I had no appetite for breakfast, still not up to par. I did go to the dining room to bid *kwaheri* to Sue and Frank who were leaving after breakfast. Sue was Putt's teacher last year and she and her fiancé came for a visit over Easter weekend. I went back to bed and was awakened by Valerie and Ron about noon. Feeling much better, I went hunting with Ron, Larry and Mr. Robinson out to the area where we had gone camping. Larry got a warthog for me and an impala and Tommy for the Robinson family. Lots of giraffe, zebra and warthogs out there. We took a short foot safari along the riverbank. Upon my return, the warthog went immediately to the kitchen to be butchered. Warthog is actually quite tasty.

Gideon had brought up his clients, the Pauers, a lovely German couple, and Michael, who is working at the camp, for dinner and invited Valerie and me to join them. He had the kitchen staff prepare the birds the Pauers had shot that day. Michael's brother Rolf showed up with his ex-wife "Mütter" and two hippies in tow. Strange group. I turned in early and Valerie stayed for B&B's (Brandy and Benedictine).

Skip and Putt left after breakfast for Nairobi. It was a short school break, but so great to meet Putt and spend time with her. I helped Valerie in the office. We are skipping dinner for the next couple of nights, must lose weight!! Plus, neither one of us was feeling well. About 10:00, Daudi came knocking on our door to see if we were all right since he had not seen us in the dining room for dinner. As Valerie says, "It's not everyone who has their own personal Maasai checking up on them." So true. Everyone around here seems to have a touch of malaria or something.

It wasn't until the last Friday of April that we went to visit the Vishnyakovs. Valerie was feeling horrible and did not think she could make it to Mwanza, a 3½-hour drive over bumpy roads. A car arrived at 1:30 to pick us up. The driver gave her a note from Yuri saying "no excuse for not coming." We both hopped in the car and took off. It turned out to be a beautiful drive. Everything was so green and we saw lots of wildebeest. Olga had dinner ready for our arrival. The menu consisted of a cold fish dish in tomato ketchup, cabbage rolls, brains and more. After dinner, Yuri drove us up into the hills of Mwanza. We learned from him that the so-called Chinese trucks are really Russian trucks, same as the weapons, and not very good. Before bed, Valerie and I played scrabble with Lyuba. Valerie had a fabulous vocabulary. Me, not so much. Lyuba spelled a word on the board and Valerie challenged her on it. Lyuba got out the English dictionary, found the word, pointed it out to Valerie and said, "It's your language, not mine." Then we all laughed.

The next day we ate, ate, ate! Yuri pulled out the Russian vodka for lunch. He kept making toasts and we had to chug each shot down in one gulp. In the afternoon we drove into Mwanza to do some shopping. I bought a couple of *kangas*. I just love the different colors and patterns. Not sure what I will do with them, but they aren't expensive and very useful. Afterwards, we drove out to Bujora where a French-Canadian Roman Catholic priest has built a church in the style of a Sukuma house. The Sukuma live in this region and the church houses a museum showcasing their styles and traditions. We found it very interesting. The priest told us that he has had much trouble with Rome because of his unorthodox ways, but he has had great success here. Friends of the Vishnyakovs joined us for dinner that evening. Carmela is Spanish and her husband Ibrahim Bhati is Pakistani. They have two young sons, Yusef and Isaco (10 months). A darling family.

Sunday morning breakfast was red caviar and vodka. Yummy! Olga cooked up some Russian sausage which is made from beef. The Bhatis came over for lunch and Olga made *shashlek*, the Russian version of shish kebabs. *Shish* in Russian means "nothing." After much wine and cognac with lunch, we all drove out to a Catholic mission where a Spanish priest lives and who Carmela needed to visit. Lovely gardens.

Not that I was hungry, but for dinner we had a Siberian specialty, *pelmini*, a Russian ravioli, only better and served with thick cream. I could eat only ten, but Olga informed us that in the Soviet state of Georgia, which must be the party capital of the USSR, one would plan 100 *pelmini* per person along with at least 5 liters of wine per person. These are the people who live to a ripe, old age. Olga said that the parties last for days and people sleep wherever they can find a spot, like under the dining room table. Needless to say, we did not go hungry!

Juma, the driver who was to drive Valerie and me back to Fort Ikoma was sick so Yuri drove us back. Olga decided to come along. We were stopping by a *duka* on the way out of town and I suggested that since tomorrow was May Day, a holiday, why not get Lyuba out of school and all of them spend the night at the Fort. They thought that was a splendid idea and that is what they did. We made a stop in Ikuzu to look at ivory jewelry (poached, no doubt) and ostrich egg necklaces. Yuri hit some terrible bumps and I thought the car was a goner twice, but those Peugeots are amazing. We were back at the Fort about 3:00. We all went swimming and then had dinner and turned in early. Everyone was tired, and probably a little hungover, too.

Tanzanian Dignitaries, History, Holidays

T uesday, May 1st is a holiday, much like our Labor Day. We enjoyed pool time with the Vishnyakovs in the morning and then they left after lunch. It had been a great visit with them, but we were beat and went back to bed, skipping dinner because who could be hungry after this weekend? Soon there was a *"hodi, hodi, hodi."* It was Peter Luhte who had arrived with a Unitours group. He had been Valerie and Linda's courier when they came on safari in October 1971. So happy to meet him!

On the 2nd, I helped Valerie with her first of the month inventory. Furniture from Seronera Tented Safari Camp arrived. It will be used in Valerie's tent. We hope to move in soon. Made sukiyaki for dinner. Always a treat to have something "off" the menu.

Valerie and I had been planning a Cinco de Mayo fiesta for this coming Saturday. On Wednesday we learned that we had to postpone it until the following weekend because Aboud Jumbe, the President of Zanzibar who, therefore, also serves as Vice President of Tanzania, would be coming to Fort Ikoma this weekend with an entourage of 50 or more.

Present-day Tanzania was colonized by Germany in 1885 and was called German East Africa. The military built an administrative fort at Ikoma, in the northern Serengeti plains. After Germany was defeated in WWI, the area became a British mandate under the League of Nations and the area was given the name Tanganyika. In 1946, Tanganyika became a United Nations Trust Territory under British administration. The leader for independence was a teacher by the name of Julius Nyerere, one of only two Tanganyikans with a university education. He formed the TANU party (Tanganyika African National Union) in 1954. Independence was achieved on December 9, 1961, but retained the British Monarch and Julius Nyerere became Prime Minister. A year later, a republican constitution was implemented and *Mwalimu* Julius Nyerere became the first president of Tanganyika. *Mwalimu* is Swahili for teacher and is how the people addressed him.

The island of Zanzibar has a very rich history. It was under Portuguese rule during the 16th and 17th centuries and then under Arab rule until it became a British protectorate in 1890. Zanzibar and the nearby island of Pemba were world famous for the spice trade and became known as the Spice Islands. In 1964, Tanganyika and Zanzibar united to form the United Republic of Tanganyika and Zanzibar. A few months later it was changed to United Republic of Tanzania. Tanzania is a blend of the two names. I never did get to Zanzibar, though I heard such colorful stories of its Arab culture and architecture. Zanzibar still has somewhat of an autocratic government.

Mwalimu guided the country to one-party rule and introduced *Ujamaa*, a form of socialism. By 1967 all companies had been nationalized and Tanzania was economically dependent on Red China (The Peoples Republic of China). The Chinese were building a railroad across the central part of the country from Dar es Salaam to landlocked Zambia. The gauge of the railroad tracks is narrower than European trains, thus ensuring dependency on Chinese manufactured trains.

Tanzania's form of government has a President, Vice President and Prime Minister. When I was there in 1973, *Mwalimu* Julius Nyerere was President. The President of Zanzibar, Aboud Jumbe, served as the Vice President, and Rashidi Kawawa was the Prime Minister. All three of these men made visits to Fort Ikoma while I was there. I did not meet any of them, but I was present.

The entrance to Fort Ikoma was all decorated for Jumbe's visit. Twine had been tied overhead from the front entrance towers to trees along the driveway. Strips of colorful *kitenge* cloth were tied to the string every 12 inches or so. In between each strip of cloth was tied a small cluster of bougainvillea flowers. It was so festive and colorful. Everybody was ready and waiting by 11:00. A truckload of school children from Musoma arrived to entertain Jumbe with singing. There were two groups, the youngest were about five and the oldest were in their teens. Jumbe and his entourage finally arrived at 2:15. David Babu was among the arrivals. After all had lunch, everyone moved onto the terrace for entertainment. The older kids sang first, then the younger ones. The final performers were the Ikoma lion dancers with our very own Rashidi as one of the six dancers. They wore headdresses of lion mane and dressed in colorful loincloths. A few of them had beaded body vests with shoulder straps. Rashidi did not have on either the mane headdress or the beaded vest, but because he is of the Ikoma tribe and he worked at Fort Ikoma, he was allowed to participate. Later, I asked Rashidi the significance of the blue paint decorating his arms. He answered, "It's what we found in the storeroom." It started to rain during the performance so everyone moved into the dining room and dancing continued. Jumbe and others gave short speeches in Swahili, then retired to their rooms. We had dinner with David Babu and David Mlongo, the Regional Director from Bunda. Joseph Nyerere, President Nyerere's brother is also here because of Jumbe's visit. He lives in Butiama, the Nyerere family village, and will start supplying Valerie with eggs and vegetables from his *shamba*.

Everyone departed the next day. The Fort had been notified that Jumbe would stay the 4th, 5th and 6th. That is why we cancelled the Cinco de Mayo party to which we had invited all of our friends in Seronera and at the Serengeti Research Institute (SRI). Turned out we could have had it anyway. Bryan Payne, manager at Seronera Wildlife Lodge, arrived at 6:00, totally unaware the party had been canceled, so we made a dance tape and danced!

This is considered the rainy season so tourism really slows down. This is good news for Bryan because he is still experiencing water issues at the new Seronera Wildlife Lodge. The story goes that there is 60 miles of PVC pipe that travels from the well source to the lodge. The Chinese manufactured the pipe and drilled the hole off center. When pressure builds up, the pipe will burst somewhere over the course of the 60-mile length. Then the engineer has to find the break and repair it. And then the problem repeats itself again, and again, and again. Bryan sure appreciated the shower he was able to take at Fort Ikoma! He left at 11:00 the next morning.

I organized the cassette tapes I have recorded for Skip and then made chili. I also tried making tarts using treacle. They were horrible! Treacle is like a heavy molasses. Mcharo and his six-year old daughter Vita flew in for a visit and left before the late afternoon rains. Mario and a lorry arrived around 5:00. There were no guests. Mario made spaghetti for dinner and then the three of us enjoyed the evening rain.

Valerie and I are enjoying the slow time. We made German pancakes for lunch. Yum Yum. Mario had left with the lorry. He returned the next day in the late afternoon with the Cold Room from Seronera Tented Safari Camp. With that safari camp being disbanded, the equipment and vehicles are being relocated to Fort Ikoma and Ngorongoro Crater Lodge. Mario will install the Cold Room here. David Mlongo was passing through. He invited us to come to Seronera Sunday night for a big dance celebrating the passing through of *Mwenge wa Uhuru*, the freedom torch.

With Mario here, we made pizza for lunch and then he left right afterwards. We sat on the terrace and watched the many wildebeest down the hill, what a noise they make! This is the time of the year that the wildebeest migration passes by Fort Ikoma, grazing in clusters as they make their way north to Maasai Mara. It rained in the afternoon. Joseph Nyerere arrived and joined us for sukiyaki which I had made for dinner. He is an interesting fellow. He is the full *kabisa* brother of the president of Tanzania, Julius Nyerere. Their father had 22 wives, and they are 2 of 6 children with the same mother. The family is from Butiama.

Sunday, May 13th was Valerie's birthday. Mushi, Dionisia, and Joseph Nyerere joined us for breakfast. I gave her a Meerschaum *kiko* (pipe). Meerschaum is mined near Kilimanjaro and Mother, Dad and I had visited the factory near Arusha. Valerie and I made her birthday cake in the afternoon during a heavy rainstorm. Once again, we made sukiyaki for dinner since there were no guests and so all kitchen staff had gone back to staff quarters. It is so easy and a great way to use the fresh vegetables being supplied by Joseph Nyerere. At 8:30 Mushi came into the kitchen where we were and said that Julee had just arrived with seven people with a booking he made in March. Julee is a local guide who brings clientele on occasion. Mushi had to go get the cooks from staff quarters to feed the group. Valerie cut her birthday cake after Julee's tour finished dinner, then we had a dance. Our dance music tape is A-OK and coming in very handy!

We had a very interesting conversation with Joseph later that evening. We had heard talk about the government requiring the Maasai to abandon their traditional dress and be required to wear western clothing. Valerie and I could not fathom this. He explained the reasoning behind it, though doubted that it would implemented. He said that the African has never had to plan for tomorrow. If he needs food, he can forage it from the land. If he needs shelter, he can build it from available materials like trees, bushes, mud. If he needs clothing, he can kill an animal and use the skin. The African does not need to store provisions for cold seasons. All these materials are available all year long. To come into the 20th century, perhaps it was necessary to adopt some western ways. It got me to thinking, the most advanced civilizations of modern times are in the colder climates where short growing seasons necessitate the need to plan ahead and store provisions for the winter. Around the equator, where the temperature doesn't vary much and might only be categorized as the rainy or dry season, a mañana attitude is prevalent. I responded that I may have a college education, but I wouldn't survive out in the bush on my own. I wouldn't know which plants are edible and which are not. Which ones can be used for medicine? The African living the way his ancestors have for centuries knows this. Who is the smarter one after all?

At 10:00 the next morning, the entourage with *Mwenge wa Uhuru* arrived. Once a year the freedom torch makes a journey through Tanzania. Today it came by Fort Ikoma on its way to Mwanza from Seronera. The idea of the torch sprang from a speech *Mwalimu* Nyerere made in 1960 before Independence, something to the effect of "Let us bring light where there is darkness, let us bring truth where there are untruths, let us bring happiness where there is sadness, etc." This was explained to us by Joseph Nyerere.

Joseph said that it was not until 1964 when he, as secretary general of TANU youth group, suggested that the youths carry a torch symbolizing the speech by Julius Nyerere through Tanzania as a reminder of *Mwalimu's* philosophy. Julius had been a teacher before getting involved with independence and politics. All the officials arrived first and immediately proceeded into the dining room for breakfast. About 10 to 15 minutes later, a group of about 30 Africans, the women in colorful *kitenges,* came up the hill chanting:

Oooh TANU, *yajenga nchi* (sung 3 times)

TANU, oooh

Oooh TANU, *yajenga nchi* (repeat).

Translated this means "TANU builds the nation," Nyerere, or *Mwalimu,* or Jumbe, or political party name, or Afro can be substituted for TANU. TANU is the national party. One member of the group carried the torch which is a gold-painted 5-pound tin can with the top cut into points as on a crown. The torch is mounted inside the can and the whole affair is mounted on a beautifully grained and polished reddish brown wooden pole. They marched around the Fort chanting and then departed. Don't know if these people were locals or not, but presumably so. Someone was selling *Mwenge* shirts for TSh 20/= so Valerie and I each bought one. On the shirt was a picture of the monument in Arusha (with Kilimanjaro in the background) which was built after the Arusha Declaration of 1967 when Nyerere announced that Tanzania was going socialist. The monument is a graceful construction of a freedom torch. Poor Joseph Nyakachara was too late to buy a shirt and wanted Valerie or me to give him ours. You are out of luck, Joseph!

It was customary that staff took long vacations since they worked seven days a week for several months straight. They would go back to their home village to visit their wives and children. Cha Cha was one of the cooks in the kitchen. He came back very distraught after his vacation. His wife and children had been forcefully moved from their home and little *shamba* to an *Ujamaa* Village, a collective farm concept that was implemented by President Nyerere's socialist government. It was not a voluntary program either. Yes, she and her children were given housing and a *shamba*, but everything she grew had to be taken to the collective market. The man next door contributed nothing to the marketplace, yet he could get anything he wanted from it. Cha Cha's wife had no more than a 6th grade education, but she could readily see the unfairness in the program and was not happy to be there at all. Maybe the accommodations were newer and nicer than their former home, but that had been their own little plot of land and what they raised was theirs.

Too Bad You Can't Make It

I t was one of those still, hot days when the only noise was the buzz of a fly. This was supposed to be the wet season when it may rain for only an hour a day, but the rains are unpredictable and they play havoc with the roads, thus it is the slow tourist season. With no tours coming through, I was bored for the first time since I had arrived in Africa. Kicking a pebble provided some diversion.

This particular day, absolutely no one was around during lunch time. The Freedom Torch had come and gone. The generators were running their customary few hours in the afternoon. Off in the distance I could see dust stirring up. A vehicle was approaching from the direction of the Serengeti National Park. With visibility of 50 plus miles, it would be at least 30 minutes before this vehicle would arrive. Fort Ikoma is very remotely located, guaranteeing that it is either the destination or at least a stop on the way to somewhere else for the vehicle approaching.

Valerie and I were going into the dining room for lunch. It was dead. Usually there weren't many tourists having lunch. Most tour groups plan day sightseeing trips and the kitchen prepares box lunches for them. But this day felt different. This day was dullsville.

As Val and I were eating, in came Mario. It was his "gypsy" truck that had been stirring up the dust. He was here to check the generators again. We invited him to join us for lunch, which he quickly did. In his Italian-accented English he proceeded to tell us about this hunting safari he would be going on in a few days with his Greek friend, Costas. Costas Zikakis was the taxidermist for Tanzania and had contracts from Japan for lion and leopard. Mario kept punctuating his conversation with, "Too bad you can't make it. It would be so much fun!"

After lunch Mario went out to work on the generators and then, as was his usual custom, he would go into the kitchen and make fresh pasta for dinner. Mario always traveled with his hand-crank Atlas pasta machine. It was great fun to watch him work the flour, eggs and water and then roll out the delicate noodles. He'd whip up a sauce with whatever was available and we would then all savor his heavenly dinner.

The next day, as Mario prepared to leave, Valerie distracted him while I snuck into "Gypsy" and pinched the pasta maker that sat beside him on the front seat. We gaily waved off Mario, suppressing our laughter until he couldn't see us. An hour later, Mario returned in a huff. He had discovered the missing pasta machine and came back to fetch it. Darn! As he drove off, he waved and hollered once again, "Too bad you can't go on the hunting safari." With that Valerie and I looked at each other and asked, "Why can't we go on the safari? What's keeping us here?"

Packing never took us more than a few minutes. Valerie and I would share four pairs of jeans and six shirts. We could pack in our camera bags and that's what we did.

A toothbrush, toothpaste, a bar of soap, contact solution for Val and we were ready. Valerie and I hitched a ride with Rajabu at 1:00 for Seronera. Raja delivered goods to Fort Ikoma and Seronera.

Once there, we went to the Serengeti Research Institute (SRI) to look for a lorry that was supposed to leave that day for Arusha. We couldn't find it. We put the ballooning pictures in Mike Norton-Griffiths' box and then went over to Ndosi's. Manka was there. Apparently Obadiah has found someone and I am ever so happy for him. Ndosi said that we could have a ride on a Serengeti National Park lorry that was going to Arusha the next day. The driver told Ndosi that Chubi, the NUTA secretary had wanted a ride, but Ndosi cancelled that because Chubi had been giving Ndosi and David a lot of *matata* (problems). Val and I spent the night in the new Seronera Wildlife Lodge in a suite next to Bryan's. Ndosi joined us for dinner.

On Tuesday, May 15th, we were at the Park's headquarters by 9:00 for our ride. The lorry didn't depart until noon. Mzee Omari was the driver, a darling little African Muslim. This 7-ton lorry was quite comfortable to ride in over the dirt roads. We stopped at Ngorongoro Crater Lodge to see Justis. We also stopped in Karatu for tea while Omari ran errands. Then we stopped in Mto-wa-Mbu for more errands. These stops, plus intermittent ones for "Joseph, *weka maji!*" (bring water!") for the overheating radiator – Joseph was Omari's helper – made the trip nine hours.

We arrived at the New Arusha Hotel just before Shakir drove up. Shakir was expecting us and had made reservations. We checked in and then met Shakir for dinner. We went looking for Mario afterwards to tell him that we had arrived and, if his invitation to go on the week hunting safari was still open, that we were here and would be ready to leave early the next morning. We found him at his friend Maurice's home. Mario was shocked, but happy, to see us and said that the safari had been delayed a day.

Arusha

Valerie and I moved over to Mario's house the next day (Wednesday), in time for lunch of fresh fish that he broiled and then served with a deliciously simple sauce made by pouring boiling water over chopped fresh parsley and chopped garlic. He then drove us out to Tanzania Taxidermy to meet Costas who has organized the hunting safari. Costas seemed okay with the two of us coming along, which was good news for us. Mario had received word in the morning that generator #3 at Fort Ikoma had gone out so he had to leave the next day to fix it. That meant that the safari had to be delayed until the following Monday. Costas came over to Mario's for dinner and then afterwards we drove out to see Kilimanjaro at sunset, but there were too many clouds. We did get a good view of Mt. Meru, though. *Kilimanjaro* is a Swahili word and means "little mountain of the witch" because of the rumbling noises its three volcanoes made while active. *"Kilima"* means "little mountain." There are actually two prominent peaks and a third smaller peak on the Kilimanjaro mountain range. *Kibo* is the snowy dormant volcano's crater rim and *Mawenzi* is the jagged peak. *Mawenzi* and *Shira*, west of *Kibo*, are extinct volcanos.

Mario left for Fort Ikoma before we got up. We decided to first go shopping in the open-air market which is so colorful! The women are dressed in the bright *kitenges* and we couldn't help but buy some *kitenges* for ourselves. Some vendors had tables and others spread *kitenges* on the ground and set up their baskets of goods. So many things for sale – fruits, vegetables, grains, herbs and potions for healing, pots, pans, dishes, baskets, *pangas*, hatchets, clothes, jewelry and more. Many of the women vendors, as well as shoppers, were carrying their babies on their backs, swaddled with *kitenges*, and nursing on demand. There were lots of Maasai women with their shaved heads and beaded jewelry. It's a noisy place with so many people talking and buzzing with activity. We lunched at the hamburger stand next to the cinema and then headed over to the New Arusha Hotel to see if anyone we knew was around. Pilot Phil Riddell was there. An acquaintance of his joined us for a Coke. Turns out the fellow knows Jogi, knew where his workshop was and took us there. Jogi was thrilled to see us and took us to his home where we met his wife, son and Charin. They invited us over for a curry dinner the next evening with the Singh family.

Arusha had a population of 43,000 in 1973 with a centralized business area so it was easy to get around. It wasn't difficult to encounter people who we knew. We had seen Azghar the day before and had accepted his invitation for dinner this evening. We went by his office to see if he was back from his overnight trip to Ngorongoro, but he wasn't. Then we headed over to the shoe repair to pick up the shoes we had dropped off the day before. The restitched sole repair was well done. The shop is pretty bare. Four men are making and repairing shoes. They sit on the floor with knees bent and holding the shoe being worked on between their bare feet. Scraps of leather litter the floor. A girl in the corner is sewing clothes on a treadle sewing machine. Azghar never made it back so we amused ourselves that evening. This is the way of Africa. Communication is difficult at best, so many times plans don't materialize because one is delayed and has no way of getting in touch with the other party. The rule of thumb is that you don't worry about someone until the person is two days late!

On Friday we met Charin at 10:00 to go shopping. I wanted to buy an Indian rolling pin, tapered on the ends and used for making chapatis, but couldn't find one. We also looked for a clay bowl which chapatis can be cooked on over a gas stove, but had no luck, supposedly available next week. Charin pointed out the four men, each sitting behind his own table filled with an assortment of bottles. She explained that these are the doctors and people come to buy different potions and herbs guaranteed to cure any number of ailments. I bought some gifts at a curio shop, including a small Zanzibar chest for Mom and Dad. It is intricately carved with brass hinges, tacks and hasp. We went by Azghar's office again and he was back so we nabbed him to take us on errands for which we needed a car. But first we had tea and samosas at the new Naaz Hotel. I had wanted to look at batiks so Azghar took us to Kantans. I decided on one with a flamingo and before I knew it, Azghar had bought it for me and then refused to leave until Valerie chose one. She selected a beautiful orange one of a

Maasai maiden. Quite stunning. After drinks at the New Arusha Hotel with Azghar, we headed over to Jogi's for dinner.

To be a dinner guest in the home of an Indian family for a home-cooked feast was a fantastic experience. There had to be 15 of us. Jogi's family included his wife, three children, parents, brothers, sisters and in-laws. The women did the cooking while the men talked. It was fascinating to watch the women prepare the meal. They all are dressed in colorful saris with arms festooned with 18- and 22-carat gold bangle bracelets. Gold rings adorn their slim fingers and gold earrings adorn the lobes. The painted dot on the forehead is cosmetic and the color is coordinated with the sari. The chicken curry had been simmering for several hours and now one of the women was seasoning it. On the counter was a brass box, approximately 8 inches x 12 inches. It was divided into 24 compartments, 2-inches square, and each holding different dried spices. She would take a pinch of this and a pinch of that to season the curry and the spinach side dish.

I loved watching Charin make the *chapatis* which are similar to our tortillas. At least two chapatis per person will be made for the evening meal. This preparation is a daily ritual. She mixed whole wheat flour with a little water. Then she wet her knuckles, formed her hand into a fist and bore down on the dough to knead it. She heated up the heavy flat griddle as she took a ball of the dough, about the size of an egg. It was like a choreographed ballet: Roll ball between palms, dip ball into flour, put on wood board, roll with rolling pin, flip, roll, dip in flour, roll, pick up, flip on hot griddle, turn over, turn over again when underside gets even brown spots. Put into oven to keep warm while rolling out another one. When that next one goes into the oven, take the previous one out of oven, put slightly undone (or first) side back on griddle to brown slightly, then store in napkin-lined tin. Repeat this procedure until all the chapatis are made. She had to make a lot because we were a big group. Her slim arms adorned with gold bangles danced as she expertly took a little flour and water and cooked up the delicious unleavened bread for the curry dinner. She shared some tips with me. When rolling, do not press hard and use ever so faintly a circular motion so dough forms a fairly thin, but not too thin, round chapati. When cooking, use a toweled hand to press down sides because dough will have a tendency to puff up in the center. She described to me other flat breads of Indian cuisine. A *purri* is a chapati that has been deep-fat fried rather than griddled. A *papadum* is made out of rice flour and deep-fat fried. A *deburah* is a chapati which is grilled about 3/4 done, then buttered on both sides before being grilled some more. The special cornmeal chapati is flattened with the hands as a corn tortilla is.

At dinnertime, we all crowded around the table and ate in true Indian fashion with the fingers of our right hand. Chapatis are torn and used to scoop up the curry and side dishes. The curry was so hot that it even made Jogi cry. As he says, that's the sign of a good curry. I must have been bawling! The cold beer was a welcome companion to the hot curry. Dinner consisted of chicken curry, a mashed-up spinach dish with peppers and lightly fried in mustard seed flavored oil, chapatis, papadums, rice for those who wanted it, and cut-up fresh vegetables. It's an Indian custom to have a sink by the table for washing hands after dinner. It was truly an enjoyable evening.

Jogi is a Sikh. Sikhs are the warriors of India. All Singhs are Sikhs and the men wear turbans and never cut their hair. Some Sikhs do cut their hair and don't wear a turban as does Jogi's brother, Jite. The Indians still practice arranged marriages by the parents and a third party. The couple must be from the same community and of course, be of the same religion. We learned that Jogi's sister lives in Phoenix and her husband manages a Truly Nolan branch there, a company that Valerie and I are familiar with.

On Saturday, I was in the mood to bake so made a cake for our safari. Mario returned about 11:00. Azghar came soon afterwards to take us on a tour of the Meerschaum factory. Unfortunately, a delegation of Yugoslavian officials arrived at the factory before us and so we decided to come back another day. We went to Tusker Brewery instead and had a tour of it. Such big beautiful copper vats. Azghar took us to lunch at the New Arusha Hotel. He entertained us with customs of the Indians such as arranged marriages. The eldest must marry first. Azghar is eldest, over 30 and not married, which means his siblings can't get married. It is a paternalistic society whereby the sons bring their wives to the family home to live. If a husband goes to live with his wife's family, it is usually because she comes from a very wealthy family. The husband is referred to as a duke in this case and it is quite an enviable position. Azghar's family comes from Punjab, the same area that Jogi does, but he is of the Muslim faith and does cut his hair.

I rested in the afternoon. Mario had his house boy Joseph wring three of his chickens to take on the safari. That's self-sufficiency! Mario has a regular menagerie - six dogs (three grown, three pups), three fish aquariums, two roosters, five hens, seven chicks. He did have five roosters but not after Joseph wrung the necks of three. He also has one cross-eyed Siamese cat and one black cat that is supposed to be a Siamese but isn't. His name is Mr. Jimmy. He has taught his German Shepherds the command *"Raus!"* which is German for "out."

Azghar picked us up at 5:00 and drove us out to Lake Duluti which is about 11 miles east of Arusha. This is the lake where Mario goes fishing and every year wins all the trophies for the record catches. I got some good pictures, including Mario's boat, but Mt. Meru hid behind a cloud. There is an old lodge near the lake which must have been quite nice in its day but is now only patronized by town people. The lake is quite a ways off the main road to Moshi and the drive took us through a coffee plantation. Afterwards, we drove out to von Nagy's Meru game sanctuary to see about dinner, but they are not serving until next Tuesday. Von Nagy's is quite a charming place and where Mom, Dad and I had stayed in January. The tiny living room/lounge is so homey with a lovely fire burning in the fireplace. Great elephant tusks straddle the fireplace and skins and trophies decorate the place. Very ranch-like in an African motif.

We drove out to Kilimanjaro International Airport which is 27 miles east of Arusha and 21 miles west of Moshi. Right now the airport is out in the middle of nowhere and the closest hotels are in Moshi and Arusha. The airport opened up a few months ago and is absolutely beautiful, modern and large. It was designed and constructed by Italians. Unfortunately, present traffic includes one plane a day because there is not enough bed space in Arusha or Moshi to handle the passengers that would fly in. Presently, plans are on the board to build a 60-bed hotel outside of Arusha and it is rumored a Japanese firm is thinking of building a 600-bed hotel at the airport. Another problem is a shortage of cement. The airport is a beauty and will have a wonderful future providing accommodations can be met.

We raced back to Arusha to grab a bite at Jambo Snack and then to the cinema to see *Fiddler on the Roof*. We arrived at Mario's just as he was returning from the Gymkhana Club. He persuaded us to go back with him, getting there at 1:00 a.m. It was still going strong – drinking, dancing, dart game finals. Jimmy who showed us around the brewery was there, a Dick, a Roland, a Barclay, and more of the "gang." I think Mario wanted to show us off. I played some snooker with Azghar. We finally left about 3:30 a.m., very tired, but not before helping Barclay find his one and a half-ton Land Rover that he had misplaced.

Thank goodness we had no plans on Sunday. I slept until noon! Azghar came over and we went out to get some chapatis to make "tortilla" chips for the guacamole that Valerie and I were making. Quite tasty! We also picked up some *pilau* (rice pilaf) and chicken curry. It was a lazy day.

Mario made stuffed pepperonis with fresh heavy cream for dinner. He stuffed the hollowed out green peppers with a ragout made of rice, minced meat, sautéed onions, tomatoes and seasonings. They were placed in a casserole dish and his secret is to add a cup of boiling water to the pan to help them steam and keep them moist while they simmer for half an hour. They were served with heavy cream. Divine!

Costas came over and we finalized plans for our safari. We are leaving early tomorrow morning.

Hunting Safari

On Monday, May 21st, we were up at 5:00 a.m. and off at 6:00 for the much anticipated hunting safari. Seven of us climbed into the short-wheelbase Land Rover, or should I say, stuffed ourselves into it. Costas, Mario, Valerie and I squeezed into the front seat. Mbangi, the gun bearer, Ndoho, the *mpisi* (cook), and Marusu, the skinner, were sprawled atop the supplies loaded into the back. Even if we hadn't joined the group, at least two of them would have been relegated to the back anyway. Costas' Land Rover was also pulling a fully loaded trailer with tent gear and 55-gallon barrels of water and petrol. Costas was the driver and Mario sat shotgun. That meant that either Valerie or I was seated next to Costas and had the gear shift between our knees. When Costas said "shift," we shifted. Team work!

In the still dark early morning we headed for Maasai land and a Game Scout Camp about 42 miles south of Arusha. Along the way we bought some fresh corn before heading into the interior. We stopped periodically so that Mario could shoot partridges or guinea fowl which would be used as meat for our meals.

At one point we passed six *sikoliu*. This is the stage before *morani* for a Maasai warrior. The stage lasts about one month and commences right after circumcision. The *sikoliu* were wearing blackish burlap-like garments

123

(caveman style) and had black feathery looking headdresses hanging down the back. Their faces were painted with a white paint in a spiderweb pattern on the forehead and on the cheeks from the nose to the ears. They looked very black and Halloweenish. Occasionally, we passed Maasai guarding their cattle. They were *morani,* distinguished by their ocher-ed hair. Yarn is braided into their hair and then the red-earthed ocher is applied. They wear only a blanket wrapped around and another over the shoulder usually concealing one arm; the free arm holds the spear. They love jewelry and wear beaded necklaces, bracelets, and belts around their stomach under the outer blanket, and earrings in their pierced ears. The women dress somewhat the same way, but wear much more jewelry. Jewelry depicts beauty and the more the better. The beaded necklaces are disk-shaped, but do not lie flat on the neck and are quite wide. They wear silver coil bracelets on the upper arm which are very attractive. Not too sure how these bracelets are put on and look as though they will never be removed. Red beads predominate their jewelry.

We arrived at our campsite about 3:00, a beautiful flat open area with several large umbrella acacia trees. We set up the tents, one for Valerie and me, one for Costas and Mario, one for the cook tent. Each tent had a large fly sheet overhang to provide a porch of sorts. Inside, Valerie and I had cots with blankets and a small canvas wash basin. The cots might have been for Costas and Mario, until we crashed their safari, not sure what they had in their tent. Had we not come along, Costas and Mario each would have had a tent to himself. The three staff slept in the cook tent. The food preparation took place under the fly sheet and cooking was done on the fire pit that was about 15 feet away from the tents, in an open area. Costas had a tent rigged on top of his Land Rover. Collapsed, it rested above the roof on a metal frame. He had designed this so that he could climb into it from the hood of the vehicle if he was at some location without adequate space to pitch a tent. We didn't need it on this safari, but he did put it up once for me to see. Small, but adequate for one person.

After setting up camp, we went looking for *maji* (water) and also signs of lion and leopard. We came across several water holes, but no usable water. No signs of lion or leopard either. The clean drinking water that we brought with us in a large drum had to be used sparingly. Two Maasai teenage *morani* came to visit us at camp and chatted with the cook. Their cattle practically walked through our camp, bringing with them lots of flies. The Maasai are a curious people and we are camping on their land so we are respectful of their ways. From them we learned of some water wells nearby which provided water that could be boiled and used for washing. "Wells" might be a little misleading. They were natural occurring sunken holes in the ground. One had to carefully climb down the steep side to reach the water level which was about five feet below ground level. Lots of green algae and who knows what else floated on top of the water, but at least there was a water source. Sponge baths would be the order of the day and we only had one or two changes of clothes. Or, as Valerie and I liked to do, "today I will wear the brown cords and you can wear the blue cords." At least that gave us a change. We could rinse out our shirts and hang to dry. One night Costas offered to "iron" my shirt by putting it under his pillow and sleeping on it.

We enjoyed a nice dinner of Mario's moussaka. He brought out the Ouzo beforehand and we all had a little taste. It is made from grapes and flavored with anise which gives it a licorice taste. After dinner we had a visitor way out here. News definitely travels fast through the bush. Young Gerald Miller, a professional hunter and son of a professional hunter, was looking for some crazy Bob Brown, a fellow of tall tales according to Mario and Costas. They referred to Miller as a cheeky bastard who hasn't learned his manners yet. We all turned in about 10:00. Valerie and I are in the large tent and Mario and Costas are in a tent that almost blew away. I fell right to sleep, but woke up and thought it was time to get up because I heard Mario and Costas' voices. I fell back to sleep, and woke up again at 5:30 to Mario and Costas' voices. Found out that they had to shoo *fisi* (hyena) out of camp at 2:00 a.m. and that *tembo* (elephant) were near camp at dawn.

Day 2 – After a cup of tea, we four plus Mbangi and Marusu took off to hunt for leopard bait and look for *maji*. Of the seven of us on this safari, I am the only one who did not smoke. Sitting in the front seat with three smokers, smoke was constantly wafting my way. Every so often I would bum a cigarette off of someone just so I could blow smoke in their faces. Apparently, I was not inhaling because the smoke I blew out was white, not the shade of gray it is after it has passed through the lungs. That was fine by me. And it turns out that having a pack of cigarettes is a good idea in case a fuse goes out in the vehicle. One simply takes the foil liner out of the cigarette box and wraps a piece around the fuse, reinserts, and it works like a charm until a new fuse can be found for replacement.

Mario got some partridges and guinea fowls. He shot a male impala with a beautiful rack, but didn't bring it down. We spent an hour looking for it and couldn't find it so we pressed on and Costas got a Grant's gazelle. He will use the cape, along with the skull and horns, to make a head mount. The rest of the animal will be used as bait. The only other wildlife we saw were a few Thomson's gazelles, but none worth using. We drove to a spot that looked like a leopard's haven with lots of bushes, big acacia trees and water holes nearby so we dragged the gazelle for about 3 miles in the selected area to make a trail of scent. As we passed a herd of Maasai cattle, the cows got excited by the dead carcass and were very curious. We found a good tree and hung the gazelle from a high branch with rope. The gazelle was hanging by the feet but high enough off the ground so that hyena or lions could not reach it. The leopard will have to walk out onto the limb and lean to the side closest to the blind to eat. We then built the blind about 60 to 65 yards from the tree. Three Maasai boys came over to check things out. The Maasai do not want their pictures taken because they feel that the camera will steal their soul. Never found any usable water, so headed back to camp at 1:00 for lunch. It was a feast and we were hungry, having had no breakfast. We ate the rest of the moussaka plus freshly made bread, and Mario's Italian spaghetti with ragout. At 3:00, the six of us left in the direction we had come yesterday to look for *pundamilia* (zebra). Found *kongoni* (hartebeest) and *punda* (our slang term for zebra). Mario and Costas shot three *kongoni* and one zebra that we never found. Marusu took the capes of the three *kongoni* and cut meat for eating off two. He also cut out the tripe (stomach lining) and liver of one to cook and loaded one into the Land Rover to use for bait tomorrow. We pulled the remains of one under a tree and covered it with thorn branches in hopes that a lion will smell it and come. The lion will not be able to get at the carcass and eat the entire thing in one night, as he could easily do, because of the covering, but, if a lion does come, he will try to eat what he can get to, then sit by it and guard it. Will check it tomorrow (site is 8 miles north of camp) to see if the lion is there. We headed back for camp, the four of us plus shotgun, .270 and 30-06 in front seat and Mbangi, Marusu, meat, one *kongoni*, guinea fowl in back, literally packed in like sardines. This morning I rode in the back with the two Africans and the gazelle after we had gotten it. I succeeded in getting blood all over one shoe.

We arrived back at camp about 6:30 and Mbangi and Marusu went off to get washing water from a newly discovered spring in the nearby hills while we sat around and drank Aquavit (a Danish liqueur similar to Ouzo).

Marusu began to *scarve* the Grant's gazelle hide. This

involves scraping the fat off the underside so that the hair will not slip. When the skin is removed from the animal, the underside is immediately sprinkled with water to remove blood and then liberally salted and folded up. The skin should be scarved within 12-24 hours (which removes the salt and about 3/4 of the skin thickness which consists of fat globules and membrane). Or, the skin can be kept for a period time without scarving if heavily salted, rolled up and kept this way for at least three days in a cool area, then opened and slowly dried in the sun. The fat must be removed or salted to prohibit deterioration which would cause the hair to "slip," meaning to fall out. Costas keeps filling up my glass with Aquavit. I am on a second tot and the stuff is potent! Mario just said, "This is the way to go hunting." He is so right.

For dinner we had Mario's pepperonis plus baked potatoes and spaghetti, and of course Aquavit. The staff heard a *simba* that undoubtedly has smelled the bait and meat in the trailer. *Mbangi,* whose name means "pot smoker," pulled the Land Rover over in front of Mario and Costas' tent in case there is any need for a quick escape from *simba*. Certainly hope not, but should be an interesting night. Aquavit put Mario and Costas in a crazy mood. Mario found an elephant dung beetle (a scarab beetle) about the size of a small tarantula and was teasing us about putting it in our tent. We turned in at 10:00, and no beetle.

Day 3 – We were up at 6:00 after a peaceful night. Tea for breakfast once again and then left at 6:45 to hang another leopard bait. We finished about 9:00. Mario found a dead turtle there and had Mbangi clean it out so Mario could keep it. Went looking for another spot to hang the other half of the *kongoni* (plus entrails which we carried on the tire on front). Couldn't use the air because the horrendous odor would come straight through the vents and blast us in the face. We headed to the other side of mountain, passing through *porini* (the bush) and by a Maasai *boma*. About 12 Maasai came over while we asked directions for the *barabara* (road) to the area we wanted to go. The Maasai are extremely attractive people with high cheekbones, tall and lean. As we were leaving, one took my hand and shook it. We had trouble finding the cow path in direction we wanted to go and ended up climbing up the mountain part way, passing some small caves. We continued on into the thick jungle through bushes higher than the car roof and through a *korongo* (gully). It was tough terrain. We finally got to a point where we could go no farther and had to turn around. Sad thing was, the campsite was just on the other side of the mountain. We had to follow our tracks back which were difficult to find, but could have gotten stuck some place if we didn't. The bush was so thick that it would be easy to get lost in it. We finally got back on the road after a two-hour, 9-mile "exploratory" mission. Made it back to camp at noon, hungry, too. Had *posho* with barbecued partridge, guinea fowl, pork and sausage for lunch. Both *posho* and *ugali* refer to the same cornmeal porridge that is a staple of Africa cuisine. It is made from white maize and cooked until very thick. It is served with the meat and vegetable stew that is typically served at meals. Using the right hand (never the left!) take a scoop of *ugali* and roll it into a ball. Using the right thumb, make a depression, then scoop up some of the stew and eat. Seven of the local Maasai came to visit us. They bring their cattle and donkeys nearby to graze. We must be the local excitement.

We took off at 1:30 to go hang a third leopard bait, using the front half of the *kongoni*, on the camp side of mountain. This should be a good spot as it is a good bait tree with bushes and rocks nearby, and a clear area between tree and blind. Leopards seek shelter in cool, dry areas because they sleep during the day and want shelter when it rains. They usually come to feed in the late afternoon and early evening. Leopards are the only member of the cat family that drag their kill up into a tree and feast on it there. They are powerful, strong animals to be able to drag a kill that possibly weighs more than they do up a tree. After feasting until full, the leopard will climb down the tree and sleep in bushes or a sheltered area near its kill to keep an eye on it and then go back to feed on it when it is hungry again. This can keep a leopard in vicinity indefinitely if we keep changing bait every eight days. If the leopard is killed, it will be nice and fat and with a glossy coat. The leopard just thinks another leopard left the bait in the tree and doesn't realize the rope for what it is, apparently. Also, there should be a water hole in a relatively close proximity. The lion eats its kill on the ground and eats until he's full (about 70 to 80 pounds of meat), then leaves the remains to the hyenas and vultures. The lion usually eats with the family – papa first, until he's full, then mama, then the cubs.

Mario did not come with us to hang the bait, instead, he took a siesta. It took us about one and a half hours. We went back to camp to pick up Mario, then off to view the lion bait. No lion in sight, but a big black mane had been feeding on the covered bait because black mane lion hair was caught in the bristles. It couldn't eat much of the bait and has probably gone off for water or to nap. Who knows, he might have been watching us the whole time, but if he was, he might have charged, thinking we were going to steal his food. We left to go get some more bait to hang in the tree and keep the lion satisfied. Costas got a *kongoni* with one shot with the .270. We took it back to the tree and hung it up high enough so that the lion, even on his hind legs, could not eat enough to fully satisfy himself and, hopefully, will stay around. If he could eat until satisfied, chances are he would move on. We removed yesterday's bait so the lion wouldn't get to that and possibly fill his quota in food, including the new *kongoni*. We will return at daybreak tomorrow morning in hopes that the lion will be there and sluggish. We headed back to camp and came across some impala. Costas got a beautiful male, dead *kabisa* (completely) with one shot. We returned to camp at dusk (6:45) and proceeded to get into heated discussions about poaching, Tanzania's government, etc. We are in *Naibormut*, Maasai land. It is a beautiful campsite with no mosquitoes or tsetse flies. We do have to contend with regular flies, ants and the Nairobi eye (beetle) which is supposedly harmful and should be killed.

Day 4 – Up at 5:00 a.m. and off by 5:45 to the lion bait. Had to wait about 10 minutes about 1 mile away until it was light enough because we could not use the headlights for fear of scaring the lion away. Unfortunately, no lion was at the bait and he had not even been there because the bait was untouched. Drove around the vicinity to see if we could find the zebra that was wounded the day we shot the three *kongoni.* Did find the bones of the zebra about a quarter of a mile away from the bait. The back bones were completely cleaned of meat but the four legs were missing so our lion must have dragged them somewhere to eat, therefore the lion was satisfied and did not need to go to our bait to feed.

Went to check leopard blinds #1 and #2. Saw wild dogs on the road, one with a dik dik head in its mouth. On the way, the road passed through a dense area, giving me the feeling of driving through an orchard. We came around the curve and six Maasai *morani,* who had been walking down the road in our direction, jumped into the bushes to get out of the way of our *gari* (vehicle). They had such startled expressions on their faces. Wish I had a picture, three Maasai on each side of the road, with heads and spears poking out through the bushes. My first reaction when I saw them jump was that we were being attacked. No bites at the two leopard baits.

Back to camp about 9:00. Had ranch-style breakfast of fried eggs, hash browns, sausage. Made curry of leftover fowl and tripe dishes for dinner. Left about 10:00 for the *duka* 49 miles from camp on the way to Arusha, to see if one of its cannibalized Land Rovers had a shaft and pinion to replace the one that broke off the Land Rover the day before, apparently when we were making our way through the thick jungle. On the way, Mario shot a young *ngiri* (warthog). It was a beautiful shot, the *ngiri* did not know what hit him. Mbangi covered him with thorny acacia branches and we will pick him up on the way back. We stopped at one of the lakes on the way and Mario wounded a duck. He will keep it alive until we want to eat it so it will be fresh. Poor duck. We carried on to the *duka* at Tinga – no shaft, no beer, no cigarettes. Onward 7 miles more to Simanjiro. *Duka* there had beer, but no cigarettes and no shaft. There were a lot of local Maasai sitting around the *duka*, apparently the only place where there is action. They most likely do this every day. All of a sudden, we heard a high wailing and looked to see two women, perhaps Maasai sisters. The first woman had her hands on the shoulders of the other woman and the other woman had her hands on waist of the first woman, their foreheads touching. Then they turned around and not facing each other, continued wailing. Apparently one was leaving. It was an emotional scene for them, but caught us off guard. We found it quite funny.

We went back to Tinga and Costas talked to the store keeper who is going to Arusha. He will bring back a shaft, cigarettes and booze for us. We tossed out the idea about him bringing them out to the campsite and we would give him dinner and he agreed. We then headed back to the reservoir where Mario had shot the ducks because before he had not been able to get Mbangi to go in the water after the dead ones. Still had no luck.

Just as we are ready to depart from the lake, we heard a toot and up drove Costas Papadopoulos, Costas Zikakis' friend who was due the day before at our campsite, and who plans to stay for a while. Valerie got into Pappas' truck and off we went. They headed for camp and we stopped to pick up the warthog, but first had to build a fire and burn off the ticks. Wild animals are covered in ticks! We got back to camp about 6:30 to find Pappas, with everything unloaded from his Peugeot truck, pitching his tent right in front of our tent, spoiling our view. We nixed that! As I walked by the campfire, I heard a clucking in the tall grass. I looked and found Mario's duck and a chicken. Apparently, Ndoho, the *mpishi,* bought the *kuku* (chicken) from one of the Maasai. The three men were full of stories and Mario told us about his duck hunting dog Rufo who always got so excited that either he scared the birds away or would knock Mario off balance just when he was ready to shoot. We ate the curry for dinner and turned in early. Valerie and I both slept through it, but learned the next day that Mario had shot at the hyenas about midnight when they were trying to get at the biltong that was drying.

Day 5 – Up at 5:00, off at 6:00 for lion bait. Mind you, this is in the dark, just at sunrise. Hooray, a lion had eaten what he could reach. But disappointingly, no sign of the lion. It must have been scared off when Costas, the driver, and Mbangi changed places. We drove around, but could not find him. For sure he was probably watching us the whole time. He must be full and therefore slow and sluggish. We know the old lion is alone and it might well have been him that we heard roar last night. We took a different route from the wells and finally reached the open, grassy *porini* that we can see from our camp. Costas *piga*'ed (hit) a zebra with his first shot. Any good hunter wants to take down the animal immediately with the first shot to avoid injuring the animal and causing it undue pain. The cape was removed for the head mount and the lower legs and hooves will be used for lamp bases. The remains of the zebra were dragged to leave a scent and then hung for another lion bait. On the road to the wells, we passed an apparent lion bait that wasn't more than 20 yards off the road and so low a lion could eat the entire *kongoni* and be off before the hunter came back. We checked leopard baits #1 and #2, no bites.

Back to camp for a "pig-roast" lunch. The warthog meat is very tender and tasty, better than pork or ham.

Three Maasai *morani* came for a visit. They just stood outside our tent veranda and looked at the five of us. Really a picture, the three of them, young, clad only in two cloths – one wrapped around and tied over one shoulder, the other blanket wrapped around shoulders – their ocher-ed hair, necklaces, earrings, bracelets, ankle straps, and holding their spears in one hand. The two *morani* on each side of the middle one each placed a hand on his shoulders. He must have been the oldest, but they could not have been more than 15 or 16. Pappas went to ask them, unbeknownst to Valerie and me, what our price was and would they like to buy us. Valerie got an offer of ten cows and I got an offer of five cows. Pretty good price considering a good wife goes for four or five cows. One saw Mario's shaving mirror leaning against a bucket and knelt down to look at his reflection, then started to fix the ocher-braided lock that hung down his forehead. Then another bent over to see himself. Their fascination with the mirror fascinated us. Then, up and off they went.

Saidi Kawawa, a black professional hunter, came by. He is hunting *tembo*. His group is walking about 20 miles a day. Elephant is very dangerous because if alarmed, they will charge and the only thing to do is stand there and fire at the elephant, hoping to dissuade him, or kill him if you want him. The hunter needs a .458 for *tembo* and one bullet costs 14 shillings. Mario and Pappas gave us demonstrations on how their rifles and shotgun work. Pappas has a Mannlicher rifle with a Schoenauer bolt. With this rifle, the bullets in a magazine are transferred to the chamber by means of a revolving apparatus. Mario has a Winchester rifle with a Mauser bolt. It has a spring mechanism for pushing the bullet into the chamber when the rifle is opened and cocked. *Risasi* (bullets) are difficult to come by in Tanzania and unavailable in many of the different sizes. Another example of Tanzania's short-sightedness. The government wants to bring in revenue from licensed hunting and yet hunters can't buy the bullets. Mario is our resident worry-wart and now something else to worry about, not much petrol left if we are planning to be here another five days or so.

Eight Maasai wandered back into camp, our three regulars plus a *mzee* (old man) plus four *watoto* (children). They just stand in the middle of camp and watch what's going on around while the cattle, goats and donkeys graze on the surrounding grass. They are so inquisitive, but don't ask questions and don't talk except maybe to one another. They keep watching Valerie and me as though they are appraising us, maybe they are serious about buying us? We don't mind the Maasai visitors but they bring so many flies with them. They love red and their clothes are always sienna or red. If they buy white material, they dye it brownish-red with ocher. Their sandals are made from strips of tire with leather straps and many of them tie spiky looking rubber tire spirals between the big toe and other toes. I offered M&M candies to the Maasai. I ate one to show that it was okay to eat. The first Maasai to try it made an awful face and then spit it out, similar to how we might react to eating a slice of lemon. The Maasai do not eat sweets and so it was a very unfamiliar taste. Their diet consists of cow's milk soured by cow urine. They also will shoot the cow with an arrow to the jugular vein, suck out blood, then patch up the hole with a mixture of mud and cow dung. Not very appetizing to us.

Valerie and I made banana bread but had no baking soda so Costas suggested that we use fruit salts like Alka Selzer. We tried it, but the bread did not rise. It tasted all right, although a bit rubbery. Mbangi came back from collecting wood and water and said that he had checked leopard bait #3 and the bait was nibbled on. Costas and Mario got all excited and grabbed their guns to go and sit in the blind. Mario told Pappas that he would have to take care of us two girls which greatly delighted him. Then Pappas went bipping off to his tent. Meanwhile, Costas came up to us and said that we can sit in the Land Rover with Mbangi to be close by when the *chui* is shot, so we grabbed our stuff and went, not realizing until later that Pappas probably wondered what happened to us.

Mario and Costas got out of the car about 50 feet from the blind and walked to it while we continued on driving up to the blind. Now the point of this is so that the hunters slip into the blind while we make noise coming and going. If the leopard is in hearing distance, which no doubt it is, then the *chui* will think all the invaders have left when the car drives off. We parked down the hill a ways and waited. Costas and Mario got to the blind about 4:30, with beer, of course. They finally returned to the *gari* on foot about 6:50, having no luck spotting the leopard. The oncoming darkness called an end to the wait. We returned to camp and Pappas was waiting.

We had barbecued pig and *kanga* for dinner. Everyone was in rare form. Costas tried to get some of the hyenas that were stealing the impala from camp with a .22. Pappas tried to seduce Valerie to his tent with a new line, "Come see the flies in my tent." Finally went to bed about 10:30. Mario's duck kept us awake half the night as he was flapping around trying to make love to the food box. We screamed to Mario to do something, but Costas said we had to wait until Mario fell asleep and then he would tell Mario to go do something about it, just as he had told Mario to do something about the hyenas the night before. That night Mario got up, got his shotgun and shot in the air a couple of times, then went back to bed complaining about his feet – he hadn't put any shoes on and got thorns in his feet.

Day 6 – Awakened at 4:30 by Costas and Mario. Costas just had to get up before me one day. We left to go find the lion and arrived at the bait at daylight. No trace of the lion, but drove around to look for him. Pappas spotted some movement in the grass and thought it was leopard. He nearly pulled the trigger of his Mannlicher when Costas said it was a mama cheetah and three cubs. They looked at us warily, didn't run away, but moved behind coverage. Cheetah are protected game as are giraffe and the penalty for shooting a cheetah is very, very severe – about in the same category as assassinating the president. We went to check out the second lion bait, but no bite. Drove around a bit to find a zebra for Pappas. Found a *kongoni*, but lost it in the thick brush. Later came across what we all could have sworn was a *simba*, then maybe a lioness with three cubs, which ultimately turned out to be a giant mama warthog and three piglets, all the color of *simba*. This really stumped us all. As we headed back to camp, we came across some zebra and Pappas got out to track them and get one. We heard the shot and drove over to the area. Pappas had downed a female zebra. Nearby was a giant hunk of elephant hide, very tough and dried. Don't understand why, but instead of skinning the zebra on the spot, we loaded the 700-pound *pundamilia* into the back. Valerie, Mbangi and Pappas' boy piled in on top along with Mario's *kikapu* (basket) with the beer, Cokes, coffee and food Mario insists we take everywhere with us, the four rifles, the bag of salt, and other various sundries. Costas, Mario, Pappas and I sat in the front. We had over one and a half tons in the short-wheelbase Land Rover and with only the front wheels pulling since the broken shaft had put the back wheels out of commission. We have been having to use high ratio 2-wheel-drive these past few days. The 7-mile trip back to camp was harrowing at times because the road has so many bad spots, deep ruts, small Grand Canyons, and very uneven. With the weight of the car, when we got caught in a rut there was a very real threat of the Land Rover rolling over. Costas kept saying, "Not to worry, we will make it." With fingers crossed, we made it back to camp all right. The zebra was unloaded and Marusu skinned her.

We had pizza for lunch and discussed the problems of petrol, beer and cigarettes. We have enough petrol to get back to Arusha, plus a little more, but for sure, definitely not enough to last until we get the leopard and lion. Pappas is going back to Arusha tomorrow, but will not be able to return with the supplies. We'll have to figure something out. We just hope Joseph from Tinga comes with the supplies Costas ordered from him, then he can go run the errands for us.

About 3:00, Mario and Pappas went to check the other two leopard baits and were going to stay if a leopard had been feeding on the bait. Meanwhile, Valerie and I had target practice with the .22. Mario and Pappas returned, having had no luck. Costas invited me to sit in the leopard blind with him so Mbangi drove us to the blind and we settled in at 4:20 with cheese sandwiches and coffee that we never touched. The blind is about 60 feet from the bait so it is very important to be very quiet. What a great sensation to be sitting in the midst of all natural Africa and to be able to really listen to the sounds. To hear the faint sound of the Maasai cowbells in the distance, to hear an occasional donkey (Maasai *punda*) braying, to listen to the birds and the insects and the Vervet monkeys, to hear the wind whistling through the bushes and trees. A few partridges pecked around the blind, never seeming to notice us. Costas discovered a leopard spoor right in the middle of the blind that must have been made within the last 24 hours. The time passed quickly because there was always the expectant hope that you would look through the peephole and see the *chui* on the branch with the bait. It got more difficult to see about 6:15 because of the oncoming dusk and the interference of a twig with leaves that fell over my peephole by the breeze. At 6:25, one bird near the bait tree began to make a lot of noise and then Costas saw the *chui* jump from one rock to another on the small hill behind the tree. We waited until 6:50, but by then it was too dark for Costas to be able to see through the scope and the *chui* never appeared, so we left. It could be very likely that the *chui* will sleep on one of the rocks and then feed early in the morning. Good news, though, to see the *chui* and to know it actually exists.

Back at camp and no more cigarettes. The smokers are very irritated without their nicotine fix. Ndoho gave Costas and Valerie some *Mbulu* tobacco (referring to the region where it is grown) that he had bought from a Maasai. The tobacco needs to be rolled in paper. Valerie rolled a smoke, took a draw and just about died on her first inhale. No kidding! She was unable to get her breath. Her eyes were wide with fear. I'll never forget that look. We both were scared to death! Finally, at what seemed like an eternity, she was able to catch her breath. Costas tried it and was very judicious with his first puff.

After dinner we fixed the *mtego* (trap) for the hyena who were after the biltong. We cut the bottom of the big shortening can with two diagonal cuts forming four triangles and buried the open end of the can partly into the ground. Then we put some of the zebra remains into the can as bait for the hyena. The object is for the hyena to put its head into the can to get to the food, but when the hyena does this, it traps its neck by the triangles and can't get its head out. Eventually the hyena can dislodge itself, but not until after it has banged the tin against trees, etc., making lots of noise. The hyena came again in the middle of the night, but unfortunately, the trick did not work because the tin triangles weren't bent down enough into the can for the hyena to willingly get its head in. Costas said he woke up three times that night, once to hear the hyena, once to hear the roar of a (our?) lion, and once to hear a herd of elephants trumpeting nearby. Darn! I manage to sleep through all this nighttime excitement!

The zebra that Pappas shot was a female and pregnant. I was interested to see the fetus and opened the uterus to find a tiny, perfectly formed zebra. It could not have been more than 10 inches from nose to tail and weighed about 1 kg. The gestation time for zebras is nine months and we didn't know how old the fetus was, but maybe a couple of months. The hooves were formed, but white and soft as cartilage is. The ears were tiny but the eye sockets were very large. A reddish-pink flesh covered the fetus. I couldn't stand the thought of a hyena eating the fetus so I asked that we bury it. Mbangi thought it a funny request, but everyone was very cooperative.

Day 7 – It's May 27th, our brother Robert's birthday and my one year anniversary of graduation from the University of Arizona. We were supposed to get up at 3:30 to run out to the lion bait and wait, but didn't wake up until our usual time, 5:00. Amazing how our internal clocks work, waking up without benefit of an alarm clock and while it is still pitch black outside. Off to the lion bait, but no sign of anything. Checked the lion bait with the zebra. Saw lots of vultures in surrounding trees, but as of yet no bites from animals. This time, Costas brought up the subject of food at 7:30 a.m asking, "What is the menu for lunch?" We decided on spaghetti with ragout, in care of Mario. On the way back to camp, after a five-minute period of silence, out of the blue Mario says, "Now you must tell that fellow of yours not to cook the spaghetti, because if he does he'll cook it for three hours and spoil it." That put us all into complete hysterics since our last mention of food had been a good one and a half hours before and our last conversation before he piped up was about *simba*. Mario has a one-track mind, "fully operational" 24 hours a day, and that is about food. Every morning, noon and night, he checks the *kikapu* to make sure it is full of goodies to eat, and beer and coffee to drink. We all laugh about Mario's obsession with his *kikapu* which must always be in the *gari* when we go anywhere in case we should have a breakdown or something. We must never starve!

Had to stop about 6 miles from camp because Mario spotted some *kanga* (guinea fowl). The boys refer to him as the professional *ndege* (bird) hunter. He got one on a wing shot and kept it, planning to take it home with him as a pet. A little farther on, we stopped and Pappas got out to shoot some birds. Costas walked over to the nearby water hole and found a bottle of snuff there, apparently one of the Maasai had dropped it. Costas and Valerie had run out of cigarettes two days before, had bummed off the boys as many cigarettes as they could, and Ndoho gave them some tobacco he had gotten from the Maasai that they had been rolling in newspaper to make their own strong cigarettes. Yup, Valerie's scare after her first inhale of the Mbulu tobacco didn't preclude her from smoking it. This discovery of the *ugero* (snuff), therefore, was a welcome discovery since they were running low on tobacco. The snuff wasn't very good and the boys were the ones who used it up. Back at camp, Mario made the ragout for spaghetti and zebra meat patties for snacking.

We all then set off in Pappas' Peugeot truck to check out the other two leopard baits and look for impala. We drove in the direction of Tarangire and kept driving until we came across an oncoming Land Rover which turned out to be Bob Brown and Gerald Miller. Bob said that he had been in a leopard blind when a lioness came to the door of his blind and he had to shoo her away with a sack. We turned back and headed for camp.

We dined on spaghetti and the last two beers of Pappas' to celebrate Robert's birthday. When thirsty, even warm beer tastes good. Discussion and debate commenced about what to do since we weren't having much success with baits and we are running low on petrol, out of beer, booze and cigarettes, and with a broken shaft. Every half hour the plans changed – from sending someone back to Arusha with Pappas to get supplies and come back, to all going back to Arusha and giving up, or moving to a controlled area for some of the game, the only hitch being no leopard or lion licenses for controlled area. While Costas and Mario were still debating about what to do, Valerie and I celebrated Robert's birthday by taking a bath. The canvas bathtub was about 2' x 2' and 8 inches deep. We had only 1 gallon of water in it. It required tricky maneuvering to get wet, but it was a bath and our first in one week.

By late afternoon, the plans were to go to the lion bait about 6:00 and wait until 10:00 to see if the lion comes, and the next morning Costas and Mario would sit in the *chui* blind. Then, success or not, we would leave mid-morning for Arusha. So, at 5:00 we piled into Pappas' Peugeot and went to the lion bait. We parked the truck behind a full bush, out of sight of the bait, and very quietly, we all crawled under the bush and sat there until dusk. Costas, Mario and Pappas all had rifles and shotguns, ready in case the lion should show up to feed. At one time, they even had considered rigging a blind up on top of the bait tree so they could shoot straight down, but that was dismissed as being very dangerous. At dusk, we moved back into the truck. Valerie and I sat in the cab, the three men plus Mbangi and Bakari (Pappas' boy) sat in the back. Actually, as we were moving from the blind to the truck, Mbangi, who has been watching from the back of the truck, spotted something moving and thought it was *simba*. Well, immediately Valerie and I jumped into the cab, scared out of our minds. It was difficult to see and after a silence of about 10 minutes, the moving object showed itself to be *fisi* (hyena). Mario then joined us in the cab and we sat in as complete silence as we could for a good hour. The floodlight from the Land Rover had been rigged to Pappas' car and about 8:00 Mbangi saw something moving in the shadows. They turned on the light and a pair of yellow eyes came into view. The first thought was *chui* and then the possibility of cheetah. The animal walked stealthily, looking at us the entire time and the light followed it. It had to be a good 75 yards from us. Then Costas shot (how loud it sounded!) and the *chui* took off. He yelled for us to turn on the lights and follow, and with the headlights and floodlight, we followed it as best we could, as the *chui* followed the perimeter of the open area. Costas shot again and hit, but the *chui* got away. We followed it and lost it in the thicket. We looked for eyes and followed one set, reddish in color, but it turned out to be *fisi*. We called it a night and headed back to camp. The stories came out. When Mario was in the back of the truck, he and Pappas were sitting opposite each other. At one point, Mario said, "Pappas, don't stand up because I have my gun aimed over your head." With that, Pappas said, "What? Have you gone mad? Are you trying to kill me?" I think that was the deciding factor for Mario to get into the cab. Then, when Mbangi saw the shadowed figure and there was a doubt as to whether it was *chui* or cheetah, they watched the movements of the cat. A cheetah would run and a *chui* would crouch. When Costas was positive it was a *chui,* he had a perfect aim and was about to pull the trigger when good ol' Pappas moved, upsetting Costas' aim which he says would have had the *chui* down. Anyway, no luck with *chui*. Pappas really has been a pain in the neck. He is Costas' Greek friend so Valerie and I are being cordial, but the unspoken sentiment among Costas, Mario and us is that he has spoiled the camaraderie the four of us had prior to his arrival. He truly is the "fifth wheel." I was dead tired so I went to bed. Costas rigged up the *mtego* for the hyena again.

Day 8 – Up at 4:30. Valerie and I went with Mbangi to drive Costas and Mario to the leopard bait. They were going to sit in it from 5:00 to 7:00 because Mbangi had checked it Sunday morning and found fresh feeding. Apparently *chui* feeds in early morning. It was still dark when we deposited them, and chilly. The three of us drove down a ways to wait for "the shot." We waited until 7:00, drove back to the blind and found no one. Costas and Mario had walked up to the bait. They had checked it out and said no *chui* had been feeding on the bait. This one bait had never been checked by Costas or Mario, only Mbangi. Not enough of the bait had been eaten for it to be *chui* and the hair Mbangi had found on the tree was questionable as to whether it was *chui*. It was a sad day for all of us.

The last couple of days, Costas, Mario and Pappas have vacillated between optimism and pessimism about getting a leopard or lion. Mario had always been pessimistic about no game in the area, no lions or leopards. He even went so far as to contradict the facts we had in hand such as a lion hair. Valerie and I continually work on keeping the spirit up. We can always counteract Mario's pessimism with humor, but we hate to see Costas get down in the dumps because he is always such an easy-going fellow. We know he really wants the lion at least, but he seems to be giving up. We keep using his line on him. "Not to worry, we will make it!" We went back to camp and packed up. Pappas had stayed until Monday, although he was to leave on Sunday, because his mother would worry about him. Maybe that was his problem. Two nights before, Pappas had told Valerie he would give all of us his dissertation on sex. When I had said that I thought he made too many references to sex, he went on babbling and ended by saying that he was twice my age and had many more experiences than I. Typical of him to say something like that, but it did shut him up on the subject. All of us were getting so tired of him.

As we were packing up, several of the Maasai came to pick up the leftovers. Two of them were *mzee* and had first choice. How delighted one was to get the *mtego* can used for the hyena trick that never worked, and an old Konyagi bottle with cap. He stuck the can on a stick and carried it over his shoulder. The other *mzee* took two empty Ideal milk tins and we gave him the plastic case that had wrapped cheese inside. Whatever else we left, if anything, the others would take, and they would take everything. We left the *Kanga* campsite (our name for it) at 10:45. I went with Mario in Pappas' truck, and with Mbangi and Bakari in the back. We were first and waited for the others at the marked tree to the lion bait because we wanted to go check one last time to see if any lion was at the bait before we left for good. Costas said that we could go, but that he would go on. He did seem awfully depressed. We went on in and about 100 yards from the bait, Pappas spotted lion heads. He immediately slammed on the brakes, threw the car in reverse, backed up and turned around. We were off at full speed chasing Costas, Pappas all the time getting excited, then telling us to shush, be quiet. We took the tight curve (Pappas corner) right before the deep *korongo* at such a speed that I thought for sure we had lost Mbangi and Bakari for good because they were standing on top of all the stuff in the back of the truck. Fortunately, we didn't. We finally caught sight of the Land Rover after about 1 ½ miles and had a hell of a time honking and speeding to get their attention and catch up with them. We were out of the car with a flash, "*Simba, simba!*" Even quicker than that Costas was loading his rifle while the boys were unhitching the trailer and unloading the back. I jumped in the Land Rover's back end and squeezed in among Valerie, Marusu, Mario with shotgun, the food box and with one leg over the box and the other one wedged in between it and Valerie who was crouched down halfway between the floor and the seat. We were crowded but had to give Mario elbow room. Pappas (who claimed half the lion because he had spotted it) and his boy were following us in the Peugeot. When we got close enough, we spotted five lionesses who ran for the bushes when we circled the tree. They had eaten the entire bait and were resting under the bait tree. Some of them ran to the same bush we had used as our own blind. At first we thought one was a male lion without a mane because it was so large, but we finally decided all were lionesses. Pappas did not circle the tree, but stayed behind because his light gray car reflected the sun too brightly. Even afterwards, he still insisted that one was a male, although we all were positive it was five females, one being very large. We returned to where we had left the trailer and Ndoho. Our spirits were raised because we had actually seen lion, even if female, but disappointing that the male had gotten away, if indeed, he had been there. Costas says that usually the male eats first and is the first one off when alarmed and then joins the females later. At one time, I thought I spotted something that could be a black-maned lion, but we never checked it out, and it was at a very great distance. Actually, I was a very good spotter.

Costas was not about ready to leave so we decided to set up camp where we were, but back away from the road. Pappas had to leave so Mario went with him with intentions to return as soon as possible with petrol, water, cigarettes, beer and other supplies. Since Joseph had not come with our supplies, Mario would check at his *duka* first and come back with him if he was there with our stuff. We unloaded the stuff at the selected spot, then took off to get another *kongoni* to use for bait. We hunted in the vicinity of camp, across the road into the interior and had no trouble finding game. We immediately took it to hang as bait at our lion tree, hoping that the lions would be back. Later in the afternoon we got another *kongoni* for food and drove by the lion tree at twilight, but no sign of lion. Had *kongoni* kidney and liver for dinner. Turned in early. Valerie, Costas and I shared the one tent we had set up. Mario never returned.

Day 9 – Up at 6:00 and off to check the lion bait. A lion had eaten some of the neck of the *kongoni*, but not much. There was no sign of him or the lionesses. Mbangi discovered *chui* claw marks on the tree and a white stomach hair of *chui* on the limb the bait was tied onto, so apparently both *chui* and *simba* had fed on the bait. As we were driving back to the road, Costas spotted a leopard running through the grass. Mbangi was driving and Costas was riding shotgun. (True definition of the expression.) We started to chase it. Mbangi must have been going about 40 mph and we were keeping up with the *chui*, but Costas wouldn't be able to aim until the *chui* had crouched down and we could stop. In a split second, while Mbangi was looking at the *chui*, we started careening toward two trees which were too narrow to pass through so Mbangi swerved to the right and had to swerve to the right again to miss a dead tree. The left corner of the roof rack nicked the tree, breaking the tree in half and we landed in a thicket of bushes, unharmed, but well aware that the situation could have been much worse. The only way out was to back out the way we came. We lost the *chui,* too. We went to check the zebra lion bait and passed warthogs and giraffes on the way. We've been seeing a lot more game since Pappas said there wasn't any around here. Nothing at the zebra bait, not even vultures this time, and that's the last time we were going to check it. Out by the zebra bait there was no game whatsoever and the grass was too tall and dry that we wonder how we ever got the zebra in the first place. On the way back to camp, we came across some zebra between the wells and lion bait. Costas shot five rounds at a reasonable distance and finally brought down a *mtoto* zebra which he had not even aimed at. All of us were rather listless so headed back to camp to wait for Mario.

Valerie, Costas and I visited one of the two derelict Maasai *bomas* nearby. The Maasai apparently had temporarily abandoned it for greener pastures but would return when the rains came. The maize field lay idle until they returned. The *boma* consisted of four huts made out of dung and mud. I went inside one. The ceiling was too low to stand up; the beds were made of branches about two feet off the ground and covered with dry grass, and a fire circle was in the center of the dirt floor. Outside, the huts circled the center which is packed dirt. This is where the livestock is kept at night. Living in a Maasai *boma* would be like living in a horse stall within a corral. Even though the Maasai had left quite some time before, there still were plenty of flies. The *boma* is encircled by bushes and calabash vines. They hollow out the ripe calabash fruits and use the very hard skin for their gourds. The maize field is outside the *boma*.

We were packing up to leave at 11:00 because Mario had not returned. We thought maybe he had reasoned we would shoot the lion early in the morning and then head back so there would be no need for him to return. Then Costas noticed that his rifle was scratched and the barrel was slightly bent. He then discovered the bent window frame of the left door and reasoned that when we had hit the tree this morning, the last six inches of the barrel had been sticking out of the window and had gotten caught between the window and tree. This explained why he killed the *mtoto* zebra instead of the one he had aimed at because the scope and the barrel were marking two different points. He thought the rifle was *kwisha* (finished) for good and that ended any more hunting because only the .22 rifle was left, plus Mario's 30-06 which was already packed away.

At this point, everyone was down-hearted and no one had any desire to check the lion bait because if the lion were there, we would have no rifle to use on him. So, at 11:00 we left *Simba* camp for Arusha and at 12:30, as we were coming around a curve, who is coming the other way but Mario in a hired truck. We screeched on the brakes to avoid a collision and jumped out. Here was Costas who wanted to just go back to Arusha and Mario laden with supplies and eager to get back to hunting. He had seen Saidi Kawawa in Arusha who had said he had seen a beauty of a black mane about 3 miles from his campsite near the Maasai *boma* by our *chui* bait #1 that had been killing some Maasai cows. We discussed what to do when along came two Land Rovers from our direction. It was Bob Brown and Gerald Miller. Out in the middle of nowhere, where one can drive for days and not see another vehicle, and all of a sudden we have four. They stopped for a while, then left and we decided to turn back and try again. I'm sure the cigarettes, beer and *bangi* (marijuana) clinched the decision. So, we loaded all of Mario's supplies into the Land Rover and trailer, and sent the hired truck back to Arusha while we headed back from the way we came. We chose a campsite on the opposite side of the road from last night's camp and dropped everything off so Ndoho and Marusu could start setting up. Then we took off to retrieve the *mtoto* (foal) zebra, if the birds hadn't already finished it off, to use for another lion bait. When we got to it, a couple of vultures flew off and it was amazing to see how much they had accomplished in a few hours. They had completely devoured the skin on the lower jaw and the eyeballs. Since the hide is so tough, they rip open the anus and enter through there. They had consumed enough meat to give the zebra an emaciated look with the hip-bone cavity very visible. It was really quite a ghoulish sight. We loaded the stinking beast into the back of the Land Rover as flies crawled out of the stomach through the bullet hole. The birds and flies had eaten most of the stomach and intestines. We took the zebra to an open spot between the other lion bait and our camp, but farther back into the interior. As soon as we could, we unloaded the zebra and dragged it because it really stunk. We drove by our other bait, but no sign of lions.

We headed back to camp for the curry Mario had brought from Naas. Mario was so concerned about the curry because he had Ndoho start boiling the rice when we left, thinking we would be back shortly and we didn't return until 6:00, a good 2½ hours later. After meeting up with Mario, Valerie had said let's pitch camp then go get the zebra and hang it up. Mario said yes, let's pitch camp, have something to eat, and then go get the zebra bait. Same old Mario, always thinking of food. We didn't go out again. Mario straightened out the barrel of Costas' gun, Valerie rolled some *bangi*, and we all enjoyed the good life with beer, booze, cigarettes resupplied.

Two tents had been pitched, but all four mattresses were in one. I turned in early and was awakened to hear the other three discussing the sleeping arrangements. Mario suggested making one a married man's tent and the other a bachelor's tent, or snorers and non-snorers. Finally, two mattresses were dragged over to the other tent and the men turned in there while Valerie joined me. Costas raised the tent on top of his Land Rover and the three *watu* slept up there. Valerie was carrying on a conversation through the canvas walls with Costas in the next tent. They got her to get up and go roll them a joint. I was asleep by the time she returned. As a joke, Valerie had wanted them to start up the *gari* while the three *watu* were asleep in the tent on top of Costas' Land Rover, but they never did. As two single gals out in the bush with six men, Valerie and I knew how to handle ourselves. Mario may have wanted things differently, but we never gave him any encouragement. Costas was a perfect gentleman. The ratio of educated men to women within our social network here in Tanzania and Kenya was about 10:1, so it was important to maintain platonic relationships only, otherwise, things could get very awkward.

Day 10 – Up at 6:00, off at 7:00 to check lion baits. The first lion bait had been fed on a little, but no sign of the crafty old lion. Nothing on the new zebra bait. We then took the old road into the interior and after about a half hour chase, Mario got a *kongoni*. We had gotten twisted and turned around chasing the *kongoni* and everyone had a different idea as to where the road was. Lots of trees and lots of cloud coverage on a very overcast day did not help us to find our way. It took us four hours to finally untangle ourselves from the bush. Costas had said that Nick DeBeer was once lost in this bush for four days. It is very easy to get lost and hard to find any landmarks. Twice Mbangi had to climb a tree to see what he could see. It wasn't until he spotted the hills Naibormut and Naiverera that we were able to locate ourselves and try to find our way out. Mario found a baby dik dik that he brought to the car, but we turned it loose. It was tiny and cute. We got back to camp six hours later, having had nothing to eat and no *kikapu* in the car for the first time. No longer will we laugh about Mario's *kikapu*! Mario and Valerie stayed at camp to fix lunch and I went with Costas, Mbangi and Marusu to hang another leopard bait and lion bait with the *kongoni*. We ended up hanging one *chui* bait and one *simba* bait near the Wells in the *korongo* and one *chui* bait in the *korongo* near camp. On the way back from hanging the *simba* bait, Mbangi spotted a tree with honey. The honey is made by very small bees that make a very light honey kept in wax sacks. Mbangi and Marusu got the little bit of honey that was left in the tree and we all ate it. It was very good. Costas re-sighted his gun using 16 rounds; it is fairly accurate now. Good news considering at one time he thought it was finished for good. We realized how fortunate Costas had been the first time he shot the rifle, totally unaware that the barrel was bent, that it wasn't cracked inside. He might have been killed if that had been the case.

About 5:00 we left to go sit at the lion bait #1 and see if the lion would come. Near the bait were three *twiga* (giraffe) and four zebra. The animals weren't interested in running away from us and into the bush so it was assumed by Costas and Mbangi that they had been chased by *simba*. Costas decided to try out his rifle on a zebra. He hit it on the first and only shot, but the zebra went quite a ways before dropping dead. His shot was only a couple of inches from where he aimed which proved that the gun was firing all right and can be used. Costas shot the zebra in a hunting block but, unfortunately, it crossed the road and dropped dead in a controlled area so we had to get it out of there fast, in case a game scout should show up. The five of us had to load the 800-pound zebra (with one testicle) into the back of the Land Rover which was a chore. We all were pushing and shoving and at one point I thought my knee was going to break because the zebra's shoulders were resting on it while Mario was climbing over the front seat to get to the back in order to lift the back end of the zebra into the back end of the Land Rover. They said my face turned bright red as I was screaming to Mario to hurry up. We headed back to camp, leaving the lion until tomorrow. Mario was going to use the zebra's skin, including the head and tail, for a wall hanging and the meat to make biltong for his dogs. Ndoho smoked *kongoni* meat for dinner which was very good.

Day 11 – Up at 5:30. Valerie and I took tea in to Mario and Costas because they had requested it in bed. Went to check baits and, lo and behold, every bait except the *chui* bait in the closest *korongo* has been fed on. When we drove out to the new zebra lion bait, Mbangi and I noticed something run from the tree which turned out to be a *chui* "*kubwa sana*" (very big). No one else saw it, but there were definite *chui* hairs on the tree. The hairs are black and white. We fixed up a blind and Costas will sit in it this afternoon. At the first lion bait, Mario had shot some *kanga*. A couple of them were still alive and rustled around the back of the Land Rover. When we had stopped to fix the blind, one of the *kanga* flew out of the window and Mbangi had to chase it a couple hundred yards, round and round, periodically throwing the *panga* at it to try to stop it. He finally retrieved it. It was a good show. Found *chui* and *simba* hairs at the respective blinds near the Wells so we fixed a blind at the *chui* bait. Drove out to the first lion bait with zebra to check it for the last time. I had a bet of one bottle of Konyagi riding with Costas that there would be no lion feeding on the bait. I won. I was happy to have won a bottle of Konyagi, but disappointed that there wasn't a lion for Costas. We cut the rope and left the zebra to the vultures. Will check it no more. On our way out we saw a family of wild pigs (forest pigs). They are different from warthogs, teeth as sharp as razor blades, very dangerous, and the meat tastes just like pork. Saw some *twiga*. On our way back, stopped by the *chui* bait in nearby *korongo;* no bites. Costas got a full grown duiker (and almost the Maasai in the distance that he didn't see). The duiker is larger than the dik dik, but smaller than a Thomson's gazelle and supposedly very good meat.

Back to camp for curry lunch. This curry was made with the fresh *kanga* meat. Boys made *kiloriti* tea from the bark of a special acacia tree. This tea is a laxative, good for constipation and also increases the appetite. This is the tea the Maasai drink when feasting because they can eat more. After lunch Costas took Valerie and me to the Wells so we could wash our hair – haven't washed it in 11 days. The level of the water is a good five feet below ground level. What a pal Mbangi is, he climbed down and filled the bucket with the green, algae-covered water and brought it up to us so that we could shampoo and rinse. That meant he had to make the precarious climb down and back up several times. Even with green water, it felt so good to wash out the dust in our hair.

About 3:30 we left camp, first to take Mario and Marusu to the *chui* bait by the Wells and then to take Costas and Mbangi to the #2 lion bait (zebra), turned *chui* bait. Valerie and I drove off into the thicket to wait. Valerie heard a noise in the bushes to the left and also in front of the car, a couple hundred feet away. About 6:00 I saw some impala to the right and front. We were going to wait until 7:00 when the sun was fully down, but about five minutes until sunset we heard a gunshot. Well, needless to say we were super excited. I started the car and zoomed on down to the bait. Just as we reached the edge of the open field, I saw Costas and Mbangi come out from the blind and they did not seem at all concerned about anything in the direction of the bait. When we got up to them they were laughing a little nervously. What had happened was a scare by an elephant. They had been watching the bait from the blind when Mbangi turned to the left to check a noise coming from that direction. What he saw was a giant bull elephant coming toward the blind, apparently, to eat the tree. But when the elephant had gotten close enough, he could smell the men and was ready to charge, trunk up and ears out. Quick thinking got the men up the tree and Costas let him have it right in the forehead with a large-gauge shell in the shotgun. The *tembo* did an about-face and ran back into the bush. So many things could have happened. The *tembo* could have gotten mad and charged. If we had the headlights on and he had seen us coming, he could have charged the *gari*. Or, if Costas used the .270, the *tembo* could have become really ferocious. Whatever, we all were saved from a terrible fate. We headed over to where Mario was, retrieved him and Marusu, then drove around lion bait #1, but saw only *mbweha* (jackals). We got back to camp about 8:15 and had duiker chops and moussaka for dinner.

Day 12 – Today is the first of June. The one-week hunting trip has turned into almost two weeks and nothing to show for all the effort. Costas brought us coffee in bed at 4:30 and we were off by 5:15 to check out the Granddaddy lion bait. He had just eaten because the meat was very red where he had gnawed. He's a very clever bugger who probably has been hunted before and he knows when to eat and when and where to get away at the sound of a *gari*. It was still dark so we shone the light around and the only pair of eyes we spotted belonged to a genet cat. We drove on down to the zebra *chui* bait and stopped the car about 1 mile from the bait. Costas, Mario and Mbangi walked the rest of the way. They saw no sign of *chui* and the *chui* had not eaten, but they did show Mario the elephant tracks. Too bad Costas didn't have an elephant license or his .358 rifle. He would have shot the elephant because it had beautiful tusks weighing a good 50 pounds each which would sell for about $10,000 to $12,000 a set. We headed for the two baits near the Wells. Mario tried for some wild pigs on the way but they got away. The *chui* had eaten on its bait, but

162

there was no sign of the *chui*. Mario, Costas and Mbangi headed toward the lion bait and in no time they were making their way back hurriedly. They had spotted six lion around the *kongoni* bait. With Mbangi driving, Costas riding shotgun, and Mario at the left rear window, we circled to the right of them. Costas took aim at a good-looking male and shot. He went down and got back up again and ran a short distance. The younger male lion with not much of a mane, plus the four lionesses also ran a distance. They kept looking at us from semi-cover and still made for an easy target. Costas shot again at the first lion and this time the lion went down, biting his paw because of the pain in his shoulder where the bullet had hit. Mario shot in the direction of the others to disperse them and drive them away. We didn't drive up to the lion until the others were a good distance away. Mario gave the lion one final shot with a shotgun as double insurance. Costas suggested we have coffee before loading up the lion into the back of the car, but we never got around to the coffee because of having to chase away the lionesses. The lionesses were looking for their male to reunite and would become very *kali* (angry) and vicious if they got close enough to us to attack. The lions really are too proud to run for their lives even after being shot at. The lion we got stood so majestically but with a very "what's going on" expression on his face after the first shot. He must have been in agony after the first shot because he bit right through his leg behind and above his left front paw. We took a bunch of pictures, then loaded him up. While the hunt for *simba* has been challenging and fun, that is where the enjoyment lay. Now that we had "bagged the trophy," the mood on the ride back to camp was somber. The sport is in the chase. By this time, Ndoho and Marusu weren't bothering to get up to see what we brought back, if anything. Costas told them to come and get the *kongoni* out of the car. The looks on their faces when they saw the lion were priceless. We took pictures comparing the size of the lion with a human. Mbangi and Marusu skinned the lion and saved the lucky bones for me to have mounted as a brooch. The lion fat was saved and melted down because it is excellent for rheumatism and muscle soreness. It sells for about 500 shillings a liter. The complete lion skin was removed and it will be made into a full mount with back legs bolted on the mount and front paws outstretched in a leap with a growling face, fangs bared. This particular lion will be sold to a Japanese firm at a price of 27,000 shillings. The boys are going to have lion fillets, but Costas absolutely refuses to eat anything of the cat family. Valerie and I want to try lion steak, though.

The lions had eaten the entire bait, leaving only the skull and horns. Our timing was fortunate because after resting they would have moved on. The lion's age is about six or seven and with a beautiful black mane. The mane isn't as full as that of an old lion, but it's still ample and beautiful. He really is a handsome lion and it's true when they say that one really appreciates the lion after outwitting him because they are a challenge. After being here for 12 days, this was the first male lion we had seen and we had baited and waited from the first day. The lion skin has to be removed and salted immediately because the lion has so much fat underneath the skin that if it is allowed to remain, the hair will slip. The lion's coat is beautiful. After salting it and folding it up, the hide is so heavy it takes two people to move it.

Duiker ragout on spaghetti for lunch and Greek Halva for dessert. It is a light candy similar to meringue and made from 50% sesame seeds and 50% sugar.

The boys melted zebra fat down into a liquid and bottled it. It is taken orally by children with coughs.

Valerie, Mario, Costas and I went to sit in the zebra *chui* bait. We got there about 5:00 and Mbangi waited in the car. The *chui* never came and had not eaten since that day we saw him at the bait so he probably had been scared away. In fact, we did not see much life at all, compared to what Costas and Mbangi saw yesterday. Only two *mbweha*, two birds and the sound of an airplane. Mbangi picked us up at 7:00 and we went to check out #1 lion bait. Mario shone the torch and we were led to a huge pair of reddish eyes which belonged to a bush baby. There was no action at the bait but as we were driving toward the road, Mario spotted a pair of yellowish-green eyes which looked like they belonged to a cat. We followed it and when Mbangi said *"chui"* everyone was all keyed up. By the torch we could see the outline and semblance of spots. Although what we saw wasn't as big as a fully grown *chui*, Costas got out of the car and gave it a show with the .270. The cat leapt in the air as he was hit and ran under a tree. Mario gave the cat a shot with a shotgun and then another one in the head because it was tough to die, but by this time we knew it wasn't a *chui*, but a serval cat. The serval cat has a spotted coat similar to the leopard's or cheetah's, but it is a much smaller cat and can be easily domesticated. The skin will be used for handbags, but everyone felt rather bad about mistaking it for a leopard.

Back at camp we had *kanga* stew and a good bean soup for dinner. We all knew this was going to be our last night at camp, but since we were out of booze, beer, cigarettes and running low on supplies, plus having gotten a lion, no one was really disappointed about leaving, although we all would love to have stayed another three months in the *porini*. Costas was already making plans for us to go to Lolkisale from the 20th to 28th of June. It is a controlled area about two hours from Arusha and is a good spot for leopard and lion. "Not to worry - we will make it!"

The Africans are known for their beautiful strong white teeth. Marusu would amuse us by removing the soda pop cap with his back molars. He would rest the fluted edge of the cap on his bottom molar and lift the bottle while slightly biting down on the cap. Off it would pop. Valerie decided to give it a try and broke a cusp off her molar. Never again! We turned in early.

Day 13 – Costas and Mario brought us tea in bed at 4:30. We got off about 5:30 and checked the lion bait. Mario had the torch (flashlight) on and as we approached the bait tree, Valerie, Costas and Mbangi spotted two pairs of eyes, but Mario and I never saw them. Since Mario had not seen them, he had trouble keeping the torch on the proper spot and we lost the eyes, which we were sure were lion, because the animals got away. When we got up to the bait, it was still swinging and red meat and blood was dripping. Mbangi was sure it was two lions, but they got away and we never did find out where they went, although we drove around a bit. We cut down the bait and drove to the zebra *chui* bait. There was no sign of *chui* or that he had eaten on the bait since the first day. We cut that meat down, too, and left the bait tree in a different direction from how we had come because Mario spotted some *kanga*. He didn't get any, but we continued on and proceeded to get lost. Costas kept stopping, refusing to drive because he was so aggravated about getting lost. Mbangi headed us in one direction and, lo and behold, we came across a *barabara*, but instead of it being the road we took from the lion bait to the zebra *chui*, the one we thought we would meet, we came across the main road instead and right between the Wells and the lion bait. A couple of hundred yards before we found the road and, still not knowing where we were, Mbangi had gotten out to look around and discovered a spot where three lions had sat. When we did come to the *barabara* and figure out where we were, we realized that we had most probably passed through the *korongo* in the spot where the lions ran to when running from the bait. No one had any idea how we had gotten to where we were because we were all thinking we were west of the lion bait when actually we were east. We drove back to the lion bait to see if by any chance the lions dragged it off, but it was still there and a few birds were feasting on it. We then drove to the spot by the Wells to look for wild pigs and on the way Mario got one *kanga*. Mbangi faked a thorn in his toe so he wouldn't have to chase after *kanga* with the probability of lions in the area. Costas got a dik dik which he will full-mount. We saw some pigs, but they got away so we headed back to camp.

Ndoho and Marusu had taken down the two tents and were packing up so when Costas got out he ordered Ndoho to "*piga hema*" (pitch a tent) "because we had come across a big lion that we are going to get." Ndoho and Marusu had the looks to kill on their faces because they had already set up camp three times in two weeks. It was more of a "I would rather walk home than set up camp again" look. They weren't really amused when they found out Costas was joking. We packed up and left "*Bunduki* (Gun) Camp" (name given to our campsite) at 11:00 and reached Tinga at 1:00 to find no Joseph and none of the supplies that he was to bring back for us. We continued on to Simanjiro's *duka* and good ol' Mzee H.... had Valerie's Sportsman cigarettes that Joseph had sent by way of another driver. He also had beer and a bottle of Konyagi which we bought. The boys had bought some Mbulu tobacco at the *duka* in Tinga so we were riding in high style. We drank some beer before getting on our way and then once on our way, we opened the bottle of Konyagi and passed it around. We were riding high. Mario kept begging us to stop for lunch since it was about 3:00, but Costas wouldn't stop until we got through the *korongo* because the road was so bad with deep, deep ruts in it. The road was so steep in some areas that Mario and the boys had to get out and push. The trailer had a broken crankshaft we discovered and Mario was certain that we would be dragging it back.

After passing through the gate of the controlled area, we stopped at a campsite where a professional hunter by the name of Keith pitches his camp when he has clients hunting in the Lolkisale area. Later on we stopped for tea by a lake and upon my request, Mario asked a Maasai girl passing by how much she would want for her round necklace. We thought 100 bob (shillings) was a little high. Although it's original, you can buy the necklaces for 5 bob. It would be neater to buy one of them from a Maasai woman, though. We stopped another time along the way because a Maasai on the other side of the road wanted a light for his cigarette. We finally reached Arusha at 6:00 and as we were entering town, Joseph in his Toyota passed us. He saw us and came back with a carton of Embassies for Costas. His car had been in the shop all week and so he hadn't been able to get back to his *duka* in Tinga and deliver the goods to us. At least we now knew why he never showed up.

Arusha and Nairobi

Costas dropped us off at Mario's then went to wake up Shagbai and have him open up his chemist shop so Costas could buy a bottle of nail polish for me. I had offhandedly mentioned that I should get some polish to put on my nails since they looked so dirty. That was a good enough reason for Costas to get his friend Shagbai to open up his *duka* because Costas loves to pull this stunt on him – tells him it's an emergency, then buys one bottle of nail polish. We all got cleaned up, got some curry, biriyani (rice pilaf), and samosas from Naas for dinner. Costas joined us after getting cleaned up, and with a bottle of nail polish. We all felt a little low about being back. We really do prefer the bush.

Valerie and I slept in Sunday morning. Mario brought us coffee in bed at 9:00 and we had pound cake for breakfast. Joseph was burdened with the chore of doing all the safari laundry. Mind you, all laundry is done by hand. No washing machine or dryer in these parts. Poor chap! While he was scrubbing away, we went to the open-air vegetable market to buy eggplant. When Valerie and I got back, we started making moussaka for tonight's dinner as we are having a little post-safari party. Mario had already made the ragout. After leftover curry for lunch, Costas came over. Valerie wants the words to the song *Malaika* and so we hopped in his car and went looking for a bar with the record so we that could listen to it. No luck finding the bar open that Costas had in mind and the other one was full of men drinking home-brewed beer. We did stop at Costas' favorite *duka* and got some ice cream – Arusha's answer to Baskin-Robbins and home of three flavors – vanilla, pistachio and melted strawberry. Back to Mario's. Out again to see about the bar, but it was still closed. Back to Mario's. Took a drive around his carport area in his Peugeot 404 which has no license plate and can't be taken off the property. Costas left and will be back for dinner and to help drink the three bottles of Konyagi he had bought. We hope he gets home all right because he had to stop seven times on the way to Mario's because water got in with the fuel. Costas returned about 7:30, higher than a kite. Instead of going home, he went to the Hellenic Club and polished off half a bottle of Haig because someone at the club was celebrating something. He entertained Mario while Valerie and I made some guacamole to go with the tortilla chips that we made out of chapatis. The men loved it. Costas wanted to go back to the Tanzania Bar to hear *Malaika*. Mario didn't want to go because he was afraid of Costas' behavior but there was no talking Costas out of it so we went. When we drove up, there was some drunk sleeping by the front door of the bar and Costas remarked, "Oh, the night watchman is on duty." The bar specializes in half a roasted chicken for 7 bob and Costas bought 2 although we kept reminding him of our feast at home. We had some watered down gin in one of the little lounges which reminded me of a bus station waiting room. One fellow was sound asleep. The waitress uniforms were like our janitor uniforms, but the girls wore colorful headdresses. The bar didn't have *Malaika* so we had the chicken wrapped up and took it home where we served up the moussaka for dinner. We only finished off one bottle of Konyagi. I got so tired, I toddled off to bed. I don't know how these people do it!

On Monday, Mario took me on some errands. He helped me with my purchase of a Zanzibar chest for Mom and Dad. The guy wanted 350 shillings and had quoted me 300 shillings two weeks ago. Mario got him down to 200 shillings. I also got the flower pot gourd for 10 shillings which had been 12. We met Valerie at the Fort Ikoma booking office. Ferdie and Azghar were there with Shakir. Ferdie is here from Nairobi for two days for business. Azghar went on to tell me how he couldn't sleep the last two weeks for worry about us and he had called the VP to see about a helicopter to come rescue us. Oh, he's such a cutie with his tall tales. Valerie and I accompanied Shakir and Ferdie to the New Arusha hotel for lunch. Met Mohinder, a Sikh who lives at Ngorongoro, speaks Maasai, and was the one who gave Babu six double brandies – the day Valerie always talks about. Back to Mario's by 3:00 to go out to Tantax (Tanzania Taxidermy). Saw Costas and met Bw. Kamaliza, a former Minister of Commerce, who is now #2 to Costas at Tantax. Costas gave us a complete tour of the taxidermy and then he bestowed me with gifts: one *chui* hatband, a warthog bottle opener, and a lion claw. Who am I to deserve such generosity? Saw Mbangi and Marusu at the plant. Even saw our lion skin. Costas told us that some hunter had a *chui* feeding regularly on a bait near our first camp so we've had a change of plans and will go this Friday to the area and shoot the *chui*, thereby canceling any need for a trip the 20th to 28th. Plans stand now to leave Friday a.m. and return Monday.

From here we had to rush to the Lake Duluti Aqua Club and meet Jack Manuel, Mario's good friend who is a Mauritian, to go fishing. Went out on a nice boat. Jack caught three and Mario got only one fish because his "glutch" wasn't working. That's the brake on his fishing rod. The lake is beautiful. It is a volcanic lake surrounded by heavily wooded hills and offers a magnificent view of Mount Kilimanjaro when the clouds move away. We had some drinks at the club bar and then Jack departed and the three of us went to the Tanzanite for dinner. Mando (von Nagy's son-in-law) was there and he sat down with us while we had dinner. He is a professional hunter and had been out hunting near our camp last week. We told him all about our safari and he said he would have loved to have been along as a spectator on our "amateur" safari since we didn't have all the hangups of a professional hunting trip. He mentioned Nick deBeer and brothers Ben and Hannis Pretorias who are professional hunters and super people. Nick is terrified of buffalo and the brothers plus Mando are afraid of *kifaru* (rhino). The four are planning to go hunting together again which, apparently, will be priceless. Mando rated Mbangi, who is Nick's gun bearer, as the #4 best in Tanzania. What his opinion is worth, I don't know, but we thought Mbangi was great! On the way home, Mario told us about his second wife whom we were not aware of. They are separated. Her family was expelled from Tanzania in the troubles of 1965 and so she went down to join them in South Africa. She is 27 and they have a 10-year-old son.

Tuesday was filled with errands. I had to get export certificates for the items from Tantax. Valerie and I bought Mario a super Swiss army knife as a thank you gift. Valerie and I each bought a white beaded necklace for TSh 8/= each (selling price 12/=) and Valerie bought a "thumb piano" musical instrument, made from recycled materials, for TSh 25/= (sell price 45/= to 60/=) at Ketan's. The guy is apparently giving us a "bargain" because he knows we are friends of Azghar. Still, I had gotten the same necklaces at the other curio shop for TSh 5/= each.

Mario had a super huge lunch for us. Since he cannot get spare parts here for the Ikoma generator, he has decided to go to Nairobi tomorrow and has made plans with Shakir. Skip is still in Nairobi. Mario made arrangements with his friends Señor and Señora Bartola and the four of us will drive to Nairobi for the day. Valerie cannot go because although she now has her proper working papers in hand since yesterday, she wasn't able to get her passport stamped because the immigration office was closed and she can't leave the country until she has her re-entry permit stamped into her passport.

We went fishing again with Mario, but stopped at Tantax on the way. Kamaliza was having Valerie and me try on the Tommy-skin coat and suede jackets and before I knew it, he was wrapping up the blue suede jacket that Mrs. Jakes had tried to sell me my first time at Tantax.

174

Valerie and I were flabbergasted. Costas had left by this time and Kamaliza was telling Mario that the coat was a gift and he would not be putting it on Mario's bill, but still I can't believe that Kamaliza would just give the coat to me. Why? Its selling price is TSh 450/=, nothing to sneeze at. I have been absolutely laden down with beautiful gifts from Tantax. I must get to the root of this matter and will certainly pay for the coat if I can.

Out to Lake Duluti. The day before, Costas had dropped off an elephant bracelet for me there and so the bartender gave it to me. Really!?! We went out in Mario's plywood Carolina IV that we later dubbed his "bathtub." He attaches the motor to the front side of the boat because it is malfunctioning and only goes in reverse, not forward. The engine must be about 1 HP because it barely propels the boat for all the work it does and leaves no wake. Valerie asked how many knots a week it does. Ha, ha! Mario was so cute, as he was paddling with the oar, helping the motor along, he likened his boat to a gondola. He caught three bass and I got some good photos of Mount Kilimanjaro as the clouds parted and the sun shone on the snowcapped peaks. Mario made *plakea* for dinner. It's a Greek dish which Mario says only about 2% of the Greeks really know how to make. One must remove the organs and scales of fish first, in this case a large bass. Then, using the entire fish including the head, tail and fins, cut up the fish crosswise. Fry in oil, adding lots of chopped onion and garlic, and continue frying. Add sliced celery, including leaves, and sliced tomatoes. Optional, add sliced green olives and capers. Bake in medium hot oven for 45 minutes. Just before placing in oven, add one cup boiling water to any casserole-type dish that is baked in the oven to prevent it from drying out. Also put some slabs of butter on top (especially for moussaka and lasagna) to prevent top from becoming too dry. These are Mario's "secrets." Serve with bread, garlic bread is good. Must be very careful when eating this because of all the bones, but the bones increase flavor and excrete gelatin to make a thick sauce. After dinner, Mario showed us some of his home movies.

On Wednesday, June 6th at 6:00 a.m. we headed off for Nairobi after picking up Ely and Mario Bartolo. They are Italian and both deaf and blind as Mario says. Nairobi is a three-hour drive, but with them it was five hours. Tarmac all the way and lots of game. Saw one cheetah, one leopard, giraffe, impala, Grant's gazelle, *kongoni*, African fox. Upon arrival, we ate lunch in the cute little alleyway of the New Stanley Hotel and ordered the specialty, half a spring chicken, salad and roll for 10 shillings. Very good. Unfortunately, after our nice meal we discovered that the car had been towed away because it had been parked in a zone that had been converted to a taxi zone the day before, but had not yet been aptly marked. It took the men all afternoon to retrieve it, costing them a 100 bob fine and the task of replacing the left wing window which had been broken in order for the tow truck driver to release the handbrake. This is Africa! Expect delays. It sure is teaching me patience.

I checked on charter flights home with Ely Bartolo in tow. Mario said she would get lost if she went alone. Difficult to get everything I wanted done and she kept saying, "Do it tomorrow morning." We were to meet the two Marios back at Brunners Hotel at 5:00. It had been decided that this is where we would stay overnight since the afternoon had been taken up with the towed *gari*. I had to placate the Missus when they didn't return on the dot. Finally, at 6:30 I went upstairs to rest. At 7:30 Mario returned and we went to the Hilton coffee shop for dinner. The Bartolos' friend, George Torch, joined us there for dinner, then we all went to the casino as his guests. Mario cashed 100 bob and at the first roulette table we hit a lucky streak and amassed 13/= above. Then the other three wanted to move to another table and there we didn't have any luck at all. When we left an hour later, we had exactly what we started with so nothing gained, nothing lost. The casino is in a very elegantly furnished club featuring the gambling hall with roulette table, blackjack and baccarat, a dining room and a nightclub with entertainment.

At breakfast, Mr. Bartolo, who has lived in Africa 43 years, stumped the waiter when he asked for *mashua moto* instead of *maziwa moto* (hot milk). *Mashua* means boat. I spent the morning running errands while Mario got his needed spare parts and went to see Skip at the Aero Club. I arranged for an airline ticket home, departing Nairobi on July 5th. Mini Cabs and Tours Ltd. features student flights for KSh 1080/= plus KSh 28/= booking fee that will get me from Nairobi to London via Copenhagen. That comes to about $150.00. Charters with other agencies are KSh 1200/= so I saved about $15. I met up with Mario and the Bartolos at the Thorn Tree for lunch. We finished errands after lunch and were off by 4:00. Lion claws with 9K gold work were 1200 shillings at one place and 600 shillings at another. Even difficult to get things in Kenya now. Mario had a terrible time trying to find a coil for a generator and had to settle for the copper wire to make it himself. A gasket he needed cost 33 bob which used to cost 6 bob. Also, the dollar/shilling value exchange rate is going down, but $1 is going for 27 shillings on the black market. Nairobi is so cosmopolitan after Arusha. Lots of young American tourists around, very social. I didn't like it, <u>much</u> prefer the bush!

Mario got some Kentucky Fried Chicken to take with us and eat on the way. The Bartolos had purchased lots of clothes for their shop and on the way to the border, Ely rearranged my Carly bag with her wadded up new purchases so I could claim them as mine if questioned by customs at the border. Mr. B entertained Mario and me with his calling out animals we saw by the wrong names, impalas for Grant's, for instance. We stopped at the Namanga Hotel which is on the Kenyan side of the border so Mario could have another Pilsner before leaving Kenya. This is the same hotel where Mom, Dad and I stopped and I had not remembered the name. We had no problems at the border. In fact, the Immigration officer had to be called from home. They didn't check anything. And, I was able to get my visa extended for one month. We reached Mario's at

9:45 with the news that Costas will be picking us up at 5:00 a.m. tomorrow morning.

Malaika is a Tanzanian love song in Swahili. Miriam Makeba recorded it.

Malaika, nakupenda Malaika	Angel, I love you, Angel
Malaika, nakupenda Malaika	
Ningekuoa mali we	I would marry you, my fortune
Ningekuoa dada	I would marry you, sister
Nashindwa na mali sina we	Was I not defeated by the lack of fortune
Ningekuoa Malaika	I would marry you, Angel
Nashindwa na mali sina we	
Ningekuoa Malaika	
Pesa zasumbua roho yangu	Money is troubling my soul
Pesa zasumbua roho yangu	
Nami nifanyeje, kijana mwenzio	And I, your young lover, what can I do?
Nashindwa na mali sina we	
Ningekuoa, Malaika	
Kidege, hukuwaza kidege	Little bird, I dream of you, little bird
Kidege, hukuwaza kidege	
Nami nifanyeje, kijana mwenzio	
Nashindwa na mali sina we	
Ningekuoa, Malaika	
Nashindwa na mali sina we	
Ningekuoa, Malaika	
Malaika, nakupenda Malaika	
Malaika, nakupenda Malaika	
Nami nifanyeje, kijana mwenzio	
Nashindwa na mali sina we	
Ningekuoa Malaika	
Nashindwa na mali sina we	
Ningekuoa Malaika	
Ningekuoa Malaika	
Ningekuoa Malaika	

Hunting Safari – One More Try

Costas arrived at 5:00 a.m. on Friday, June 8th. Mario woke up not wanting to go, but we talked him into it. This time we were traveling light, no trailer, minimum supplies, no *mpishi*, just Mbangi and a skinner named Stanley. We were off by 5:30. Right before the Game Scout Camp we saw a Greater Kudu which was absolutely mammoth – he couldn't even get through the bush, his horns were so big. We were supposed to have driven in caravan with Alexander, an African farmer from Moshi, but he had gotten a head start. We stopped at Joseph's *duka* and had *chai* there with him. *Chai* is the Indian tea with milk and flavored with spices, especially cardamom. From there we took a different road and headed for Loborsoit, the area that Costas had heard about with a leopard feeding on a bait. This place is about 80 miles southwest of Arusha at a higher elevation, about 4000 feet. We will set up camp near a Maasai village with a *duka*. Mario is happy because the *duka* has plenty of beer and Konyagi. Valerie bought a red bead necklace off one of the Maasai girls for 5 shillings, but the necklace I wanted, the girl wouldn't sell for less than 20 shillings. Will try again later. After hunting around for a site, the only place which was clear of dry grass was along the stream on low land. Mario insisted on setting up here although there is another campsite only a stone's throw away. On top of that, seven *wazungu* are camping there, including the American ambassador to Tanzania, so we heard. We are not too excited about the site although it is beautiful, but Mario can be difficult and we must conserve on petrol rather than running around trying to find an oasis in the middle of hazardous dry grass. We unloaded Mario and the three of us took off to look for another site, but only got as far as the *duka* when we had car troubles. Out of gas. Had to refill using one of the jerry cans of petrol strapped above the rear bumper. Swallowed our pride and went back to Mario's campsite which does have lots of neat climbing trees. About 4:00, Alexander, his wife Jean, a Goan friend Sonny, another African friend Sako and two helpers arrived in their Land Rover and Peugeot. They set up camp with us. Then we all set out in two Land Rovers to go hunt for bait. We lost one impala in the tall grass, but Mario got some *kanga* and on the way back to camp Costas got a Grant's gazelle to use for the *chui* bait and the Maasai who knew where the *chui* tree was showed us to the spot. Supposedly, nine *chui* have been shot in this tree and one man got two *chui* there in one day. Hope we have good luck.

We returned to camp after sunset to find a big party going on. A fellow from the camp next door came to visit. His name is John Speed and he is an American working for the Game Department. He clarified that it's not the American ambassador, but the Spanish ambassador who is at the camp. John is quite an interesting person. He has been here for two years and was very open about the problems here in Tanzania, about the wild game situation and the poaching, especially that done by people working in the Game Department. I slept through most of the partying and woke up at the tail end. I talked to John for a while and found out that he is from Tucson, at least his parents live there. Small world! He knows Doogie Douglas.

Day 2 – Everyone slept in, did not get up until 7:30 and had posho porridge for breakfast. Since we had to conserve on petrol, the men were all going out in one Land Rover so Valerie and I stayed at camp, as did Mario. Valerie and I fixed up the tent. Also repaired the chairs that needed some tightening. About 10:30 we heard the sound of Maasai cowbells. A couple of *morani* had brought their cattle to the stream to drink. The *morani* walked into camp and I thought for sure all the cattle were going to follow them. Our nice semi-clean stream became a muddy mess with 100 cows trampling through it. The cattle moved on to graze, but the Maasai stayed on to stare and a few more joined them. Valerie played doctor to one who had done something to his shin. Looked like gangrene was setting in, the sore had gone quite septic.

The men returned with a beauty of a Greater Kudu. They had checked the *chui* bait but no bite. For lunch we had antipasto. The men had also grilled a delicacy, *mapumbu,* and served it with lemon. It was delicious and tasted like mussels. The men had thought that they had pulled a fast one on us, serving us the testicles of the Greater Kudu. What they didn't know was that Valerie and I grew up eating "mountain oysters."

After lunch, Valerie and I joined the men. They were going out for bait for the lion that has been raiding a Maasai *boma*. The lion had gotten a donkey two nights ago. Valerie and I sat up front with Alex, who was driving, and Costas. This was a mistake because Alex uses half the seat when driving, so I had to scrunch on Valerie and she on Costas. In the back was Mario, Sako, a Maasai who apparently lived at the *boma* in question, and another Maasai tracker, Doublelip, who has been the guide here, more or less. Not sure if Doublelip was his real name or just how we referred to him. We first drove to the *boma* and all the men got out to go by foot to where the lion supposedly dragged the donkey. Valerie and I stayed in the car, ready to drive in case of a shot. Since we were only about 20 feet from the *boma*, all the women and children came out to talk to us, touch us and look at us. They were fascinated by our long nails, our braided hair, our palms, apparently because the color of our palms and theirs is about the same. At one time I counted 10 women and 20 children. The little children are adorable. The Maasai girl from whom I had wanted to buy the necklace was there, but she didn't have the necklace on. The men came back without the lion but they had seen where the lion had lain.

I had spotted a necklace on one of the young girls that I liked so Mario and Alex asked her about the price, but her mama came in and handled the financial end. Alex offered 10/= and they wanted 20/= and it went back and forth. Finally Alex settled on 15/=, gave her the money and took the necklace. We piled into the car with the woman still hounding about more money. Before giving up the necklace though, the young girl asked for the two keys that had been hanging from the front of the necklace and I gave them to her. They love to put all sorts of trinkets on their jewelry and I'm sure she figured she could always make another necklace, but finding more keys was something else.

We carried on to look for bait, not finding much game in the area, and finally settled for an ostrich. Costas had aimed for the male and got the female. These wingless birds are so ugly up close. Their bare legs look like that of a plucked chicken and the foot is actually an 8-inch long toe with a super giant toenail on the end. The bottom of the foot is heavily padded with a thick skin, looking like the skin of a tongue. We dragged the ostrich to the vicinity of the lion, but could not find any good bait trees in the area and finally had to settle for putting it under a thorn tree and covering it with thorn branches.

We drove back to the *boma* to drop off the Maasai. All the women and some of the *morani* who had come home after a day of grazing the cattle were waiting for us. Mama was still screaming about more money for the necklace. I let Alex handle the affair and he finally shelled out 15 bob more, making the total price for the necklace TSh 30/=. They had wanted TSh 40/=, but as Mario says, they don't really know the value of money and so they can be very unreasonable in the prices they ask. Their only gauge of value is cattle since that is how they calculate wealth. They can buy a cow for 400 to 600 bob and will sell it for about 1000. This money most likely will be used to buy another cow. Although I do not in the least begrudge the 30 bob for the necklace, converting it into US $4.00 makes it an expensive necklace for the standards here. The beads probably cost about 2 bob and the labor cost is practically nil so Mama made a huge profit. If we go by the *boma* tomorrow, she'll probably ask for more money so we'll simply tell her we don't have it anymore. The Maasai who had been with us in the car (and bringing all his flies with him, of course) had been fascinated by my watch with the spandex band. He took it off my wrist and tried it on. Sonny made a deal with him, 200 cattle for the watch, but the Maasai wanted me, too, in the deal. That way the guy gets the watch and never loses his cattle and gains me for his domestic help. Not much of a deal for me!

We came back to camp and a little while later the men went out again. Valerie and I walked over to the campsite next door that had been vacated this morning so that we could talk in peace. Stanley came looking for us because Mama Jean and Sonny became concerned about our safety. We are still not Africanized enough to realize the possibility of a lion or leopard, a buffalo or rhino, or an elephant coming upon us.

Mario came back with 18 *kanga*. We had heard gunshots and that's when we headed back to camp because we didn't want to be mistaken for something else and get shot.

For dinner the men cooked shish kebabs of pork and kudu. The kudu was very delicious and tender. Everyone turned in early. Since the four of us have to share a tent, Valerie and I have to put up with Mario's suggestive commentary which we ignore and pretend we have fallen asleep quickly. In the middle of the night I woke up to hear Costas asking Valerie if she heard the lion outside. The sound was imaginative for sure. Lions typically avoid populated areas. He did hear a laughing hyena though. The biggest concern is having to get up in the middle of the night to go pee. Fortunately, that usually wasn't a problem because we weren't drinking that much water. There was beer or soda pop to drink, but since there wasn't a cold box, it would be warm. But, if you are thirsty, a warm beer hits the spot!

Day 3 – Up at 5:30 and we all went to check the lion bait, picking up Doublelip on the way. We parked at the *boma* again and Valerie and I stayed with the car while the men went on foot to the lion bait. No lion had been there, only *fisi*. It was too early in the morning for the Maasai to come bothering us, but three *morani* did pass by. Checked the *chui* bait and only *fisi* again. On the way back to camp, Mario got some *kanga*. We ate breakfast while Mbangi replaced the shackle pin on Alex's Land Rover. It had broken the night before during the men's last jaunt out so they had to use Costas' Land Rover this morning with Alex driving and only three in the front this time. Valerie and I crawled under the *gari* so Mbangi could explain to us what everything was. After it was repaired, we took off again and this time Mama Jean joined us. We headed in the direction the men got the kudu. Saw lots of eland but too far away.

Costas got a zebra. The zebras here are not as attractive as those at our other campsite. Their coats are very scarred because they are always running through so much brush. Sonny got a Grant's gazelle and we left Doublelip with the gazelle while the rest of us went with Alex to find a zebra or something. He had no luck and when we returned to the gazelle, Saidi Kawawa and his men were there. Saidi had gotten a small elephant in the area of *Campi ya Kanga*. Since we left, he has seen both lion and *chui* in our former area. We should have stuck it out there because we knew the area and we were going by hearsay to come here.

Back to camp. Mario had not come with us because he was sleeping when we left. I had a bet that Mario would have prepared something for lunch although Valerie and Costas figured that he had resigned from any managerial duties on this "camping trip." He had the most delicious lunch of spaghetti with stewed meat and green beans. We also have fresh tomatoes, cucumbers and green peppers which Alex grows on his farm, absolutely beautiful vegetables. They have also brought homemade butter which is divine. Everyone took a siesta after lunch. Later on, a fellow came by the camp and it turned out that he was the one who knew the proper *korongo* for the *chui* bait. We all got up to go with him but he had left. Costas and Alex then took off on foot looking for him, with no luck, and were gone for at least an hour. As Valerie had said, she wouldn't have come down from her tree if she knew this would happen. In the meantime, though, she shot Sonny's

187

.375. Valerie said the sound hurt her ears more than the recoil hurt her shoulder.

Mama Jean taught me how to wrap the *kitambaa* (fabric) around my head. For height, wrap another *kitambaa* around the head before putting on the desired *kitambaa*. The women usually use two meters of *kitenge,* or one piece. Overlap one of the raw edges to shape the *kitambaa* into more of a square, then fold into triangle. From here, wrap the triangle around head in any desirable fashion.

After Costas and Alex returned, all the men took off to look for buffalo or something. We were not invited to go along. Mbangi wasn't going either. In fact he hasn't gone on any of the outings except for the first day and this morning when the three of us were under the car, Valerie asked him if he would go on the next outing of the day and he said no and had no interest in going. This certainly isn't like our last safari. Valerie and I walked over to the other campsite. She climbed up a huge tree to sit in and I wrote in my journal. Mbangi came later and he scrambled up the tree that Valerie was in, about six times faster than she had climbed up. Shortly after he came, one of Alex's men came over and he was up the tree in a flash. Mbangi told me to write in my book that there are three baboons in the tree. Ha, ha! Mbangi really is a cutie. I think we have made this trip halfway bearable for him. He had told Valerie he wants a penpal in the United States and so I offered to look for someone. Also, I'll correspond with Mbangi. He wants copies of some of the pictures and made a special request for a pair of Levi's and a cowboy belt. The boys had another bottle of *pure* which they said was much better than the one bought at the Game Scout Camp. Mbangi went to get it. By this time it was getting dark so Valerie and I came down and we sat on the rocks and drank *pure*. It is raw Konyagi distilled from bananas and molasses. No wonder you can't buy molasses in Tanzania. *Pure* is homemade and illegal. The penalty is about three years in prison if caught drinking it, but all the Africans drink it because it only costs 4 bob a bottle. Don't know what the alcohol content is but after two tots my head was swimming. It absolutely fractures me, the boys had the *pure* in an old Vat 69 bottle and used maize husks for the stopper. The *pure* had a very smooth taste, but a different flavor from Konyagi. Valerie likened to it quicker than I, but I would enjoy it in small amounts.

We heard the *gari* and so made our way back to camp. This interlude has been the most enjoyable, relaxing part of our trip. Heard Mario and Sonny singing. They surely sound as though they are in a good mood and I wonder if they had hit the bottle while out.

The big meal of the day was at lunch time so we had some pickings for dinner and then Alex and Jean toddled off to bed. Sonny stayed, Valerie brought out the *kiko*, and Mario and I got into a big discussion about souls. Are there X amount of souls or are there an infinite number of souls? Hmm? Back to the original question.

Day 4 – Up at 5:30 and all the men, except for Sonny, went to check the baits. Valerie and I are not

189

included. Costas no longer insisting we come because he's perceptive enough to know that Alex's group thinks of us as "excess baggage." Valerie and I went to our spot after Doublelip had taken me to find a *mswaki* (or *gigé* in Maasai.) This is the Salvadora persica tree from which the Maasai cut the straight branches and use as toothbrushes. The bark is scraped away and the fibrous inside is chewed, forming a brush and then rubbed over the teeth. The juice is very refreshing. Makes a great pacifier.

The men returned about 9:30 with no news except that they had seen elephants. We broke up camp and a couple of Maasai came to collect the remains. All of us left by 10:45, but we set our own pace and did not keep up with Alex's two cars. Every time we saw cattle, they were right in the middle of the road. They must think the road will lead them somewhere. One large herd of cattle was being herded from Dodoma to Arusha for slaughtering. They were poor contrasts to the nice looking Maasai cattle in this area and these were the cattle that would be supplying the Arusha butchers. We had a leisurely picnic lunch between Joseph's *duka* and the Game Scout Camp near Lolkisale. I supervised the cutting down of a couple of branches for Costas to use at his shop in window displays. We tied one to the front fender, making for a strange sight.

Between the Game Scout Camp and the beginning of the tarmac (paved road), along the Infantry Training Ground, we saw groups of Tanzanian soldiers practicing maneuvers in rocketry, camouflage, etc. and saw a few of the Chinese military advisers in their blue pajama uniforms and sombrero-type hats.

We arrived in Arusha at 5:00 with plenty of stares at our tied-on branch along the way. We invited Costas to come back for Mario's famous black bass curry that Valerie and I had insisted Mario make since he had talked about it so much. However, Costas had seemed rather down for the latter part of the trip home and he didn't seem too keen about coming back after getting cleaned up. I think that Costas was sad that our good times had come to an end and that I would be returning home within a month. It would be easier for him to make the break then and there rather than to drag it out. Costas is such a super fellow who has a genuine and warm nature. Never once on the safaris did he make Valerie and me uncomfortable the way Mario sometimes did. Costas always behaved in a perfectly decent manner and is truly a gentleman and good friend. I never heard him berate anyone.

Valerie and I had to go into town for shampoo, etc. and so we walked down the driveway as Costas, Mbangi and Stanley got in the Land Rover to turn around and head out. As they passed us on the driveway, we were on Costas' side of the Land Rover. Costas put his arm out and grabbed us each by the shoulder, giving it a gentle squeeze. That gesture said more than any words ever could. As they waited to turn left, Valerie went up to Costas and said, *"piga hema."* That put a humorous touch on the situation which was desperately needed at the time. It was sad to look at Costas' and Mbangi's faces because I know we mean a lot to them and by the same token, they mean a lot to us. Initially, I am sure that Costas was apprehensive about two women joining this hunting safari; he had never met Valerie or me. But by the end, we had become great friends. Valerie and I added to the fun. We were always ready for adventure, never complained, and kept a sense of humor when things went wrong. Strangers a month ago, very good friends now.

As we walked into town, both Jogi and Shakir passed by going the other way and waved. On the way home, we ran into Jogi's sisters and sisters-in-law. Back at Mario's, he helped me wrap the Zanzibar chest and suede jacket for mailing. Then we dined on his delicious bass curry and learned that he had made plans for us to go as far as Ngorongoro tomorrow with Jack Manuel.

A Circuitous Route

I had to mail off my souvenirs before leaving with Jack at 10:00. Now that I have a reservation to depart July 5th, it was imperative to ship what I wouldn't be able to carry in my backpack. Not only did I have to find boxes, brown wrapping paper and string, but the knots have to be sealed with hot wax. The problem, though, is that if I seal the boxes before taking to the post office, then the clerk will want to know what is inside and instruct me to unwrap. If I take the box unwrapped, then the clerk gets pissed. I've spoiled his fun. The clerk had glasses like Joseph's, window glass with no curvature so the light reflected off the flat surface. After he was satisfied, he took his fountain pen and with a flourish, signed off on the customs form. I wrapped up the boxes again, tied them with string, melted the knots with sealing wax and off they went. For a total of 54 shillings (or about $6.00) the two boxes would travel by ship and reach Tucson in about four months. The Zanzibar chest, *kitenges* and batik were packed in one box. In the other was the beautiful blue suede jacket, my *Mwenge* (torch) shirt and a small gourd. I do hope that they reach their destination undamaged.

Jack picked us up at 10:15. Mario was not coming with us because he couldn't find all the necessary spare parts he needed for the FIL generator. We stopped at Lake Manyara for lunch. Just before the Mbulu turn off, Jack asked us if we would like to go there with him today and then he could take us to Ngorongoro the next day. He had to check the area and this would give us the opportunity to see Mbulu. It was a climb through beautiful vegetation to 6000 feet. Since there are no eating places in Mbulu, Jack bought a rooster along the way. He will have someone kill it and roast it for us. As we made our way up, we stopped to look for rubies in the eroded sand cliffs by the side of the road. I took pictures of the houses which are mud huts built in the side of the hills. The front height of the hut might stand all of three feet above the outside ground, but the ground inside is dug out to make a sunken floor. The huts are probably 10 feet by 10 feet and people bring their goats, cows and chickens inside at night. Each day, the manure would be removed from inside and was piled outside. A *mzungu* (white person) most probably would get sick if he ever smelled the inside of a hut. Jack tried to buy some tobacco from a fellow at one hut, but it wasn't ready. Mbulu tobacco is what the Maasai smoke and what nearly killed Valerie.

We reached Mbulu at 5:00. Jack is in charge of the roadworks for the northeastern part of Tanzania so we stayed in the spare bedrooms at the "comwork" yard. Valerie and Jack went out for a walk and I wrote some letters to friends. He took us to a bar for drinks and there, had the rooster prepared and brought to us. Then we went to another bar, with four Africans piling in along the way. A cute little Mbulu gal was working there. Her name was Vicki also. She showed me how she wrapped the *kitenge* around her head which was a different style than I had seen before.

The next morning we headed for Dongobesh to check the roads and passed more interesting houses. We stopped to watch some cattle-dipping. It is done once a week and free of charge. Cattle are dipped for protection from fleas. Saw lots of wild lovebirds in Dongobesh, too. We also went to the open-air market there. The big once-a-month cattle auction was starting. It was a neat marketplace and I was able to get some good photos. I bought two *pangas* (machetes) at 7/= each and a double *kitenge* for Mom. A popular item is the 10,000-mile sandals, as we jokingly called them. Old tires are cut up to form the sole of the sandal. The sidewall is cut to form the straps. A great way to recycle, but don't count on any arch support with these sandals as the sole is concave from the curvature of the tire. Deep-fried balls of dough were for sale, but we didn't dare try them. The area is so off the beaten track that the people are not accustomed to seeing *wazungu* (white people). They wear their *kitenges* in an Arabic fashion, by draping it over their heads. (There are several words used for the colorful print fabric and as I recall, were interchangeable. The *kanga* – not to be confused with the guinea fowl, same spelling – and *kitenge* refer to the colorful fabric sold in panels, typically 1 meter x 1.5 meters. Then there is the *kikoi* cloth which is striped and what is used to make the *kanzu*. *Kitambaa* typically refers to a smaller piece of fabric such as a napkin. In this journal I add an "s" at end of some words to make plural, but Swahili would add a prefix to denote plural. For instance, the "m" of *mzungu* denotes singular. Replace the "m" with "wa" (*wazungu*) denotes plural. As we drove back to Mbulu, Jack told us that the road from Dongobesh to Arusha had been used in the 1971 and 1972 East African Safari Rallies. Lunch was out of tins. Vicki came by to pick up the *kitenge* we had promised her since she had taken such good care of us the night before...and because her name was Vicki! She was quite sad that we would be so generous and then leave. She really was a sweet and appreciative girl.

We left at 2:30 for Ngorongoro, arriving at 5:30. First we stopped at the Forest Lodge and dropped off the rooster that Jack had bought today for the cook to make chicken curry and chapatis for us for dinner. Mohinder Mahendra, the owner and chap I had met at the New Arusha hotel with Valerie, Shakir and Ferdie, was not there, he had gone to India. We checked in at Ngorongoro Crater Lodge. Unfortunately, Justis was not there, but in Arusha. It felt so good to get a bath before dinner after all we had done the past two days. From the window I saw an elephant about 100 yards away, and as I was taking a picture, zebras ran under window. We had a drink at the Lodge and then headed over to the Forest Lodge for a brandy and dinner. It is freezing cold here at this 7000 foot elevation. The chilly mountain air definitely warranted the fires that were burning in the fireplaces. After a delicious curry dinner, we went back to Ngorongoro Crater Lodge and to bed.

Valerie and I slept late. We woke to a great mist outside so we lingered in bed. We haven't had this luxury in a long time. Jack left about 10:00 for Arusha. He had only come to Ngorongoro to bring Valerie and me. We did not get dressed until 1:00, after a good sisterly talk about all we had done since my arrival, and then we walked over to the dining room for lunch. Julee, a local guide who comes through FIL with clients frequently, was in the dining room. He looked like he was on a very private tour. After lunch we sat by the fireplace in the bar, keeping our eyes half open for a ride to the Fort. We are in no hurry to get back. Later, the desk clerk sent a fellow to our room who has a kombi and room to take us to Seronera tomorrow at 7:00. We had beef fondue for dinner which was very good. The new manager, Biba from Moshi, introduced himself and bought us a drink. Tomorrow is an early day, so we toddled off to bed and a good night's sleep.

We met Willie, the German fellow who was giving us a lift to Seronera, at 7:00. His kombi is a super Volkswagen van with two beds and is equipped like a boat with a sink, table and booth seating. There was a heavy mist around Ngorongoro, but we drove out of it as we descended down the escarpment. I never get tired of this view of the sweeping Serengeti plains in the distance. We passed Idi in the Ngorongoro Crater Lodge lorry going to Ikoma. The road between Ngorongoro and Naabi Gate is still being worked on, with big red piles of murram in the road, so we had to follow the track along the shoulder of the road. Jack had told us he has only four graders for his entire region. No wonder the road hasn't been worked on since we last traveled it. The cost is 14,000 bob per mile to grade the road. We got stuck in some loose fine dirt. Idi stopped and helped us out. In the process we got filthy dirty and were completely covered in the fine red dirt. We reached Naabi Gate, the entrance to the SNP, a little after 9:30. Willie needed to be out of Ngorongoro before 9:30 or he would have to pay for another day. Getting stuck didn't help our timing. I had to pay 20 shillings entrance fee. The only other time I have had to pay was when Mom, Dad and I came through, at this gate too, and David had issued orders to give us comp entrance. Valerie says we'll simply go to David or Ndosi and get my money back. I got sidetracked to look for *chui* on the way to Seronera, but did see thousands of zebras, huge herds.

Willie dropped us off at Seronera Wildlife Lodge. Bryan Payne was there, fortunately, and also Tony Wilkes and his wife. Tony is the manager at Lobo Lodge and they had come for lunch at SWL, before driving to Ngorongoro. We ate lunch with Bryan, but had no luck finding a ride to Ikoma. At 4:00 the three of us went on a game run toward Moru Kopjes, driving through unfrequented areas of the park. We passed some large herds of zebra and wildebeest and saw a lone elephant near one of the hills. We noticed a very stagnant smell as we drove by Lake Magadi (not to be confused with the lake by same name in Ngorongoro Crater). The area was beautiful and green, green, green. The hills were covered with flora, not a lush vegetation, but a plentiful plains vegetation. In fact, all around Seronera it is very green, the greenest I have ever seen it. We turned back about 5:30 and passed our lone *tembo*. Bryan drove up close to him to get a picture. The young male obviously had something wrong with his right foreleg which might have been congenital because the muscle of the upper leg looked shriveled. He was definitely favoring the leg and couldn't move fast. He did feel endangered by us and when we got within 30 feet of him, he faced us, spread out his ears, lifted his trunk and trumpeted, but couldn't really charge because of his leg. Nevertheless, I was scared. There were lots of zebra, wildebeest and buffalo around the lodge. All of a sudden, about 200 zebra ran across the road in front of us, giving me a dizzying back-and-forth sensation of black/white black/white. Because of the contaminated water problem, Bryan has had to close the lodge except for lunches. Valerie and I stayed in his spare room and had omelettes à la Bryan for dinner. Omelette *baveuse* is one that is not cooked completely through. Bryan and David have had a tiff brought on by this water problem and aren't speaking to each other so we didn't want to make a big deal about having him take us over to David's. Therefore, neither David nor Ndosi know we are here.

The next morning we got a ride with two folks in a van to Park Headquarters. Neither David nor Ndosi were there. Some big fish from Arusha had come and so they were out on a game drive. I wanted to go to the game scout post to buy some park books and a national park pin. A Parks Land Rover gave us lift back to the lodge. Valerie and I toured the construction areas, new bar and swimming pool. The pool is being built among the natural rocks so concrete forms only a small portion of the pool. At this point, it looks as though it would be a dangerous pool.

Bryan, Valerie and I were the only ones having lunch inside the big, empty dining room. Bryan, being British, had scones served as part of the meal. He educated us on the proper pronunciation of the word. They are called scones – with a long o sound – until eaten, then they are called "scawns" because they are "gone." As we were lunching, David arrived with a visiting Parks accountant, a Mr. Babu, but no relation. David and Bryan ignored each other, but Valerie did go over and talk to David. David said he would take us to Retima Springs (hippo pool) that afternoon if we were still here, but Bryan had found us a ride with a UTC tour and we would be leaving at 4:30. Bryan took me on a super tour of kitchen and construction areas. We left with the UTC tour. I shared a seat with a cute couple my age, Joan and Jerry. Earlier, Valerie had spotted Rojabo in the tractor so we had him take most of our luggage in the trailer. We arrived back at Fort Ikoma about 6:30, after being gone a good two weeks longer than we had originally planned. It was good to see everyone. Caroline was in the bar and shared the good news with us that she and Jurgen are getting married July 18th. Gideon came up later and had dinner with us. All rooms occupied so we slept in tent 46. Still haven't moved into "our tent" because the bathroom is not finished.

The Taj

About 8:00 the next morning, Sherlock, now sporting his very own window-pane glasses, came into Valerie's office to announce that we had visitors from Mwanza. It was Yuri and Olga with a Russian friend, Igor Anisimov, who was with UNESCO headquarters in Paris. They had arrived from Mwanza that morning and were taking Igor on a sightseeing trip. Yuri had been to Moscow since we last saw him and brought us some Russian chocolates and a whiskey-colored vodka. He had hoped to go hunting. The Fort needed the Land Rover for other purposes and so we went down to Jurgen's camp to check with Gideon. There was a problem with their Land Rover so they made plans for Yuri, Olga and Igor to go on a Serengeti game run and then possibly go hunting in late afternoon providing Gideon's clients had not arrived. The three took off and Valerie and I spent the day getting organized and cleaned up. We had not washed our hair since before the second leg of the hunting safari!

Unfortunately, hunting in the afternoon never worked out for Yuri. I took photos out on the terrace of Yuri, Olga and Igor. Sadly, this roll of film must have gotten lost because I have never seen the photos. The roll also had photos taken yesterday of the lame elephant and the green, green plains. Too bad. I used slide film and it had to be mailed to London for developing and then we had it sent to our parents in Tucson for safe keeping since we had no way to show slides. Film was not always available. For the most part, the gift shop at Fort Ikoma kept rolls on hand for tourists, but many were either beyond the expiration date or hadn't been stored properly. Some of the rolls I purchased resulted in slides with a green tinge. This particular roll must have gotten lost somewhere between Fort Ikoma, London and Tucson. Oh well.

David Babu had arrived earlier in the day. Valerie took him out to the Taj for a long talk. I think she's trying to help patch up the rift between Bryan and David over the water issue in Seronera due to the PVC pipe that keeps bursting because the hole was drilled off-center.

Neil Outram arrived with a family of four private tour and Patrice DuFar with his four kombies of New York tourists. Patrice would greet his group in Nairobi with the perfect spiel. He announced that if anybody in the group was afraid of snakes or spiders, didn't like dust or delays, they should stay in Nairobi, but if they wanted the adventure of a lifetime, board the minibus...and no complaining!

Valerie and I enjoyed a lovely dinner with Yuri, Olga and Igor. Lots of toasts! Neil and Patrice joined us for after-dinner drinks. We were up early the next morning to see Yuri, Olga and Igor off, but they had already left. After breakfast I chatted with a woman on Neil's private family tour. She is associated with a public relations firm in New York City. When she found out I was a Home Economist she gave me the name of her associate whose client is Johnson

Wax. The company is looking for people to represent Johnson Wax in various sections of the country. When she left the States on June 1st, he was looking for someone to represent the southwest area. She says he is very aggressive so not to be modest, but very conservative so dress Midwestern. Out in the middle of Africa and I have a job lead! I'll be home in a few weeks and will have to hit the pavement and look for a job.

Neil and I spent the morning on the terrace discussing and recommending books. We then climbed the water tower to get an unobstructed view. As far as the eye can see to the horizon, north, south, east and west, the plains are a beautiful green. Too bad the pool is empty because of generator problems. It was the only thing that spoiled our view. As we were climbing back into the car, Patrice arrived with his four kombies and in a loud voice asked, "Oh, is this Honeymoon Safari?" Typical Patrice.

I rested after lunch. Asinta, the new young *ayah* for Judy, kept bringing over little gifts, some candies, a packet of cookies, bananas, oranges. She wants to make friends; undoubtedly, she is very lonely. Asinta is all of about 10. She and Judy came over for a visit. Shy little Judy rarely makes eye contact. She barely looked up at me, yet her first real response was when she was leaving. Asinta had her by one hand and Judy turned around and waved bye-bye with the other. That warmed my heart.

Gideon came over with clients and sent the two ostrich eggs he had found to our room with Daudi. By the time we got to the bar, he was gone. Neil's group had left after lunch. Before he left, Neil left his phone number with us and explicit instructions to call him when in Nairobi. He and three others have started their own tour group called Game Trails Tours, Ltd. We invited Patrice to come to the room after dinner where we watched the moon rise at 9:00 from Skip's terrace with *Atom Heart Mother* playing.

Patrice's group left after breakfast. He won't be in Nairobi around July 4th so this was my last time to see him. Valerie and I made serious attempts to move into the Taj. I definitely want that experience before I leave. She asked Norbert and a few others to hang things and make the necessary repairs in the bathroom. We took a picnic lunch out to the Taj and enjoyed the peace and quiet. The three cranes bothered us and one took a nip at my elbow while I was eating. After lunch we found all three up on the thatched roof. We went back out to the Taj about dinner time. Gideon came by to see if we were moved in. Valerie asked Daudi to deliver a message to Peter, the cook, to fix two shish kebabs and for Daudi to bring them out, but Daudi misunderstood her and sent Peter out instead, in his all whites, no less. Anyway, Peter did bring out two shish kebabs. We dined alfresco, truly a relaxing, enjoyable evening even though it took us 45 minutes to get the fire lit in the fire ring. It is June 19th and we spent our first night in the Taj!! Hallelujah!! We were awakened about 3:00 a.m. to find Daudi making a big fire from the coals. The night watchmen like to sit by the fire early in the morning to ease away the chill. We keep the flaps of the screened windows open for the fresh night air.

Arusha

I ate breakfast with a fellow named Colin who was hitchhiking through and an American couple who were traveling by bus when I heard a plane which looked as though it were lost. Could it be Skip? Ha, ha! No, it was the Flying Doctor to pick up a tourist about which I knew nothing. A little later I heard another plane. This time it was the Robinsons giving us quite a show with their buzzing. Mr. Robinson and Larry were on their way to Nairobi by way of Arusha and offered to let me come along as far as Arusha so I jumped at the opportunity, grabbing my Carly bag. Colin hitched a lift as far as Arusha, too. This reminds me of the adage I learned from Larry. "It's not who you are and what you have, it's who you know and what they have."

Flying over the Serengeti, we saw the albino giraffe that lives in a particular area and I was able to get a photo of it. We flew over Olduvai Gorge and Ngorongoro Crater. To see these two landmarks by air was quite a thrill. We landed in Arusha about 12:30 after a flight which took a little over an hour. Larry, Colin and I lunched at the New Arusha Hotel while Mr. Robinson took care of his business. We bumped into Shakir as we were leaving the hotel. The Robinsons left at 2:30 for Nairobi and now I had to work on a ride back to Fort Ikoma. I went over to Mario's but he wasn't home although all of his cars were there. I went to

Shakir's office and a few minutes later Jack Manuel walked in. He said that Mario was in Dar. Then I went over to see Azghar at his office. He arranged for me to stay at his Uncle Grewal's house that night. Then I saw Beryl, Charin and Meet before going to the Gymkhana Club with Azghar. On the way, we passed Shakir and so we had a drink at the New Arusha Hotel with him and Eve who is from Nairobi, but has been living in San Francisco for the last two years and is involved with a travel agency there. We spent the entire evening at the Gymkhana Club. Where else? I did see Bryan Payne who is in town on business. Beryl came late, after her play rehearsal. Azghar arranged a tennis game for me the next day at the Gymkhana Club. Then Azghar, Bryan, Beryl, Shakir and I went to the hamburger stand next to the Metropole for a midnight dinner.

The next morning Azghar took Beryl and me to the Meerschaum Kiko factory. I bought three *kikos*. All the pipes sold at the factory are rejects and therefore much less expensive. I stopped in at the East African Airways (EAA) office to reconfirm my flight, then zipped across the street to see the recently opened Tantax shop. Costas came in while I was there. Bryan was there also. I had lunch with Beryl, Bryan and Salim, Hallmark's (travel agency) financial manager. I heard Mario is back in town so I went over to see him. The tennis game was scheduled for 4:30 with Annabel, Jackie and Chris, three people who I only met last night. But before the game, Azghar had to take me to buy a pair of Chinese tennis shoes for 18/50 shillings. After playing not too badly, given I hadn't played tennis in years,

I met up with Beryl and Bryan at the Gymkhana Club. The three of us decided to go see the movie *What's Up Doc*. It was funny. Beryl invited me to spend the night at her house to which I eagerly accepted.

On Friday, Mario picked up Beryl and me and took us to Tantax. Costas had the certificate of ownership for the lucky bones from our lion that he had given me. I took some pictures of a mounted lion; it was not ours, though. Costas told us that he and Nick DeBeer are going out Tuesday for *chui*. He invited me to go along, but I had to decline. We headed back into town so that I could run some errands and ran into Costas a few times. A Land Rover with a bunch of Africans carrying beer overturned but landed back on its wheels while going around the Clock Tower round-about. Big commotion. The *mpishi* from Kirawira stopped me and asked me where Gerard was, as if I would know. Arusha is a small town. It's amazing how many people I saw who I had met elsewhere. For her kind hospitality, I treated Beryl to lunch at the New Arusha Hotel. I had first met her over dinner in Arusha in January. We went shopping in the open-air market and I bought a few silly souvenirs and then I kept Beryl company at the beauty parlor. Mario invited Beryl and me over to his home for dinner and then I went to rehearsal with Beryl for the play she is in and spent the night at her place again.

Mario picked me up at 6:00 a.m. as he will drive me back to Ikoma. We stopped at Ngorongoro Crater Lodge and picked up a Land Rover there for the rest of trip to Ikoma. We had to wait 2½ hours for it, though. First, a hole in the radiator had to be repaired. We took Rojabo with us and finally left at 1:00. He had to keep refilling the radiator. Then we discovered a flat tire while we stopped for a picnic lunch so that had to be repaired, which involved removing the tire tube, patching it, putting it back in the tire, and pumping it up. It takes at least half an hour. Rojabo showed me the *mirungi* he had brought along. It's a stimulant. One eats the reddish stem and leaves. I certainly did not try it. And then a rear window broke while we bumped over the terrible road between Olduvai Gorge and the Serengeti. After a 12-hour journey, we reached Ikoma at 6:00. Julee was here with Margaret and Elizabeth. Don't recall the drama of all this, but do recall that there was some. Rahemtulla, the refrigerator man was also here to do some repairs. We had sukiyaki for dinner which was a lovely way to end the day.

Fort Ikoma Lodge in the Serengeti Plains, Tanzania
Our tent, the Taj Mahal "Taj" is at left of photo.

The main compound. Dining room is adjacent to the terrace.
Original towers of the German fort are upper left and lower right.

Mother, Dad, Valerie　　　　*Putney and Skip Leavitt at front entrance*

Larry and Ron Robinson;　　*Ruth, Freddie, Eddie and Leonard*
Vicki and Valerie　　　　　*Robinson; sugar cane*

Olga, Lyuba and Yuri　　　*Robinsons' airplane – Cessna 206*
Vishnyakov　　　　　　　*Maasai women seeking shade*

First ever hot air balloon ride in the Serengeti; Obadiah, Mike, Valerie and David. Vicki with Jerry Rilling.

Hunting Safari with Costas and Mario. Seven of us in short-wheelbase Land Rover. Costas and Mbangi with lion.

*Lisa with Coen; with Valerie at Taj;
joyful reunion with Vicki;
posing for an FIL publicity photo;
on steps of Dumas Den.*

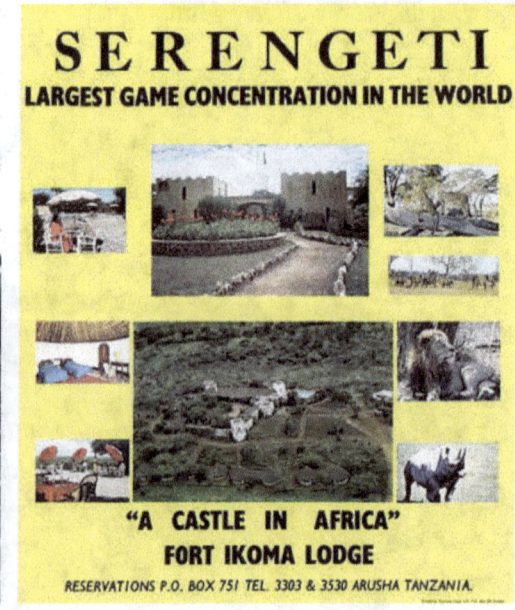

Kenya Safari first night campsite. On equator with Gideon.
Soaking wet tent and Gideon working on Esmerelda. Mount Kenya.

Climbing Mount Kilimanjaro. Spent New Year's Eve at 15,000 feet.

Mother, Shakir, Dad in Arusha

Mario, Valerie, Dad, Grant

David, Jogi, Obadiah, Valerie

Ikoma Lion Dancers

Annalise (green top), her 3 children, Putt

Lisa, Vicki, Jack hiking to Heliograph Hill

Valerie's Staff Soccer Team

Departure Day

Olduvai Gorge – Zinjanthropus
Man discovered by Mary Leakey

Joseph Nyerere, brother of President
Julius Nyerere, with Valerie and Vicki

Maasai girls shrieked when feeling
Vicki's hair for the first time

Polisi training session at the Fort

Aerial photo of the Taj taken by Vicki from helicopter

Lisa released to the wild at Gol Kopjes, Serengeti National Park – March 31, 1975

Excerpts from **Swift & Enduring** by
George & Lory Frame

Last known photo of Lisa. With Bill Hurst at
Ngorongoro Crater – March 1976

Skip Leavitt's visit to Tucson – September 1999

Reunion in Big Bear, CA – April 15, 2000

Reunion with Mohamed Ismail and son Naheed
The Grand Canyon – July 22, 2009

Reunion with Lyuba and Chris Pawlik
Alaska Cruise – August 2014

July 5th, Where Are You?

A group of locals in the travel business descended on the Fort about 11:00 a.m. the day after I returned from Arusha. Alan Brown, Salim and Danny from Hallmark, Janis Wilkes, the wife of the Lobo Lodge manager, and Bill with Rhino Safaris Ltd. They had stopped by to see Fort Ikoma, a lodge none of them had ever been to before, and then were off to Seronera for lunch and then on to Ngorongoro, but we convinced them that they should go to Seronera for lunch and then bring Bryan back with them to spend the night because we were having a super party. Off they went with the promise to return. Meanwhile, Valerie and I enjoyed an ostrich omelet for lunch. Someone had found some eggs in an abandoned nest. I spent the afternoon making tortilla chips, moussaka and Sherry trifle in the kitchen. It's pretty much me alone in the kitchen as the staff doesn't arrive until later in the afternoon to begin the dinner preparations. I want to be done and have the kitchen utensils and work areas cleaned up before they arrive so as to not be in their way. Patrick Duncan arrived about 6:30. He's leaving the Serengeti in two days to travel through southern Tanzania before departing for home from Nairobi. His stint at SRI is up. We will miss Patrick and his "dung" conversations. We talked him into spending the night so that he could attend the "tent warming" party we were throwing for the Taj Mahal, Valerie's (and mine while

I'm still here) new abode. The Hallmark troop arrived with Bryan in tow and then in Bryan's honor, the water went off. Turns out the pump wasn't running properly, but Mushi was able to have it fixed so Bryan, indeed, was able to take a shower. Poor guy, he has to live the nightmare of no water every day. The party got underway about 8:00. We brought the food I had prepared out to the Taj. A big fire blazed in the fire pit, music was playing, good food and good company. Patrick felt he had to get back to Seronera so left at 10:30. He got a great sendoff. During our revelry, someone noticed that we have our very own bat who hangs upside down from a branch on the tree that Fred, the Cape buffalo skull, is hanging from.

After a delicious breakfast of an ostrich omelet, our Hallmark friends, Janis and Bill left. They were glad they had changed their plans and had come to the party. I tried to get organized for leaving. Skip returned about noon after his two-month safari. He had spent the night at Lobo last night with Tony Wilkes and about 7:00 they had gotten the message that Janis would not be returning that night because of a big do at Ikoma. Skip said they would have come had Lobo not had a new assistant manager. This, after the former assistant manager was sacked because he had fiddled 1400 shillings worth of liquor. When I told Skip I was leaving July 5th, he took on such a shocked look and said I couldn't possibly leave. "Cancel the reservation! Quarantine! Quarantine! Cholera epidemic! The tanks are coming over the hills! (So I could barely get through.) Siege! Siege!" Well, talk about not wanting me to leave!

Skip came out for drinks at the Taj about 4:00. Later, Valerie and I discussed my staying. As far as she is concerned, I'm a fool to want to leave, she sees no reason for me to hurry back. Still later, Skip, Mario and Rahemtulla came out to the Taj for cocktails. Valerie brought up again the subject of my staying and Skip said, "What? I thought that was settled." Guess it was! On future occasions, if I would make a terrible pun like the "spoors car" one, Skip would famously exclaim, "July 5th, where are you?"

Julee tried in the morning to get Mini Cabs over the radio in order to postpone my reservation, but couldn't get through. He sent a message that he would try again at 1:00. Therefore, since there was no need to pack, I spent the morning making a Quiche Lorraine for lunch. Julee tried again at 1:00 and Skip recorded the conversation on tape. Success! My reservation has been postponed until September 19th. This gives me plenty of time to think about what to do. The first thing I planned to do was make lasagna for dinner, but Mario was in a nervous twit so I made spaghetti with clam and tomato sauce instead. A tour is here with Carol Perkins. Her husband Marlin is the host of the American TV show called *The Wild Kingdom*, a show I have watched *mingi* times. He is with the other half of the tour and will be coming to the Fort at a later date. Tor Allen, Finn's brother was one of the guides. One of the topics discussed was the U.S. banning of spotted cat trophies that went into effect February 28, 1972. It's a big *matata* though, because the countries of origin say it is in direct conflict with their internal affairs. The law might be repealed allowing importation of personal trophies only, but no commercial importation.

Mario and Rahemtulla have finished their work on the generators and refrigerators, respectfully, and left before lunch. The Cold Room is running and, a victory for Valerie, the fridges will be on 24 hours a day! I made an apple crisp as a trial for dinner desserts, then made chili for dinner. Julee's brother, Ahmed, and an English fellow, Peter, are here for the night. They, plus Margaret and Elizabeth joined us for dinner. Margaret said her problem has been resolved and she is to be out of the country in 24 hours. Apparently, Ahmed brought her the news. Peter teaches at a missionary school in Mwanza and we listened with interest as he discussed teaching methods.

Julee, Margaret and Elizabeth left after breakfast for Mwanza. Julee will try to have Margaret and Elizabeth's visas extended. Apparently, Margaret's husband informed immigration that they are no longer dependent on him. Marital difficulties, me thinks.

Skip left soon afterwards for Arusha, taking my passport to have it stamped. Ruth Fletcher, the other American part-owner is here and Skip has to be in Arusha while she picks through the account books. Pity. None of us enjoy being around "Aunt Ruthie" so I took a nice morning nap. Joseph Nyerere, his wife Dolores and son stopped here for dinner on the way back to Butiama from Nairobi where they've been for seven weeks. Later, Valerie and I went down to Saidi's bar at staff quarters to collect two beers which are partial payment for the safari vest Valerie sold

Saidi. We were given beers by the dispenser Peter, and then by Rashidi. Gideon came by later on. The three of us were invited to join in the *ujamaa* dinner where everyone eats from the same pan. The *nyama na ndizi*, essentially a meat and plantain stew was served with *mkate* bricks (deep-fried bread). After eating, it feels like you have a brick in your stomach. We all have to "hunker" around the low table. Most Africans don't use chairs so they squat when eating or resting. Once I got used to it, it wasn't so bad. Before we left, plans were underway for an African lunch for tomorrow.

We went back down to staff quarters for lunch the next day and I took some pictures of Daudi in his *shamba*. I also got a photo of me with a bunch of the staff on the tractor. Benjamin made the lunch, *kondoo na viazi* with *posho*. Basically, it is boiled meat and whatever else you desire or have available. Again, we ate *ujamaa* style. Mrs. Robinson, Eddie and Freddie arrived in TZ6049 – Ron's Peugeot. They had come to wish me farewell only to find out that I wasn't leaving. They gave me a *Makonde* figurine as a going away present. This carving style originated in Mozambique. Body parts are connected in unusual combinations. Word is that these carvings inspired Pablo Picasso in his artwork. After two meals, *ujamaa*-style, Valerie and I relished the BLTs we had for dinner. Peter Joseph had brought fresh tomatoes. We have been without tomatoes for ages! Six very unconventional Roman Catholic nuns from the Mwanza area were here for the night. They wore slacks and were drinking. Were they "off duty"?

We had BLTs again for breakfast; we can't get enough of those fresh tomatoes! Jerry Rilling's Lindblad group arrived after lunch. Lindblad is now flying into Ikoma, but stopping in Seronera first to be stamped in at Immigration. He has a small group this time, and a courier trainee by the name of Ann Morson. It's a super group, a family of four from Guatemala and a female biochemist from U.S. We all trooped out to the terrace for the solar eclipse (June 30th). We were 5 degrees too far south to see the total eclipse that was visible at Lake Rudolf in northern Kenya. At the maximum eclipse from our angle, at approximately 4:00, the sun was a small crescent fingernail visible from behind the moon. Since we could not look directly at the eclipse because of the danger of retina sunburn, we did not see the moon, only the reflection of the crescent shape. Comparing the sun to a clock, what was visible was a thin sliver from 8:00 to 1:00. We viewed it two ways. The first was by making a pinhole in one piece of paper and holding the paper over the shoulder with back to the sun. The sun will cast the shadow of what's happening onto another piece of paper. The other way was to angle the wide end of the binoculars toward the sun and the shadow will be projected onto a sheet of white paper. Although most of the sun was covered, it never got very dark, more like late afternoon. And, it cast a slight pinkish tint to everything.

Sunday was the first of July so I helped Dionisia with inventory. Plus, there were *mingi* guests so the gift shop was busy. Trudy with Lindblad, with cameras around her neck, safari suit, the whole bit, asked the question, "Do I look like the typical American tourist?" We chuckled.

On Monday, Jerry, Valerie and I made pizza for lunch for the Lindblad group before their departure. The Trislander arrived with Dicky Bird as the pilot! Dionisia and I continued with inventory. All the trinkets need to be counted! Joseph Nyerere brought a delivery and stayed the night. It was his birthday so we invited him out to the Taj for a Brandy. He over-welcomed his stay, though, and we had to politely but firmly send him on his way. We are good at this. Sitting around the fire pit at the Taj is mesmerizing, but when Valerie and I are ready to hit the sack we have to send the guests on their merry way.

I slept in. As I crossed the parking lot on my way from the Taj to the dining room, I noticed a green snake poking its head out of a hole in the hubcap of one of the tour minibuses. I reported it to the bartender so that he could alert the driver. I wouldn't want the driver to be surprised by a snake should he need to change a flat tire. Dionisia and I finished the inventory after lunch. I was pooped so took a nap in the afternoon. Skip returned before dinner and Valerie's tour guide Peter Luhte arrived with a Unitours group. We made plans for big doings tomorrow for the Fourth of July.

I spent all morning in the kitchen preparing food for an indoor picnic lunch. It would be a typical American menu beginning with "Yankee Doodle" noodle soup. Elphas roasted hotdogs on the grill, chili dogs too. Peter and Elphas dished up the hot dogs and the guests served themselves baked beans, potato salad, coleslaw and watermelon. After lunch, I was back in the kitchen to prepare *chakula* (food) for tonight's "Big Doin's in the Ruins" in *Dumas* Den, so made guacamole and fried bread rounds for that. I also baked a huge sheet cake and decorated it like the American flag.

The Independence Day dinner menu featured George Washington cherry tomato soup, Barbecued Richard Nixon shish kebab, Big Ben Franklin rice, Beans Benedict Arnold, Aubergine à la Lafayette and Betsy Ross flag cake. I was in the kitchen until 7:30 so I never made it to Dumas Den. Instead, I went to the Taj to shower and no water! I had to find Mushi and have him show me where to turn on the valve for our waterline which someone had turned off.

After dinner we had a big dance on the terrace. A lot of people pooped out, but those of us who danced had a good time. Gideon, Jurgen, Caroline, Annalise (Jurgen's ex-wife and mother of his three children), Coen, and clients from the Hunters Camp came up too. The brothers West, two bachelor doctors from San Francisco on Peter's group were chronic complainers, real drips, some egotistical hangup. Skip was drunk and funny. Gideon was funny. Skip, Gideon, Kitia (regular game officer from Musoma), Valerie and I were the last to leave. Skip walked us back to the Taj, but we probably should have walked him back to room 11. Everyone was in rare form after celebrating my departing flight with me not on it.

Better than leaving East Africa on July 5th, Valerie and I took the "sports car" to Seronera to have my visa extended. This is the Land Rover that had been stolen by poachers and later recovered after they had cut off the roof. Rojabo came with us and brought his wife and child to put them on the bus to Ngorongoro. Valerie drove to Seronera. At Ikoma Gate who should we meet but David going to Fort Ikoma. We made the bus in Seronera in the nick of time. Valerie and I lunched with Bryan at SWL while Rojabo had some part on the sports car welded at the SNP garage. Still no water in Seronera. I got my visa extended to September 19th. We found David in his office. He was back so we visited a little while and then left about 5:00 with me driving. We passed Larry Robinson and a friend going the opposite way. They had been at the Fort for lunch and were on their way to Dar. We stopped in Robanda and picked up Peter Joseph with all of his vegetables (he takes the bus from Arusha every Thursday). We loaded everything in the back of the sports car and continued on until we ran out of petrol going up the driveway to the Fort and had to coast back down. Gideon came just then and gave Valerie and me a lift up to the Fort. We heard that John Capon had arrived and went directly out to terrace to see him. He was notified about Kirawira closing the night before, just as he and June were on their way to manage it. Raw deal for them. Lyuba also is here. Olga and Yuri have gone to Nairobi and left Lyuba here for which we are delighted.

FIL Guests and Friends

L yuba had brought along a spoon and beads for me so I could learn how to do bead work. To begin, wrap nylon thread around handle several times to make it tight. Then string a bead, go under strands of wrapped-around thread and back through bead again. I never finished the beadwork, but the spoon is displayed in my Africa souvenirs. The Vishnyakovs had also sent along a box of chocolate wafers and Russian cognac.

Saturday, July 7th is *Saba Saba* Day. *Saba* in Swahili is the number seven. This date annually celebrates the formation of TANU in 1954. Everyone from the staff village paraded through the courtyard and terrace singing "Oooh TANU..." and carrying sprigs of bougainvillea, branches etc.

Dionisia and Mushi left on a two-month leave so I ran the shop. No wonder Skip wanted me to stay! There were no *wageni* around after lunch so John, Skip, Valerie, Lyuba and I went on a *recce* into SNP to look for a possible tented campsite on the Orangi River. Valerie, Lyuba and I rode in the back of John's Ker, Downey and Selby Toyota truck. We came across two lions mating and a couple of *kali* (angry) buffalo. We got out at one point to collect *kuni* (firewood) and startled a lion that was resting just on the other side of a small bush. Luckily for us, the lion ran away when we started breaking branches. On the way back we got a *kanga* by hitting it with the truck and then had to help a minibus in distress. It had a broken steering shaft. After all of this, I didn't get back in time to open up the shop.

Yuri and Olga returned from Nairobi on Sunday, bringing with them fresh strawberries, cakes and a bouquet of carnations. They planned to spend the night, but will have to sleep in the office because the Lodge is completely full. I thought I saw a familiar face in the crowd. It turned out to be President John Schaefer from the University of Arizona! He was with Ted and Mary Ann Nichols and Dr. Mays, all from Tucson. Dr. Mays is one of the scientists from the U.S. to study the eclipse. They had all been at Lake Rudolf on June 30th. Mrs. Nichols said they had met Milt Strauss at Keekorok and he had asked to be remembered to Valerie since he wouldn't be coming to Fort Ikoma. Mr. Strauss is the next-door neighbor to the Fred Vance family in Tucson! Forty Germans traveling by Rotel, a hotel on a bus, arrived at 7:30 without their hotel trailer on wheels, expecting rooms and dinner only to find out that the Lodge was completely full. They ended up sleeping in their chairs at the dining room tables so we couldn't resist having a little dance while the oldies tried to sleep.

Yuri and Olga left the next morning, leaving Lyuba here until Saturday. David Babu came by to check out the Park's damaged Land Rover, the one that Fort Ikoma rented for a Lindblad group. The first version of the story was that the driver had an accident on *Saba Saba* night when a rhino ran into him at our very own petrol station. The story later was changed to "swerving to miss a rhino and ran into a tree." No one has seen a rhino in these parts for years. And it stands to reason that the driver was no doubt drunk on *Saba Saba* night. Aquila Mcharo and son Lokiko, whose 6th birthday is today, and an American friend by the name of Pam came to go swimming. Aquila was full of news. No water at Seronera. Mike's balloon landed in a tree and was ripped to shreds. Alan Root's ballon was dragged for 40 miles behind the Land Rover from Olduvai Gorge to Ndutu with the driver not realizing it. Alan was not with the balloon. Both these balloonists must be a tad upset.

On the 10th, David Babu and two other fellows dropped by in the late afternoon. David and John were able to have a talk. Big breakthrough! John had mentioned about a possible tented camp on the milk run and David suggested Banagi. Skip had cooked a special chicken dinner for us to eat at the Taj. Gideon and a group from the Hunters Camp came up just in time for dessert – ice cream and strawberries. Earlier in the day, Lyuba had shown me how to make ice cream from a tin of evaporated milk: Whip milk to increase volume and thicken. Add several tablespoons of sugar and flavoring (1 tablespoon instant coffee powder is very good). Continue beating. Then add 1 tablespoon gelatin dissolved in warm water. Whip until fluffy and thick. Freeze. Serve. It really is quite ingenious how one can improvise. Jurgen and Caroline are leaving tomorrow for Nairobi and will be married next week. Jurgen's ex-wife, Annalise, and three children have flown in from Germany and will be here for a month at least. Annalise brings Frank, Biggy and Simba every summer to see their father and so Putney and they have forged a close friendship. They are so much fun and Putney will be home from school soon.

The next day I went with John, Skip and Valerie to check out Banagi. Super exciting about the possibilities of John establishing a tented camp here. After checking it out, John left for Ngorongoro Crater Lodge and the three of us had lunch at Seronera Wildlife Lodge with Bryan. Still no water. Back to the Fort before dinner and in time to open up the gift shop.

At dinner, Skip introduced Lyuba to someone as his wife. We decided to have a dance. I met a young fellow from New Jersey who knows Dave and Jeff Bush very well, brothers of Lesley Bush Hickcox. I asked Joseph (the head waiter who is a pain in the neck) why he wears glasses. His answer, in all seriousness was "to keep dust out of his eyes." Skip has been in rare form. This time Skip introduced Valerie as a sister-in-law and me as his mother. He called for the gopher (that's me – "go for this, go for that") and Valerie said that's Hawaiian for mother. We met a very nice family traveling with Abercrombie & Kent, Mike (the wife) and Jim Stapler from San Francisco with their son Sam and learned that their daughter went to the University of Arizona. The courier was Ken Sheldrick, whose father David is Chief Park Warden of Tsavo East. His parents are divorced and his mother is now married to Bill Woodley, another well-known game warden. Mike taught us the hula. She and Skip did a number very well. A letter from Costas had arrived that day inviting us on another hunting safari.

Skip and Valerie were off early Friday morning to pick up Putney from her boarding school in Nairobi. A telegram from Costas arrived about the hunting safari planned for the 18th. How do I send a reply? Lyuba left for Mwanza the next afternoon and I sent a letter to Costas with our regrets by way of her.

David Babu, with Mike Leach and three others, arrived at 4:30 on Sunday. Mike is a civil engineer from Arusha and is working on new gates for Naabi Hill and Klein's Camp. They left about half an hour before Valerie, Skip and Putney returned, and bringing with them a couple from Palo Alto, California – Brick and Donna Stange – friends of Skip. Brick has a conservation program going in Zambia and is very interested in game preservation.

Putney, Frank and Simba are having a great time together. Biggy is in Nairobi because she is a bridesmaid in Jurgen and Caroline's wedding. Brick and Donna went on a game run in the Serengeti and came upon a cheetah with a terrible gash in the right forepaw, showing three inches of bone, apparently caused by a snare. So awful what these poachers will do! I was alerted that there was a radio call from Costas about the safari. Because of our regret, the operator said Costas was about ready to cry and asked Cephas (who was talking for me) if he was my husband.

We have been dining quite well now that Skip is back and he has good friends visiting. Last night we had delicious grilled lamb chops. This evening's menu will feature eland steaks and chateaubriand out at the Taj. Peter and Elphas, dressed in all whites, grilled our dinner over the fire. I tried some time exposures. These photos must have been on the roll that was lost.

On Wednesday, Larry Robinson arrived about 5:30 in a brand new Range Rover. It's a beauty. He brought with him a mail bag with super letters from Mom and Dad, their first response to my staying here. They have no problem with it. We celebrated with a sukiyaki dinner out at the Taj.

Up at 5:00 the next morning and off with Larry to follow Brick and Donna to the wild dog hole. The five adult dogs arrived about 8:30 after they had been out hunting. They came tearing over the plains and the 20 puppies raced out of the hole to greet them. The adult dogs regurgitated their food to feed the young puppies. There was a lot of game in the Sabora Plains. Larry and I continued on to Musoma, but first checked out the dead rhino we had heard had been poached by the turnoff to Fort Ikoma, and evident by the missing horn. The skin looked to be at least an inch thick. Maybe it wasn't such a crazy story about the SNP driver who smashed the Land Rover by running into a rhino. Guess there have been some rhino in these parts recently. Back on the road to Musoma, we spotted a cobra crossing the road and it lifted its head to strike the car. He got the raw end of the deal, though, when Larry gunned the motor and ran over it.

In Musoma, I met up with Valerie who had driven in with a staff member to do some shopping and then we had lunch at Raja's house. Afterwards, we went to Mokoko and met Father Jones who might supply the Fort with rabbit and duck. While there, we got a bunny as a surprise for

Putney. We stopped by the Robinsons after leaving Musoma and didn't get back to the Fort until 9:30. Franz Lang had come in that day. I finally got to meet him after hearing so many stories about him! He's a professional hunter who is quite a character. Caroline and Jurgen got married today in Nairobi.

Valerie and I had breakfast by the pool with Gideon and Franz. We met a cute couple from Cincinnati, Randy and Gail North, who were traveling privately with a driver. Through conversation we learned that Gail is a Pan Am flight attendant and several months pregnant. They had decided to go on this safari before the baby was born. However, driving over the rough roads was too much for Gail and they wanted to get back to Nairobi as soon as they could and fly home. Caroline and Jurgen had returned with wedding guests in tow. The plane was heading back to Nairobi with some of Jurgen's clients. Valerie learned that there were two available seats on the plane and arranged for Gail and Randy to fly back to Nairobi with the clients. Gail and Randy were so very appreciative and we kept in touch for many years. I would even see Gail in toothpaste commercials. She was also a model and had a beautiful smile. Shakir and a fellow by the name of Paul arrived about 7:30. David Babu brought them because they had car troubles in the Serengeti. News at dinner was that the sports car had been stolen from the front parking lot. David insisted on driving back, but he had no spare so we followed him as far as Ikoma Gate at midnight. This is what living in the bush is like. Always something. Never boring.

Breakfast by the pool again. This was the day of the big party at the Hunters Camp for the newlyweds. David and Ndosi came for it, but none of us ever made it down. I was disappointed because I really wanted to go. However, there was plenty going on here. It was a full house with overflow. David had brought a film so we had a movie hour after dinner. He showed Brick's film shot in Zambia on elephants and Part II of *Serengeti Shall Not Die* which included footage of the old Fort. It was a late night with lots of action, but I was feeling out of sorts. Then Mario tells me that he loves me. Oh, brother! He's old enough to be my father and I have never shown any interest in him. It's the liquor talking.

Sunday, July 22nd is Dad's birthday. Valerie and I couldn't call him, of course, but we did sing Happy Birthday to him and hoped the sound waves would carry halfway around the world. Caroline came up and told us all about the party that we had missed. It had been a great party and had disbanded about 10:00. They even had the Ikoma lion dancers perform for them. Mr. Robinson flew in for the day, bringing Terry and a German couple with him. Then the Mcharo family arrived with their friend Pam. Mr. Robinson took Donna and Brick, Pam and me up in his plane to get some aerial photos of the Fort. That afternoon, I went on a game run to Sabora Plains with Mr. Robinson, Larry, Terry, the German couple, Mcharo and Pam. On the way we stopped by to see the rhino carcass, which was determined to be a female, and got some pictures. We saw the pack of adult wild dogs. Mr. Robinson was able to call a few of the puppies to peek out of the hole. We also saw one rhino and found two ostrich eggs in an abandoned nest. Tumaini Mcharo gave us permission to take the eggs because there were no ostrich in the area and the eggs would become food for predators anyway. I toddled off to bed early that evening, but Valerie, Shakir and a few others stayed up to be entertained by a Unitour client who has recorded his own album titled, *Buzz Siler - Through a Window.* I did get to hear Buzz play his guitar and sing the next evening. He had been requested to play at an after dinner party in one of the Unitour rooms. About 11:30, Andy, the Unitour leader, and Buzz came out to the Taj. Valerie and I got up, built a fire and Buzz played and sang for us songs from his album. It was lovely. Andy headed off to his room and I turned in about 1:00 a.m. and soon fell asleep. Valerie and Buzz kept the fire going and stayed up until 4:30 a.m.

Being as quiet as I could so as to not wake up Valerie, I got up at 5:00 to go with Skip, Putney, Brick and Donna to the Sabora Plains to see the wild dogs again. The five adult dogs took off to hunt about 15 minutes after we arrived. They headed for the nearby wildebeest herd, but got sidetracked by a jackal which they chased to no avail. They seemed rather disorganized, chasing different members of the herd, but finally one got a hold of a young wildebeest and all five attacked it with vigor, tearing it apart, the young gnu bleating until its organs had been ripped out. The hunt had taken all of five minutes and the dogs consumed the animal in about 15 minutes, then trotted back to the den and regurgitated the food for the 17 puppies. The adult dogs gulp the meat and so when they regurgitate it, they are regurgitating chunks. They make no discernible noise when vomiting, food was out before one knew it. Couldn't easily see the adult dogs regurgitate because of the puppies crowding around them, blocking the view. Puppies would tug on the same piece of meat which was cute. The only time the dogs seemed to mind our presence was when they were feeding puppies. One growled at me when I stuck my head out the roof hatch. We headed back to the Fort to have an ostrich omelet for breakfast. Brick had found the abandoned egg yesterday. The egg shell is very hard so the easiest way to remove the egg is to puncture a hole at one end with a sharp object such as a screw driver to make a hole about half an inch in diameter. Then, shake the egg out of the shell into a container. It will yield about a quart, or the equivalent of two dozen large chicken eggs. One needs a big pan to make an omelet. Donna and Brick left for Manyara after breakfast. They may or may not be able to make it back to the Fort before returning to the States, so we said our sad farewells just in case.

We were awakened by a commotion coming from the impala grazing on the Water Tower Hill. Two jackals had chased a baby impala and the impala took refuge in one of the tents. The room steward found the jackals running around the tent, shooed them away, and then discovered the baby impala inside the tent. He brought it to the old birdcage in the courtyard where the impala could rest protected. Skip and Putney named the baby impala

Blackhoof and took charge of feeding it milk and grass. We guessed the age to be about three weeks old as it had no upper teeth yet. The next day I drove ARF682 to the Serengeti Research Institute (SRI) to find out about what to do with Blackhoof. Philip accompanied me. Philip is one of two scouts who work for FIL, the other being Ernest. Both are extremely knowledgeable about the flora and fauna, and excellent spotters. They lead walking safaris around the Fort and when a Lodge Land Rover is needed for a tour group, one of them will drive and be the guide. We talked to Mcharo. He said best thing to do is to reunite the *mtoto* with the herd as the mother is no doubt looking for her baby. If the herd should not accept it, then bring it to SRI. We were up at 6:00 the next morning to take Blackhoof back to the herd. We drove over to the Water Tower Hill and let him out near the herd. We returned 45 minutes later and Blackhoof was still standing right where we had left him. The herd was still down the hill where they had run to when we first drove up, but a stag was standing about 20 feet from Blackhoof and had been on the spot a good 30 minutes, because we had seen them through binoculars from the terrace. The stag ran off only when we got very close. Skip easily recaptured Blackhoof and took him closer to the herd and then immediately left. We checked half an hour a later and we think we saw him with the herd. Yay!

Valerie and I both took thyroid medication. The Armour brand that we were used to taking was in grains, Valerie took two grains and I took one grain. On one of our trips to Arusha we needed to get a refill. The Asian pharmacist explained to us that the thyroid medication he carried was in grams, not grains, and one grain equalled two grams. Therefore, Valerie started taking four pills a day and I took two. About a month later some American doctors were at the Fort and we asked them about this. They said that a grain was equal to a gram essentially. In their defense, we may not have told them why we were asking and so they never advised us to titrate down. Instead, we abruptly halved our medication doses starting the next day. As a result, both of us started getting sick frequently. Valerie had no energy and would go into Musoma and Mwanza to get Vitamin B12 shots. I would get sore throats and take tetracycline. One did not need a prescription from a doctor to get pills at pharmacies in Tanzania. However, one did need a written script for Milk of Magnesia because the Maasai would drink the entire bottle. I was having some female issues, most likely due to taking the tetracycline. Fortunately, a Polish friend of Skip's came for a visit with his daughter and friends. He was a gynecologist working in Nairobi with the World Health Organization and so Skip arranged for me to have a "field examination." Luckily, Dr. Wicinski could send me some topical medication for my problem. It's a good thing he had explained how I should use the medication because when it arrived, all the instructions were in Polish.

Skip left for Arusha, taking Daudi with him to look for some more *WaArusha* (people from Arusha area) for *askaris*. Daudi is all duded up in his brand new blue

Chinese tennis shoes and a floppy safari hat. The Robinsons stopped by in the afternoon. They are camping nearby. Putney is spending the night with the Josch kids down at the Hunters Camp. We noticed a brushfire along this side of the river between Jurgen's camp and the road. We were concerned, but it turned out that no one was in danger.

I met a nice couple on tour, Frank and Doris Brown from Riverside, California. The Robinsons came for lunch and I introduced the Browns to them and we all sat down to eat lunch together. I was wearing the 24-strand elephant hair bracelet that Costas had given me. Frank asked to see the bracelet and so I took it off and passed it down to him. I was called away from the table; lunch was soon over and I didn't realize until getting ready for dinner that I didn't have my bracelet. I asked Frank; he panicked; apparently it was left on the table after being passed around. I asked the dining room staff. Of course, no one had seen it. I learned a valuable lesson. Never remove jewelry to show someone. Or if you do, sit right next to the person and put it back on immediately. One of the staff later explained to me that an item to be stolen can be moved around a few times before being pinched. It wasn't "seen on the table" because it had been moved to another table, and then perhaps to a window ledge. Had I come back right after being called away, not seen it on the table and asked, it very likely might have been returned to me, after having been surreptitiously moved to the other table or window ledge. No staff would have wanted it in his possession that soon. Frank felt so "awful" about the bracelet that he insisted on giving me 100 shillings to be used as a reward so he would only feel "bad" then. And if the bracelet was not returned, to use the money to buy another one and have 25 strands, the extra one for his broken heart. Sadly, the bracelet was never returned and I never did replace it. Too bad the bracelet didn't have the identifier that Africans will write inside a book, "Stolen from (name)." It's not unusual for possessions to get pinched, but no one can rob one of a memory or an experience and it is the experiences and adventures that are my riches.

Mr. Robinson took Frank, Valerie and me up in his plane after lunch to look for the albino giraffe and we found him. Mcharo had told us that the giraffe resides between the Nyaraswiga and Kubukubu hills. He is an outcast because he would draw attention to the herd and therefore must fend for himself alone. He is perfectly capable of defending himself. A swift kick can kill a lion. As tall as giraffes are, it is amazing how well they blend into their environment. So many times we would spot one giraffe, and then another one, and another, and pretty soon you count 10 or 12 where at first you had seen only one. When flying over the terrain, it's movement that catches the eye. If someone on the ground needs to be spotted by someone in a search plane, move to an open area, wave arms and run around. Conversely, the poachers will lie still under a tree so as to not be noticed. The land is very dry right now and there are lots of burned areas. The Grumeti is dry, but the Orangi River has some water flowing. In one jungle area near the Orangi, we spotted about 400 *tembo*.

We were invited to dinner at the Hunters Camp. Gideon picked us up and we had a puncture in the Ikoma parking lot. He got Pete from staff quarters to fix the flat and kept referring to him as the "manager." We dined with Annalise, the French professional hunter Mark and his wife Christian, his clients, and Willie and Friedl who have come to Africa for the last 17 years. Gideon did Coen's steel pipe through ears pantomime which was a gas and a half!

The Robinsons were camping until the end of the month, but came up every day for lunch and a swim. Mike Norton-Griffiths and two others from SRI flew in for tea. They are doing burn mapping. On the 31st, the Robinsons departed for Busegwe, some flying, some driving.

Skip and Daudi returned with two new *WaArusha askaris*. Also with Skip was Susan Waldron, a friend of a friend of Skip's that he had run into it at Ngorongoro Crater Lodge. She's from Long Island, New York. Mary Ann and Joe von Zastrow arrived before dinner. They are setting up camp near here with clients arriving tomorrow. We all had dinner together. Mickey and Arnold Fletcher also arrived in the evening, but fortunately, they kept to themselves. Skip does not want to socialize with the other owners of Fort Ikoma and Ngorongoro Crater Lodge if he can avoid it.

On the first of August I did inventory all day. Jerry Rilling and Fiona arrived with Lindblad. Peter Joseph Masawe arrived with *kuku* (chicken) and the mailbag which carried a good letter from Mom and photos that had been developed. And Ruth Fletcher's son and his wife left.

It's early August and the rains have started. John Capon arrived at lunchtime, having flown in with Jurgen's group. While in Nairobi, John had a big confrontation with Block and gave his three-month notice. He is eager to open his own tented camp and so the next day he and Skip went to Banagi to take pictures. Ann Morson arrived with her own Lindblad tour. She is now a full-fledged courier. John hitched a ride on the Trislander back to Nairobi at 5:00. The Trislander does milk runs for Lindblad, dropping off one group and picking up another at each location. If there is space on the 12-seater, the pilots are usually pretty good about shuttling someone back to Nairobi, John in this instance, if that is their route. I had a nice chat with Sue in room 11. We watched the storm draw near. Putney, Biggie and Simba came in full steam. I was in the dining room when the kids arrived for dinner before Skip and Sue arrived. Biggie was dressed in her boots, shorts, T-shirt and a 6-foot bow in her hair. All three were hyper energy, playing tag and hide and seek in the dining room and bar. Skip and Sue finally came, then left because Sue had drunk a little too much. It was somebody's birthday and the kids were the first up there for cake.

The clients of Mary Ann and Joe von Zastrow are a strange family. The parents and two daughters came up to use the pool. Mary Ann invited Sue and me down to the camp for lunch. The Mr. and Mrs. stayed up at the pool and the two young daughters went down with us and had about two bites to eat. Glamorous Mrs. apparently wants to call off the whole safari because she bumped her knee in the

Land Rover yesterday. She must have married him for his money! Poor Joe and Mary Ann. Mary Ann said the woman had a tantrum the night before, woke everybody up by her noise and they thought she was going to slash up the tent.

We had some fresh spinach so Skip made sukiyaki for dinner. It was delicious. Then I learned how to play backgammon, which means "toward the light" in Egyptian.

J.P. arrived with a Travelworld group including a family from Mexico City. I met Luis and Javier that evening at the dance we were having in honor of Annalise, Frank, Biggie and Simba who were leaving the next day. Boo hoo!

The big news was that Annalise had been on a game drive the day before and had rescued a baby cheetah found by the carcass of her mother. I had so much fun dancing with Luis, Javier, Simba and Frank. I told Simba (age 5) that I was going to marry him and make him my husband. All he said was *"zu kleine, zu kleine!"* (too small). Then Putney stole my "hubby" from me, but I would settle for Frank (age 11) any day. This was the best dance we've had yet. Lots of people dancing on the terrace to the record player. Luis and Javier were so much fun. Javier gave me his address in Mexico City.

Lisa

Annalise had brought Frank, Biggie and Simba to the Hunters Camp for a month-long visit with their dad, Jurgen. Now it was time for them to return to Germany. On Thursday, August 9th, we went down to the airstrip to bid them farewell. The three children were dressed in vests and bottoms made from Tommy gazelle skins. Coen was holding the cheetah cub that Annalise had found two days before while on a game drive and of which we had been told about. Coen had named her Lisa after Annalise. The orphaned cheetah had been found by the carcass of her mother who had been killed by poachers. This was evident because the head and skin were gone. In addition, a grass fire had swept the area, probably set by the poachers. Lisa's whiskers, the tip of her tail, the fuzzy hair on the ears and scruff of her neck had been singed off. Despite all this, she had fared well. Sadly, her brother had not survived. It was guessed that she was about 3 to 4 weeks old as her eyes were open. They gave her an arbitrary birth date of July 13. The Cessna 206 finally took off about 5:00, loaded to the gills with them, two clients, baggage, and the baby Vervet monkey the clients were taking to Nairobi. Oh, how we will miss them! Last night's dance on the terrace was a terrific end to a great visit, but still, we were sad to see them go.

Coen was given the task of caring for Lisa. Baby bottles with nipples were nowhere to be found out in the bush so he improvised. Goat milk was readily available and he used an eye dropper to feed her the milk. He even crushed egg shells as a calcium source. Her eyes had some kind of infection, possibly from the smoke of the fire and he would rinse them out with boiled water. He was so gentle with her.

Jurgen contacted his friend Dr. von Nagy who had a small zoo in Arusha. This was the zoo that Mom, Dad and I had visited at the Tanzanite Hotel when we stayed there in January. Jurgen had decided to send Lisa there. Coen was adamantly opposed to this. He and Annalise had envisioned Lisa being returned to the wild a la *"Born Free,"* the Joy and George Adamson story of returning young lion cubs to the wild. This created tension between Coen and Jurgen, his boss.

After he had been taking care of her for a week, Coen brought Lisa up to the Fort for a visit. This cute little cub, probably only a month old, followed Coen all the way up the hill. The Robinsons showed up the next day and we couldn't wait to tell them about Lisa. We all trekked down to see her. She is so cute and tiny and at this point so very dependent on humans for survival. A couple of days later, Lisa escaped from Coen's house in the late morning. Coen was a wreck until she was finally found about 4:00 p.m. This was especially nerve-racking in light of the letter Coen received the day before from Jurgen saying that a plane will come Sunday (August 19) to pick up Coen and Lisa and take them to Arusha where Dr. von Nagy will meet them and Lisa will be placed in his Meru game sanctuary. We all are vitally opposed to this and are standing behind Coen to keep Lisa here so someone radioed a cancellation for the plane because Lisa was "not fit for travel." A few days later we got word that Jurgen was furious. Dr. von Nagy had been waiting all day at the airport on Sunday for the plane that never arrived.

Jens, a friend of Coen's, had arrived a few days earlier. Jens came to tell us that Jurgen had sent Michael and Daniel from Nairobi with orders to take Lisa to Arusha. Fortunately, a regional game officer was here. He sided with us and said he would go down to the Hunters Camp the next morning and issue an order that the cheetah had to stay in the Ikoma region.

On the 22nd, we learned that Coen and Jens will be leaving tomorrow for Nairobi and then Coen will head on down to South Africa. Coen has been disobeying his boss' orders about Lisa's fate and, therefore, could no longer work for him. He had spoken to Skip about Lisa and it was agreed that she would come into our care. Coen brought Lisa up after lunch; this will be her new home. It tore Coen's heart to leave her, I know. Lisa's story weaves throughout the rest of my stay and beyond and will be recounted chronologically. But, of all my wonderful adventures and experiences the year I spent in Tanzania, none compare to the joy and privilege of helping to raise an orphaned baby cheetah that ultimately was successfully released to the wild.

Rafiki

Some *rafiki* (friends) leave, others arrive. The day after the departure of Annalise and kids, Ruth, Eddie and Freddie arrived before noon. They were to meet Mr. Robinson and the Vishnyakovs here and then all were going camping nearby. Soon Yuri, Olga and Lyuba arrived and then Mr. Robinson flew in. We all had lunch together and then they left after lunch and took Putney with them. Lyuba stayed here with Valerie and me. Skip burrowed away, working on a manuscript of the history of Fort Ikoma. Shakir and "Auntie" Ruth Fletcher arrived in early afternoon. (Another reason for Skip to have a project where he could avoid his business partner who he referred to as the EOB.) Mario and Rahemtulla arrived at 6:00. Perfect timing because the cold room motor went out at noon.

We all had dinner together and Gideon and Coen joined us. Everyone was in a gay mood, drinking, dancing, Coen doing his pantomimes. He amused us by sewing his fingers and elbow together and pulling the thread; sliding a pipe through the ears; then bicycling. Skip kept saying he didn't like Gideon's hair, it was too long, so Skip decided it should be cut, with me as the barber. "Auntie" Ruth had gone to bed and Skip was high because he had been drinking away Ruth's presence. At 11:00, Skip went to get scissors, a mirror and camera. He came flying back, started removing everything from one of the tables, and with just the flower pot remaining on it, he whisked away the tablecloth out from underneath and the flower vase came crashing to the floor. Well, that put everyone in even more hysterics! He got Gideon seated, a tablecloth wrapped around his neck and the mirror angled so Gideon could watch. Gideon didn't think he needed his hair cut, but with a cigarette in his mouth and beer in hand, let me proceed. The first thing I did was cut off his cigarette that he had been twitching around. That drew even more hysterics. Gideon wouldn't sit still, he kept moving his head to look in the mirror, his eyes going a mile a minute. Shakir was literally on the floor holding his sides with laughter, and then pulled Valerie down. Coen couldn't control himself for love or money. Unfortunately, I missed half the goings-on because I couldn't see Gideon's face. Poor Gideon, I don't think he ever really wanted his hair cut, but he was such a good sport about it and kept us in stitches. With the beer bottle always to his lips and crouching down in the chair to get a better look, he would move his head sideways and back-and-forth, while his eyes darted around. Then he got up and danced on the terrace with bottle still in hand and cloth still around his neck. Then he came back and sat down. For all his moving around, the haircut turned out pretty well, surprisingly enough. I pulled one strand straight and it came down to his chin. When it recoiled, I could press it down. Kinky hair hides a lot of barber goofs. He was a panic!

Lyuba, Susan and I made gazpacho for lunch, delicious. The campers came back for lunch. Too bad we didn't have enough gazpacho for them. I had all of us write a Happy Anniversary chain letter to Mom and Dad. Putney was scared by the lions so she didn't go back with the campers. She and Lyuba made spaghetti with scrambled eggs for dinner. Mario and Rahemtulla went back to Arusha to get a motor for the cold room and plan to be back tomorrow night.

The campers were back for lunch on Sunday. This might be the last time we will see the Vishynakovs because in the coming week they will get final word from Moscow about Yuri's plans. Tanzania wants Yuri to stay until 1976, but Russia might say "no, come back now." The Vishnyakovs left at 4:00 for Mwanza. Mr. Robinson, Eddie and Freddie went with Putney and me down to the Hunters Camp to see the baby cheetah. She is adorable and Coen takes such good care of her. Back up at the Fort, we bid *kwaheri* to the Robinsons and then Putt and I went swimming with Shakir before dinner. Mario and Rahemtulla had not returned, no surprise.

Shakir and Ruth left after breakfast. Raja arrived with supplies, among them the cassette player Valerie had ordered. I'll be busy with more taping!

At dinner I thought I saw a familiar face. Could it be? It was! He was shocked when I inquired, "You look familiar, could you be Dave DuVal?" Dave was a classmate of our brother Robert at Tucson High School and a senior when I was a freshman. He is here with his wife Trish and Harry Atwood from the University of Arizona. They are filming a cultural sequence in East Africa using only native music for audio, no script, and are here to film the Ikoma Lion Dancers and will be staying at the Fort for two nights. They departed on August 16th, Mom and Dad's 31st wedding anniversary. Dave very kindly agreed to carry four boxes of slides back to Tucson and deliver them to Mom and Dad – photos of Lisa, Kirawira, Lake Victoria and more that will give a pictorial view to the stories we tell in the letters we write. [Unfortunately, none of these letters were kept. Without the capability of making photocopies, Mom and Dad, no doubt, sent them on to relatives to read.]

I went down to the Hunters Camp with Coen to feed Lisa and while there discovered that Coen had some fantastic tapes so he brought them up for me to copy onto cassette tapes. Coen is a real *fundi* (expert) when it comes to electrical equipment. After taping *Get Ready*, he showed us how to get reverberations by playing two tapes one beat apart. *Get Ready* is fantastic with reverberations.

Coen, who is Dutch, had a German friend visiting from Nairobi. Jens is the Agfa film representative. We thought his name was Ian. A day or two later, Coen asked us why we called him Ian. Valerie and I answered, "because that's his name." Coen corrected us saying it's Jens (pronounced Yense). Jens, good-naturedly, answered to anything. Actually, Valerie and I called Coen "Conrad." That is because Valerie and I had difficulty with the Dutch pronunciation of "Coen" and were very sensitive to the similar sounding derogatory term for American Blacks. That, and when we first met Coen, we actually thought his name was Conrad! He good-naturedly answered to whatever we called him, too. Coen has won awards for amateur pantomiming in Holland and kept us in stitches. He did a fantastic one of a man driving an old, dilapidated car with doors opening, steering wheel or gear knob coming off. Another was Atlas holding up the world and trying to scratch an itch. Then there was the one of a drunk trying to fill his glass.

Skip had Julia Child's cookbook and wanted me to make the 13-page recipe for French bread. This shouldn't be too hard, right?   Well, the flour and climate are quite different here and we ran into some issues. First, I needed to add two plus cups of flour to achieve the right consistency. Most likely, that was too much because it took triple the time to rise, each time! This wasn't taking a day, it was taking several days! Skip made a delicious beef casserole with wine to go with the bread. I put the bread in the oven at 6:30 with Skip and Valerie in attendance. Skip had been taking photos throughout the process. We were like expectant fathers waiting for it to bake. When we opened the oven at 7:00, we all fell into gales of laughter because it was so peaked. What an anti-climatic ending! It tasted fine, but had no volume to it. Coen and Jens were here for dinner. The casserole was delicious and no one laughed at my bread attempt. So few guests tonight and they left the dining room early so we put on *Get Ready* right after dinner – full volume – and danced for 22 minutes straight – right after a full meal! The entire bar was filled with Africans and they were absolutely entranced by our dancing and the music. Skip got up on one of the tables to dance. We all followed. Later, Coen did his falling down as stiff as a board trick. Then I said I would fall straight back if he would catch me, but I lost my nerve halfway down. Then Susan tried it and she bent her neck. Coen lost his grip and she bumped her head on the floor. Party broke up shortly thereafter. Off to bed!

Putney, Susan, Coen and I piled into Jens' kombi and went to Sabora Plains to see the wild dogs. When we arrived, only the five adult dogs were in sight. Almost on cue, the mama dog went to the pups' den and enticed them out for us to see. The pups have doubled in size since I last saw them. We came across an abandoned nest of ostrich eggs with only three eggs and the shell of a cracked one. Maybe the hyenas or mongoose got it. There were some ostriches off in the distance so maybe the eggs belong to them. We left them undisturbed. Being the Agfa dealer, Jen's had good camera equipment. His lenses fit my Pentax camera and so I was able to take photos with his 200mm, wide angle and fisheye lenses.

Gideon's new clients have arrived and they are royalty – Prince and Princess Oettingen who live near Munich. They are a cute young couple who I was introduced to as Moritz and Lioba when Gideon brought them up for dinner. The Drowns, Putney's former schoolmaster and his wife, have also arrived for a two-day visit. It was Cephas' birthday and he gave me a bottle of wine. Apparently, Africans celebrate three birthdays: on the actual day, baptism and circumcision.

Big doings are going on with the staff. Skip was tied up in meetings all day with the workers organization, acronym TANU. Shakir flew in for another meeting with TANU. Ross, the Boscovic pilot who flew Shakir in is a nice chap. Apparently, some of the questions being raised by the staff are: "Why are Valerie and Vicki and the boss here? They need to leave." "Why does the boss have a woman in his room?" There was a big conference on the terrace with Skip, Shakir, Haunga, Sherlock, and Joseph. No doubt Joseph, the head dining room waiter, is instrumental in stirring up the commotion because he is very political and is president of the TANU chapter at Fort Ikoma. Sherlock is in charge of the room stewards and Haunga is in charge of the facilities and maintenance. I was not privy to the problems, but these meetings went on for several days. Meanwhile, Ross joined Putney and me in the pool for games of keep-away.

We received a letter on the 20th of August from Lyuba with the good news that they will be staying in Tanzania one more year. Yay! On the 21st, Gideon and Coen came up at lunchtime. "Beer Bottle" Peter, the manager at the Hunters Camp, had not locked up the guns the night before and the big elephant rifle (.458) was stolen. Gideon and Coen had to go to Mugumu to get the police.

Jens came up before dinner to tell us that Michael and Daniel had arrived from Nairobi with orders to take Lisa to Arusha. Fortunately, the regional game officer who happened to be here agreed to issue an order saying that the cheetah had to stay in the Ikoma region. Jens joined us for dinner and later others came up. Skip and Shakir had another meeting with TANU officials at 10:00 p.m.

After lunch, Coen brought Lisa up to her new home. I made a trial leather collar for her so that we could keep her on a leash when taking her out on a walk. Though cheetahs are part of the cat family, they have non-retractable claws like a dog so carrying her around came with some risks of scratching. Mike Norton-Griffiths came by in the afternoon. He will send *dawa* (medicine) for Lisa.

Shakir and Ross took off at 3:30. Coen came up for dinner. Putney wanted a picnic dinner in room 11 and so we did. She wanted to be by her Lisa who is sleeping with Putney and Skip at night. Afterwards, Coen and I joined Jens and a group from the Hunters Camp in the bar. Coen regaled us with stories about when he had been a race car driver for five years in Holland. He had been number 1 with a black car number 30. Both are bad luck but he proved the superstition wrong. He had long hair and a beard and after winning his last race he was dragged on stage and shaved. He will be 25 on October 7th and has done quite a lot in his life thus far. Both Gideon and Coen were so entertaining. What a great act they would be, thought Valerie and I. We would bill them as Gideon and Coen.

On Thursday, the 23rd, Coen in his little Citroen, and Jens and Susan in Jens' kombi planned to leave at 10:00, but the Hunters Camp manager Peter had staged a big car search somewhere between here and the Ikoma gate for their two vehicles in case they had stolen the guns. The search ended up in our parking lot. The Ikoma mayor (from

Robanda, I'm guessing) came here to interrogate Coen. Peter brought up some big deal about a mattress that Coen had taken to Nairobi, but didn't ask his permission. That delayed their departure by 45 minutes At I1:45, Jens and Susan returned because Ikoma Gate had been ordered not to let them through. Jens and Susan had brought the Ranger back with them to certify that they indeed had been searched and were allowed to leave. They left Coen at the gate with the condition that they would take the responsibility and to let Coen go on ahead since he travels so slowly. Skip accompanied Jens and Susan to staff quarters to get everything squared away and then be on their way. What a hassle! It's all power plays.

I'll miss these blokes. The one sad thing about living here is the fleetingness of friendships, not that they turn sour, but that no sooner has a real friendship begun, then one of the party leaves with the possibility of never seeing each other again. Of course, we all exchange addresses, but none of these people here are really "writing" people. Every time someone leaves, a part of me goes with him or her. But as it has been proven time and again, no sooner does someone leave than someone else pops in on the scene. What will tomorrow bring, I wonder? It is the suspense and not our losses that makes life worth living.

I finished making Lisa's leather collar out of Skip's discarded leather hems, then Skip, Putt and I took Lisa on her first walk around the grounds. The three crested cranes didn't know what to make of this cheetah. They stalked her and then when she gave them a bit of their own medicine they scurried out of reach. They know who the predator is. Coen gave us explicit instructions for Lisa's diet. She is to be fed four times a day a menu of meat, liver, hair, calcium syrup, ABCDE vitamins.

Valerie was not feeling well and confined herself to bed. Jerry Rilling arrived with a Lindblad group. He brought us French's mustard, Cadbury chocolate bars, some boxes of Jell-O, and delivered some blank cassette tapes from Alma. Tumaini Mcharo stopped by to spend the night and will continue on to Kirawira tomorrow. I showed him the slides of the rhino carcass and gave him two of the slides and one of him on the terrace.

On Friday, Isaac helped me cut out a butterfly sleeve dress from a striking black and white double *kitenge* and sew it on his treadle sewing machine. I made it that afternoon and wore it that evening. It's super simple and quick, took three hours max from start to finish, though I did need some help from Isaac. He is so patient with me as I try to master the rhythm of the treadle. Jerry came out to the Taj after dinner. Valerie and I both worked on braiding his *kikoi* fringe as our payment for his gifts of goodies from Nairobi and answers to all the questions we save up to ask him on his visits.

Putney and I took Lisa for a walk after lunch. We headed down the hill leading from the swimming pool and towards Water Tower Hill. Lisa was really frisky when we started out but she pooped out halfway up Water Tower Hill. Putney and I took pictures of each other with Lisa, especially when Lisa was hiding under my bended knees.

Putney wanted to go for a swim so she headed back and I continued on to the Water Tower Hill with Lisa. She was not in the mood to walk, only to sleep in the shade. She was enjoying the fresh air so we stayed out for 45 minutes or so and then I had to carry her as far as the Taj because she wouldn't follow me. When I would put her down, she refused to walk. She would invariably run to a shady tree or just sit on her haunches with forepaws outstretched and planted. She immediately took to the cool concrete porch of the Taj and we leisurely relaxed until Putney came to get her for her 4:00 milk time. The *dawa* Mike Norton-Griffiths promised has arrived. One is calcium lactate to supplement nutrition and the other *dawa* is for diarrhea which is plaguing Lisa, and consequently us. I will have to bring Lisa out to the Taj every day because she enjoys it out here where it is peaceful, breezy and no people.

Lioba, Moritz, Dr. Hoff, Gideon and the new hunter, Paul, came up after dinner. Moritz shot a bushbuck today; they are very rare in these parts.

On Sunday David Babu stopped by after checking the road he is building from Ikoma Gate to Fort Ikoma. We checked it, too; it's *mzuri sana*.

Later in the afternoon we had a big football game on the airstrip, or what we call soccer, between Yanga (coached by Elphas) and Simba (coached by Saidi). Valerie's staff plus Reception staff were on Yanga and all others were on Simba. Valerie, John Wangere, and Cephas are the honored guests of Yanga. Skip and two others are the honored guests of Simba. Valerie, Skip, Putney and I grabbed our Cokes and headed down. The other two honored guests for Simba didn't show up so Cephas rooted for Simba, but Putney rooted for Yanga with Valerie, John and I. A Peugeot pickup brought six chairs and 11 members of Saidi's team while Yanga had to walk to the field from staff quarters. It was a fabulous game, especially because Yanga won. George, the dining room waiter, made the two goals for Yanga and Simba made none. For Yanga, George, Maishek, Boscal, Peter, Hezron played a good game. Rojabu, Sherlock, "white shoes" played a good game for Simba. We heard some life from Joseph when he out-yelled Sherlock in some dispute. I explained American football to Cephas, Fidelis and Saul before dinner while waiting for Valerie. They know nothing about it, have never seen a picture of an American football player, and have never heard of Joe Namath!

It was late in the afternoon when I had big plans to put contact paper on the bathroom shelves in the Taj. I wiped down the shelves and while waiting for them to dry, it started to rain. It was a neat rain with the sun shining and yet a gray sky to the north. Rain came through the wire mesh window in the bathroom, thwarting my attempts for the time being. This rain storm reminded me of my camp days at Cimarroncita.

Lioba and Moritz, Dr. Hoff, Gideon, Stefan and Paul came up for dinner. Gideon was in a strange and intoxicated state, not his usual self. He's really concerned about his .458 rifle that was stolen. As he says, anything stolen is bad, but a gun is far worse because a stolen gun can really damage a professional hunter's reputation.

It's the 28th of August and I am thinking of Lyuba as she celebrates her 15th birthday today. I had sent her a card. There were no *wageni* booked for today so Erasto and I thoroughly cleaned and organized the *duka* storeroom. What a job! But when it was finished, I spent a good half hour in there just looking at the fruits of our labor. Larry Robinson popped in at lunchtime. And just last night Valerie said it was about time for Larry to pop in. He is on his way south, past Moshi. Lioba and Moritz came up and invited me to come down to see Moritz's trophies. He got everything he wanted, bushbuck, reedbuck, waterbuck and a record topi (18 inches) among them. Gideon drove me back up to the Fort, letting me drive. Then I went bird hunting with Skip and Putney. It was a big fiasco from start to finish. In 1½ hours we saw only four birds worth shooting, three Franklin which flew away when the car stalled, and one lesser bustard which avoided the shot. We did see a honey badger though. They are rare to see. Skip had never even seen one before. This badger seemed to be an old *mzee* with a few cogs loose. When we got about five feet from him, he let out a very annoying squeal and hustled off in a semi bear, semi pigeon-toed old man run. We were treated to a beautiful sunset. Lots of fluffy, elongated clouds and one transparent cloud partially covering the sun, giving the giant orb varying hues from top to bottom. The spectrum of colors turned from yellow to a deep pinkish red. The clouds behind the sun picked up the deep colors also. We were southeast of Ikoma Hill, and at one point the sun was framed by the shadowed hill to the left and hovering above two huts to the right. The sun looked so huge and rich. It was one of the most exquisite sunsets I have ever seen and I did not have my camera with me! Then we had a puncture 2 miles from the Lodge and couldn't budge the lugs so we had to drive back slowly on a flat right rear tire. Help met us between the petrol station and the Lodge. Valerie had spent the day taping cassettes for her new player. The hunters group came up. All of them are leaving tomorrow. Gideon will be driving to Nairobi and he has our shopping list and a thank you note to Dr. Wicinski for the medicine he has sent me.

I slept in because there were no guests. After a late breakfast I went into the kitchen and John Wangere had me make a fruit steamed pudding. I must say, it turned out pretty well. He has shared with me his recipes for coconut steamed pudding and marmalade steamed pudding. I always enjoy watching John bake.

A day later Lisa followed Skip and me out to the Taj without a lead. About 10 minutes later Putney came out to see Lisa and had all sorts of suggestions for me about how to handle her. Lisa stays in their room 11 and sleeps with Putney every night so it is understandable that Putney would be very particular about her care. Soon, though, Putney and Skip headed back to the Lodge and Lisa and I spent the next 1½ hours sitting under a tree. I would read while she snooped around. She is very playful and will chase a butterfly, or cock an ear to a sound and then look for a high spot to ascend and stare into the distance. She and I got along very well because I would let her explore in a safe environment.

A plane arrived to pick up hunters, but to our dismay, it brought Rolf who was making another attempt to take Lisa from here and deliver her to Dr. von Nagy. No luck for him though. Also on the plane were lots of goodies from Susan including a camera for Putt, and peaches and cantaloupe for us. A lorry came bringing mail for us and developed film. We retired early to enjoy the photos, news from home and newly recorded music.

Joseph Nyerere brought a delivery. Valerie wasn't feeling well and had gone to bed early so I had dinner with Joseph and then he insisted that I have <u>one</u> drink with him. All the Africans were up at the bar. They put on a dance tape so I <u>had</u> to dance. A Kimbla group was here with a good-looking leader by the name of Rob. I finally got away at 10:00. A huge storm was brewing with lots of lightning, flash lightning and thunder. It was really eerie walking back to the Taj, especially because none of the tent lights were on and there was only a sliver of a moon. I was so very relieved when I was safe and sound inside the tent.

Valerie received a letter from Daudi. He's in the hospital in Moshi with a bad chest x-ray. His letter was all in Swahili and near the end he mentioned he needed something *haraka sana* (quickly). Val asked Cephas to translate. It turned out that Daudi was asking for cigarette money from Val's pocket, not his salary! Oh Daudi!

We were expecting only four guests, if they come, so we had the Lodge to ourselves all day. I spent the day taping more cassettes and jazzing up the bar with a stunning double *kitenge* that features an aqua on white keyhole design. I taped the cloth onto hardboard (42" x 70") and then nailed it to the wall behind the coffee bar. It looks super. I also hung a green and yellow *kitenge* between the windows. It is dressing up the bare walls without taking away from the wonderful "cave drawings" that adorn the other walls.

A huge rain stormed in at 5:00. The lightning was so close and thunder so loud. It reminded me of the summer monsoons in Tucson. The hard rain pounded on the thatched roof, yet Valerie and I were so cozy in our tent, the Taj. We blasted *Atom Heart Mother* so that we could hear it over the rain. *Pictures at an Exhibition* was good, too. The rain continued for a good 1½ hours. I ran up for dinner. Stefan, one of Jurgen's hirelings, joined Skip, Putt and me. The bar looked hideous with its ghastly red and green lights. In there were some clientele and eight Africans. Looking through the archway and seeing 11 men seated on the settee under the windows was a photo-op that Skip couldn't resist. An album cover, so true. I headed back to the Taj and grooved out on Santana, the Rollings Stones, and the Beatles.

The first of September and inventory took all day long. As much as I loved the rain storm yesterday, it caused a lot of work today. The gift shop store room is inside the original north tower. Rain had come in through the arrowslit windows, completely soaking boxes and all the goods sitting on the floor. All that wet merchandise had to be schlepped outside to dry in the sun. Twenty-two boxes of Kleenex were a complete write-off. Carvings were not damaged, but I had to dry them with a towel to prevent water marks. The 80 rolls of film in cardboard boxes were completely drenched. The outer boxes will dry stiffly and, hopefully, still legible as to what kind of film. Fortunately, the film itself is wrapped in waterproof packaging. Just hoping the film won't be ruined by the sun, counter to the instructions, "store in a cool, dark place." We will never know because it will be bought by a tourist for photos of a "once-in-a-lifetime" experience! Storage here is not ideal. Some of the rolls I have bought had green tinges to the photos when developed. Oh well. At least out in the middle of nowhere one can get a roll of film if needed. Inventory took me as long as usual, even though I had completely organized the store room a few days earlier so that it would go quickly.

There was another light rain in late afternoon. Julee came from Ngorongoro Crater Lodge bringing mail which included a gigantic manila envelope from Bill Ballance including a letter, a tape of one of his shows, and lots of articles about his provocative call-in radio show, *The Bill Ballance Show,* in Los Angeles. Bill grew up on the same block as Dad in Peoria. Can't wait to hear the tape. I talked to Skip at dinner about Valerie going to the doctor. She has not been feeling well for several weeks. I'm worried about her.

Claus from Mwanza and two others have been here for two days. Claus and his mother own an island in Lake Victoria near Mwanza. They recommended a doctor for Valerie. Julee was driving straight to Mwanza so Valerie went with him. Skip and I listened to the Bill Ballance tape at lunch. It was entertaining...and raunchy! Another big rain storm came in the late afternoon and completely flooded the Taj bathroom. The Kimbla tour group had gone to Sabora Plains after lunch for a game drive. Coming back, they got stuck about a mile from here. One of the vehicles made it back and alerted Skip, so Skip, Putt and I went to help about 7:30 p.m. As we reached the bottom of the hill, the Kimbla truck was coming up, but now a Peugeot was stuck in the same spot so we had to go get them. And what a treat to end the day, Gideon brought me a toothbrush and some Cadbury candy bars from Nairobi.

A very nice Swiss family from Nairobi spent a few days at the Fort. Mr. Richard Wolf is the Charges d'affaires for the Swiss Embassy. Mrs. Wolf invited me to stay with them and their sons Mickey (15) and Richard (18) whenever in Nairobi. Their oldest son is away at school in Switzerland. Putt, Skip, the two Kimbla tour guides Keith and Ian, and I played keep-away in the pool. Putt wouldn't give up ball so the three men ended up tossing her back and forth while she held onto the ball. So much fun! A light rain in the late evening closed out the day. I love the sound of the rain on the thatched roof. The tent windows are kept unzipped and such a nice breeze and the sweet smell of rain wafted through the mesh screen.

Skip and Putney were going on a two-day camping trip. Putney explained to me all I needed to know about how to take care of Lisa and her bunny, Bunts. I took Lisa for a walk after they left. She was very difficult to get out of the office, but was very good about following me to the water tower. Once up there though, she wouldn't leave and really put up a fight all the way back to the Taj. I think she knew Putt and Skip had left and wasn't too sure about me. She did follow me from the Taj to the office fairly well, though. I fed her, carried her to room 11 where I will be staying as well, and fed Bunts. I got cleaned up and it started to rain just when I was to leave to open up the shop. Forget the shop; played with Lisa instead. She is accepting me more. I went up to the dining room about 7:30 although it was still raining. Only four *wageni*. Unitours with good ol' Peter never showed up. Gideon was at the bar. He offered me a drink and I was in the mood for something really exciting so I had a Pimm's Cup #1 (a gin sling with lots of fresh banana and pineapple cut up in it). Gideon invited me down to the Hunters Camp for dinner. He has only one client, a brewer from Bavaria. There was still a light rain as we drove down the hill to the camp. After dinner, while still in the mess tent, water started to seep in and within seconds it was 2-inches deep. We went to check the tents. Gideon's was about four inches deep in water and while we were salvaging shoes, etc. the water rose to my mid-calf. Gideon, Mr. Viederhuffer and I went back up to the Lodge for drinks, then I headed back to room 11 after offering

Gideon and his client the Taj for the night because they would be gurgling all night long down below.

I woke up with Lisa between my legs. I got up for a second and when I came back, she had piddled on the blanket. This is her feeding schedule: breakfast – a handful of freshly ground meat, some Thomson's gazelle hair, 1 teaspoon calcium syrup, a drop of ABIDEC vitamins, a pinch of salt. Midmorning snack - six chicken wings. Teatime – milk. Dinner same as breakfast. I took Lisa for a walk out to the Taj. She followed me very well. She played around while I did other things. It is always hard to get her to leave the spot where she is. I must carry her for a distance and then put her down; only then will she follow me.

Later, I supervised Tadaio's picture-hanging in the bar. He really makes beautiful frames. Then I went into the kitchen and demonstrated to John Wangere how to make banana bread and guacamole. I owe him some of my recipes for the ones he has given me. In the afternoon I taped records to cassettes for Skip. Gideon and Mr. Viederhuffer came for a swim so I took Lisa out by the pool so that she could run around. After they left we stayed out. I wasn't watching her, but all of a sudden I heard a splash! Apparently, she had tried to get a drink of water and fell in the pool. She instinctively knew how to swim and swam to the side where I picked her up. I dried Lisa off and took her back to the room. That evening I had 1½ beers and two Tia Maria's with Gideon at the bar. I initiated him into the Cardinal Puff drinking game, although I helped him along the way so he would finish his beer because I was oh so tired! Either I was hungover or sick because in the course of three hours starting at 1:00 a.m. I threw up six times and was also afflicted with the trots. I was miserable and very weak so the next morning I stayed in Valerie's office with Lisa where I could doze on the bunkbed. Everyone was so nice, concerned and helpful. I asked John to make some fruit jelly. Gideon came up to see me. I felt strong enough to take Lisa out by the pool for exercise while Gideon and Herr Viederhuffer were there. It was an overcast day and I lay on the lounge all the while. Putt and Skip returned from camping because Putt had bad, bad tummy and trots. Maybe some bug is going around? I toddled off to bed in the Taj at 5:00. I was awakened by Elphas at 8:30 bringing the fruit jelly (like jello). I was awakened again at 10:00 by Coen! He looks great. He is here for three days, then he will head back to Nairobi before taking off for South Africa. He's had a big run-in with Jurgen's company about the *duma*. He doesn't dare stay at camp so he is staying in room 12. It drizzled all evening and night.

Still overcast and drizzling when awakened by Gideon at 8:30 a.m. to see how I was. He drove up here just to see me. What a sweetie. Then Juma and Rashidi came to check on me. Feeling much better although I still ache all over. I must get up but don't want to. It's so peaceful in the Taj with all the flaps down. I can see almost all around – the gray and white water tower straight ahead against a blue-gray sky, the grass so green from all the rain. A herd of impala are grazing up near the water tower. How I love the open spaces where I can see for miles! Listening to the birds, the doves cooing. Such a tranquil, beautiful feeling. I love life! I dreamed about Mary Sue last night. Wonder how she is? She is such a good friend. Hope she enjoyed our four months together traveling through Europe as much as I did.

I enjoyed the morning with Coen and Putney. Coen took pictures of Lisa and Bunts in Room 11. I was starved for lunch; my first real meal in 48 hours. Then I went hunting with Gideon in the afternoon. After all the rains, the plains are lush and green. Mark and Christian returned to the Hunters Camp and mentioned rumblings they have heard about banning all hunting in Tanzania.

When I got back I found Valerie at the Taj. She looks great and healthy and was full of information about acupuncture done with silver needles. She had stayed with the Vishnyakovs in Mwanza. Yuri had left Wednesday for Dar es Salaam and Olga and Lyuba left today (September 7th) for Dar. Olga had received a call yesterday saying that Yuri wanted them to come but she couldn't understand why the immediacy of them having to go down. She hopes it isn't about Lyuba and her age. By USSR standards, she is too old to be living outside the USSR.

Saturday was a lazy morning. About 10:30 Coen came up and was hungry so I offered to go into the kitchen and fix him some bread and jam. He joined me. Because he was hungry and trying to hurry up, he grabbed the knife from me, cutting the index finger on his right hand almost to the bone. It shouldn't have happened. We were both to blame. I bandaged up Coen's finger as best I could. I thought he might need stitches.

News came that trophy hunting has definitely been banned in Tanzania until further notice, as of yesterday or today, at 13:00 hours. Apparently, this is to stop the full-scale poaching that is going on. Fortunately, the Tanzania Game Department makes an exemption for non-commercial hunting, such as Fort Ikoma, which hunts plains game as a source of meat. David Babu came for a visit and he had not heard about the hunting ban. Also, the government has banned indecent dress. Therefore, short shorts (poor Skip and his hems), bellbottoms, dresses above the knee, hair below collar for men, and wigs are considered indecent dress.

Shakir and Ruth Fletcher flew in to spend the weekend. Finn Allen was the pilot. The hunters flew out in the afternoon because of the hunting ban. What a pity because the clients had arrived two days earlier to spend two weeks here and then continue on to the Selous, a large hunting district south of Dar es Salaam. Herr Viederhuffer also left. Gideon was going to fly to Nairobi with them, but pain in the butt Michael nabbed his seat. So, we all went swimming in the afternoon. Skip gave Coen a rubber tip to put over his finger to keep it dry. Valerie and I invited everyone to the Taj for cocktails. Dionisia, and Mushi returned after a two-month holiday. Oh, how little Judy has grown! It's good to have them back. We had a big dance after dinner. It's the best dance we've had so far. Shakir really is a hoot on the dance floor. Jack and John of the

Lindblad group were up and dancing too. John and his two sons are on a scouting trip. He's a travel agent in Pennsylvania. Two cool fellows, doctors from Buck County, Pennsylvania also joined in the dancing. Didn't toddle off to bed until 1:30 a.m.

Gideon left for Nairobi early in the morning. Coen left later with Mark and Christian. Coen is having a big party in Nairobi on the 15th but I doubt I can make it because of Lisa. Coen is planning to leave in a week or so for South Africa. I'll miss him. He's got his finger to remember me, though. I spent the day by the pool. Patrick Duncan passed through. He will be at the Serengeti Research Institute for a little longer while finishing up some work. Later in the day, Finn, Putt and I took Lisa for a walk to the airstrip. Finn had mentioned that he was a semi-professional photographer so he was given the task of taking the photos. The airstrip is so green.

Finn came for cocktails at the Taj. Shakir never made it. About 7:00, out comes Skip with Larry and Terry. They had stopped by on the way back to Busegwe, but said they could not stay. Skip left them with us with instructions to talk them into staying. We tried but they had to get back. Larry leaves September 19th for school in Beirut. After dinner, Val, Finn and I stopped by Shakir's tent 37 to chat. Finn was sleeping in tent 40. Except for those two, we thought all the tents were empty. We started telling the filthiest, crassest, dirtiest jokes we knew. All of a sudden from tent 38 comes the voice of a very irritated woman, "Can you quiet down and let a body get some sleep!" You've never seen four more surprised people get out of a tent so fast. Off we went to the Taj to listen to some music. Finn told me about the days when he was young during the emergency. This refers to the Mau Mau rebellion in Kenya prior to independence. His father was a police officer during the emergency and quite the crack shot, I gather. His parents are now in Rhodesia at Victoria Falls where his father is to watch for troublemakers from Zambia.

First thing the next morning, Valerie told Skip that if he should get a complaint from a woman in tent 38, to tell her that "he will look into it." We overheard the woman mention to the couple that happened to be in tent 39 that she had never stayed at such a noisy place before. She did mention about the people in 37 who were talking so loud but apparently she didn't hear what we were saying because she didn't mention anything about dirty jokes. Also, last night road crew vehicles were driving around at midnight and the police that had come to investigate the $1,000 that had been stolen from John's (Lindblad client) room that day. The police were in a nearby tent and making lots of *kelele* (noise) too. Finn and I took Lisa for a walk to the new bridge that is not yet completed. Valerie made pizza for lunch for the Lindblad group and us. John and Jack left with their Lindblad group after lunch. Shakir, Ruth and Finn took off after lunch, too. Finn said he didn't want to leave and told Shakir, "If ever you have to make another trip like this, just remember the name Finn." It had been so much fun with them here that we hated to see them go. After taking off, Finn came around and buzzed us in the

Land Rover so low, 15 feet above the roof, that I jumped off the hood. I went to the Taj for a nap because I was so pooped. Valerie and I went to dinner because it is Putney's last night, but she and Skip ate in the room. Instead, we ate with Rosemary North-Lewis, the courier who was with the Lindblad FIT (Fully Independent Tour), a couple from Delaware.

Skip and Putney left for Nairobi late morning and took Bunts with them. A teacher at Saint Andrews has bunnies and Bunts will live with them. Three Sunbird pilots flew in together, Doug Byrd, Tony Lutyens, and Viscount Andrew Cole. I taped some LPs and relaxed. Also chatted with Jerrie Trotter, a freelance travel writer, but who mostly works for *Town and Country*. She used to write for *Harper's Bazaar*. Valerie and I moved into Skip's room to take care of Lisa.

Eileen Marshall, a woman in Bill Hurst's Lindblad group, lives in Paradise Valley, Arizona. She told me about feeding time in the nursery at the Phoenix Zoo. She will call Mom and Dad for us. Bill's group left and Ann Morson arrived with the next group. I took Lisa for a walk at 4:00 and brought her back to the Taj about 5:30. She loves the Water Tower Hill and refuses to leave. However, today it was easy because Ann's group came up and she felt as though her territory was being invaded and, therefore, was happy to follow me back to the Taj. I represent security. She kept stopping and looking back up the hill, though. We played and played at the Taj until 7:00. She climbed lots of trees. Then she followed us back to room 11, in the dark, too. Stephan, Mark and horrible Rolf had arrived the night before to completely close up the Hunters Camp. John Wangere had heard on the radio that the hunting ban is for six months. They had also heard that. Stephan and I talked about it and he said that Jurgen had mentioned something about lots of activity in the south, of lines of lorries filled with Chinese moving south. Maybe the Chinese are putting pressure on the government to clear out hunters in the south. It's a known fact that the Chinese are behind a lot of poaching, especially for the horn of the rhinoceros which when ground up is considered an aphrodisiac. Rolf was at the swimming pool in the afternoon. He was playing too rough with Lisa. When I told him, not too politely, to get his hands off her, he said she is "our cheetah," meaning von Nagy's and his, and they had a permit from Mehina, some top official in the Mara region. I told him he couldn't touch Lisa until Mehina personally came to claim her!

It's the 13th of September. I left for Europe one year ago today. I've seen a lot and done a lot in this past year and had no earthly idea at the outset that I would be celebrating the anniversary here. What serendipity! I brought Lisa out to the Taj in the morning to play around. This is the best way for her to get her exercise. Stephan came by at 11:30 to say goodbye. He's off to Arusha. He thinks this might be the end of Jurgen's company. Jurgen is in Rhodesia checking out possibilities and will do so in Zambia too, but this will entail more money than his company probably has. The Robinsons flew over and dropped a message tied to a rock to alert us that they will be by on Sunday for lunch. Cathy Potter arrived with a Lindblad group and brought us a Toblerone bar. So nice of her! She had clients from Los Angeles whom we enjoyed meeting. Always fun to have something in common with a guest.

Saturday turned out to be a stormy day with rain. JP Antoine is here with his Travelworld group. He fell in love with Lisa. JP came before and after dinner to play with her. Daudi is back, too.

The Robinsons, Leonard, Ruth, Eddie and Freddie flew in from Manyara for lunch on Sunday. I gave Mr. Robinson my passport to have it extended as it expires on the 19th. Skip and Valerie continue to say that there is no hurry for me to leave and now Valerie and I are planning a safari to Kenya when it is her vacation time. Nick Spree, the electrician at Lake Manyara Wildlife Lodge came for the night. Bryan from SWL also came. Ann Morson's Lindblad group left and Jerry Rilling 's group arrived. This time Jerry brought us bags of oregano. The Lodge is full. Since Valerie and I are sleeping in Skip's room to take care of Lisa while he is gone, Nick and Bryan are going to sleep in the Taj. We built a fire, although it was still light, and decided to bring out shish kebabs for dinner. Party at the Taj! Got some good black-and-white pictures of JP with Lisa so he has offered to get them developed in Nairobi for me. It was a relaxing evening, but when Valerie and I got back to room 11, I discovered that Lisa had piddled on my bed...twice!

Very Sad News

V alerie and I heard a plane approaching from Busegwe. We had to walk down to the airstrip because no *gari!* We were thrilled to see that it was Larry with Eddie and Freddie. They had brought my passport with the visa extended to December 31, 1973. Yippee! They had also brought their Super 8 camera. It was so good to see Larry once again before he leaves for school in Lebanon. They were staying only for lunch so we first went out to the Taj to take movies of Lisa playing around. We got some good film. She fell out of three trees, three different times. We had lunch on the terrace and shot another roll of Super 8 movie film of Lisa. Eddie and Freddie got up to play with Lisa. Larry then got a strange look on his face. I asked him if he had forgotten what to say or if it was bad news, in a joking manner. In Larry's quiet way he said he had some bad news, it was about Yuri. The first thing that went through Valerie's and my head was that they have been sent back to the USSR. Larry said, "Yuri is dead." Valerie and I were completely stunned. Not Yuri who is so full of life and laughter. Larry explained that he had been in Mwanza on Thursday and Julee told him. The only information he had was that Yuri had been killed in a car accident. The car had run into the back of a tipper (dump truck) about 4:00 a.m. Thursday, September 6, on Oyster Bay Road in Dar es Salaam. That meant that Val was still in Mwanza trying to ease Olga's fears about why Yuri hadn't called. Yuri had left for Dar at noon on the 5th and was to call Olga that night or the next day, depending on telephone lines from Dar to Mwanza. When he didn't call and didn't call, Olga got very worried. Then on Friday morning, Yuri's secretary called to say that two tickets had been cabled to Mwanza on East African Airways for Olga and Lyuba to fly to Dar that noon. No explanation. Olga kept saying to Valerie, "He's dead and they won't tell me." Valerie kept saying, "Olga, don't be ridiculous," offering many possibilities as to why Lyuba and Olga were to fly to Dar, even though Olga said that they always take the train because it is too expensive to fly. Also, Lyuba wouldn't be finished with exams until the 22nd. Olga and Lyuba left for the airport the same time that Valerie left for Ikoma. According to Larry, when Olga and Lyuba arrived at the airport in Dar es Salaam, Yuri was not there to meet them but were met by some other fellow. Olga asked where Yuri was. When the man didn't say anything, she said, "He's dead." The man answered, "Yes." How horrible that must have been! I can just envision Olga crumbling inside. We don't know anything else, but I assume Olga and Lyuba have gone back to Moscow with the body. As sad as we were, we were glad that it was Larry who had delivered the bad news to us. It was considerate of him to save the bad news until after we were done with the filming and had eaten lunch. We walked them down to the airstrip and waved goodbye. We won't see Larry again until Christmas.

275

Valerie and I went to the Taj down-spirited. We really couldn't believe it. Valerie wrote Mom and Dad about it and I started my letters to Olga and Lyuba. Thankfully, the rains came and closed out the rest of the world. Tchaikovsky was a comfort to listen to, appropriate, I guess. It drizzled onwards to 7:00 p.m. Valerie made pizza for dinner. She needed to do something therapeutic. After we ate, we went to room 11 to listen to music. A sad day, indeed.

What Will Tomorrow Bring?

After receiving such sad news yesterday, Valerie and I were awakened by Mushi at 7:30. He had been awakened at 6:00 a.m. by the *jeshi* (army). About forty soldiers descended on the property. Some searched his house and then they ordered him to open the stores so that they could search them. After that, they went down to staff quarters for a search, not letting any of the *watu* (staff) come up. Guests were waiting in the dining room for breakfast but there were no kitchen staff or waiters to feed them. Mushi explained to the guests what happened. Valerie and I made a beeline to the dining room. Then seven of the army personnel came to the dining room and asked to see Valerie and me. The only questions they asked were how long I have been here and how long my visa was good for. They didn't even ask to see my passport. Actually, they were very nice about it, but no explanation was given as to what the search was about. It is very disconcerting though, and incidents like this always seem to occur while Skip is away. Ultimately, the guests were fed and we were back in our routine. I wonder what the guests thought? I went to get Lisa and feed her. I wonder what the army would have done if they had seen Lisa?

Jerry left, taking our letters to mail and Fiona arrived with the next group. While Fiona's group was out on a game run, they saw a big *ngiri* (warthog) caught in a snare between the road to Musoma and the airstrip. Rajabu, Philip, Fiona, two Lindblad tourists, Isaac, Valerie, and I jumped into the Land Rover and took off to see if we could release it, equipped with *pangas* and no real plan. When we first approached the warthog, it got scared and ran to the end of the wire, falling down hard when he reached the end. Then he got up and ran again, this time snapping the wire by brute force and taking off at a dead run, with no apparent limp. He had been very aggravated by the snare, as we could tell, by how he had plowed the patch of terrain within the radius of the snare. He severed the wire near the slip knot, taking the loop with him. Hopefully, he'll be able to work his way out of it.

Mike Norton-Griffiths and Patrick Duncan flew in to see Lisa and have lunch. As they were leaving, Val grabbed Patrick to come to Skip's office where there were some men from the game department who had come to take Lisa away. Patrick convinced them of the need for special medicine and attention. They had come expressly for Lisa and said a leopard cage had been brought to the game post from Musoma two days before. The tide kept turning, take her, leave her, take her, leave her. They finally decided that she's getting the best care here and the chap from Bunda wrote a letter to support the letter written by Palangyo, the regional game warden, that she is the property of the Mara Region Game Department, but we are the legal custodians. Valerie did tell them that Lisa doesn't like small children and eats chickens. That could have convinced them.

Anyway, fortunately, Lisa is still here where she will get proper care, attention and *dawa*. The Game Department is concerned about her being removed by the *jeshi* when and if they make another raid, but the letters should be enough.

David Babu came in the evening but we didn't see him. He has closed Sabora Plains completely. Why? Because when Cathy Potter's group was out with Philip they came across an ostrich nest. The female ostrich feigned an injury to ward off danger to the eggs. Against Philip's protests, Cathy let her group get out of the car and touch the eggs. This is a big no-no. When Jerry's group came through and visited Sabora Plains two days later, they found seven of the eggs and three of the chicks had been eaten by hyenas. Jerry said he would not go within 30 feet of a nest with eggs because the human scent will keep a mother from her eggs and young. Repercussions from this incident have since forbidden anyone to go to Sabora Plains.

I have been suffering a sore throat the last few days and now it has turned into a cold. I kept myself busy by painting the bedroom shelves and outside tables at the Taj a bright green. Ronald Harris, president of Travelworld is here. Skip is gone and Valerie doesn't want to get cornered by him.

It's always something. We woke up to no water one morning. It finally came on at 8:30. Then we learned that someone sabotaged the petrol tank by putting water in it. I made *nyama na ndisi na nyanya* (meat, bananas and tomatoes) with Dionisia. I am starting to call Dionisia Mama *Sijui* because she is pregnant and doesn't know if she is having a boy or a girl. Everyone in the kitchen is starting to call me Mama *Duma*. I love it!

David Lockwood is here with two clients. He has a tented camp on the Tana River in Kenya near George Adamson's place. Lindblad groups stay at his camp. Poor Lisa has been cooped up inside all day long. The only exercise she had was out at the Taj for about 1½ hours. She even stayed in the office while we were in the kitchen fixing dinner. Poor baby. She is not used to this change in routine. She starts to chirp when we leave her. From the dining room we could hear her loud and clear so since we only had seven people in tonight, Valerie brought her into the dining room. She was good until Foya brought out the *nyama na ndisi na nyanya* and put it on a nearby table. While Valerie was dishing up the stew, Lisa kept jumping up trying to grab it and nearly brought the entire tray with bowl and plates down.

Earlier this afternoon, while we were writing letters in the office, she kept entertaining herself by jumping onto the narrow window sills and peering out. Then she would have to jump up on her hind legs to do a quick twist to get out. Her last time up she got stung by a bee. We never saw anything move so fast in our lives. She turned around and was off the window sill lickety-split, groaning and kicking on the floor, trying to make the pain go away. So sad and pathetic a sight, yet amusing too. Earlier today she was able to extricate herself from one of the trees by the Taj where she had climbed really high. Good! Because I wasn't going to climb up to get her. After the bee sting, I took her back to room 11 with me and she was up a nearby tree lickety-split. She must have been trying to blow off her anger at us for keeping her penned up all day because this time she went way up, twice as high as she has ever gone before. I was still suffering from my cold and feeling miserable and in no mood to play. She wouldn't come down, defying my vain attempts. I finally got so mad that I started screaming at her and then crying. I stomped back into the room. Thirty seconds later I went back outside to check on her and she was five feet from the door. To get down that fast she had to have jumped – a height of a good 15 feet. She was good after that, and yet, I could see how mixed up her emotions were. She was being defiant, yet knew I was sick and she shouldn't be so thoughtless. Or on the other hand, she wasn't ready to be outside at night on her own.

I took Lisa out to the Taj to spend the entire day because yesterday wasn't good for her to be cooped up for so long. I was feeling much better, too, and need to get the Taj ready for Skip. He had radioed that he wants the Taj when he is here and we are to stay in room 11 with Lisa. "Repeat, with Lisa." Skip has been in Nairobi taking flying lessons and is bringing a lady friend back with him. Valerie hung up the blue and green curtains around the shelves in the bathroom. With the freshly painted furniture and colorful *kitenges*, the Taj is looking really good. The man who we thought was the Travelworld president, and who we had been successfully avoiding, cornered us at the Taj. He introduced himself as Jack Wolf, a banker with United California Bank in Beverly Hills. Jack was traveling alone.

Not many tourists travel alone with a driver, so our confusion was understandable. He wanted to get some photos of Lisa.

Lisa has developed quite a purr. It comes from within her chest but sounds like someone with a cold who is snoring. She loves jumping onto my (or anyone's) head and gnawing on the scalp while clutching the victim around the neck with her front paws. Yow! I call it her "love bites." This must be how they play with their siblings.

Peter Greaves arrived with his Club Tour group. Eve Daniels, Skip's lady friend, arrived with Travelworld. Martha Bell was the tour leader and brought with her the music cassette tapes from our cousin Pamela. It's always a treat for us to see the tour leaders who regularly come through the Fort. Many times they will join us for dinner and regale us with stories. I remember one tour guide complaining about a client who kept pestering him for the names of every bird she saw and then writing them down in her journal. One bird he couldn't identify so he made up a name – the double-breasted, yellow-titted *sijui* bird. She dutifully wrote it down. Good luck looking that one up in a bird guide. *Sijui* means "I don't know." And then Ruth, Eddie and Freddie came for the night. Ruth said she told the boys, "Everyone's gone and I feel so lonely so let's go visit Valerie and Vicki." Julee is here, too. What a crowd! We settled Eve in the Taj. Eve is a sweetie and so appreciative of all we are doing for her.

Terry and Veronica Joshua and Helen and Valerie Martinsen came for the day. With Ruth, Eddie and Freddie here, we all spent the morning around the pool. I had Lisa out with us to let her run around. She came tearing over to our table but misjudged the corner at the deep end and went plunging into the water. She managed to get halfway out, with her head and forepaws on the coping, but would have had problems getting out completely because the water level was low and her hind end and tail were waterlogged. We helped her out. She didn't seem very afraid this time.

Sharp ears Ruth heard a plane about 12:30. I had my camera ready and got a picture of Skip flying overhead. Ruth, Terry, Valerie and I raced down in the Robinsons' Range Rover. Mushi followed us in ARF121 and Cephas and Saulo in the Volkswagen bug to give Skip a big welcome. Eve wanted to wait for him at the Taj. By hanging out the window, I got some super pictures of him taxiing up. I thought for a minute that the licensed pilot with Skip was Finn, but it turned out to be his brother Tor. Skip is training in a Cessna 150. Skip told us that Ndosi is also taking flying lessons now. Skip did the unforgivable, he put his "fat hairy legs" in the Robinsons' Range Rover, something he had vowed never to do, to drive up to the Fort. Guess it's all right, though, because he flew the plane here.

Peter Greaves and I took Lisa for a walk in the afternoon to the Water Tower Hill. Peter got me interested in looking for old German relics lying around. Blue glass from medicine bottles, thick black glass from beer bottles, green glass from wine or liquor bottles, all the African pottery pieces. He found a 1906 1 Heller coin and gave it to me. He says a lot are lying around. He found a 1907 1 Heller coin also and said to look for ½ Heller coins, 20 Heller coins, ½ and 1 rupee coins. Heller coins were minted out of copper (J meant it was minted in Berlin) and rupees were minted from good quality silver. I found a button which was imprinted with Buttons Ltd. B'ham. It must have been off a WWI British uniform. He also encouraged me to keep my eyes open for bright blue beads that were used for trading.

The Robinsons and gang left. A super duper party for two was planned for Skip and Eve in Dumas Den, such a romantic and intimate setting amidst the ruins. Valerie and I helped. The salad was avocado with a vinaigrette dressing. The main course was a chicken and wine casserole. The side dish was a vegetable plate accompanied by a Ranch dressing dip served in a hollowed-out tomato. Dessert was a choice of fruits – pineapple, mango, papaya, bananas – attractively arranged in a basket made from dried banana leaves, along with cheese and crackers. Quite elegant for these parts. Wine flowed and music played. Valerie and I had dinner with Tor and Jack Wolf that evening. The four of us went to room 11 to listen to music and play with Lisa. We heard through the grapevine that Sabora Plains might have been closed because President Nyerere's sister died and he attended the funeral in Butiama. Who knows?

Eve is leaving today, which happens to be her birthday. She wants to send Valerie and me something from San Francisco. So cute, "do you like Villager, Peck and Peck...?" Skip gave her a beautiful, heavy, silver Ethiopian necklace. At breakfast, after she left with Travelworld, Skip told Valerie and me not to peek. He then clasped a necklace around each of our necks. We each were given a beautiful orthodox Ethiopian silver cross. Skip said, the cross is from Ethiopia and the chain is from Woolworth's. How sweet of him. He raved about the great dinner and atmosphere last night. This was a token of his appreciation. Then we jumped up from the table to witness all the minibuses crossing the river over the new bridge. Good thing because the old bridge was deep under water. We didn't know that the bridge had a top on it yet. Skip and Tor flew out after lunch with Skip at the controls. We could see heavy rains in the northeast so they got away as quickly as they could.

I went out with Jack in the afternoon with Julee's driver, Ibrahim, who asked me if I could drive. I confirmed that I could and then he invited me to get behind the wheel. I don't get to drive too often and thoroughly enjoy driving a Land Rover. I have adapted well to the steering wheel on the right and gear shift on the left. We checked the river at the old bridge. The water had gone down to about an inch below the top, but so much debris was cluttered up against it. Jack joined Valerie and me for Sundowners at the Taj. We got the fire going, rigged up two cassette recorders and four speakers so we had quadraphonic sound. I brought Lisa out from room 11, but by tent number 43 she went bounding off. We spent a good 15 to 20 minutes looking for her and finally found her stuck up in a tree she had never climbed before, amidst all sorts of sticky branches and twigs. Her chirping led us to her but she was really frightened and stuck. I got on a stool to help her down but she kept clinging onto the mat of thin branches for dear life. I finally got her untangled and she held onto me for dear life until she was safe and sound in the bathroom. She found security on the bathroom shelf protected by the curtains, but soon wanted to come out again. The fire scared her though, she tries to get far away from it. Most probably she has a tortuous recollection of the brushfire which passed over her. I finally took her back to room 11 so I could enjoy the evening. I slept in 11 with her; Val stayed in the Taj.

Elphas told Valerie that the only Africans who wear crosses like the ones Skip gave us are the witch doctors. Hezron, Boscal and Japani also commented on the crosses. When I asked them if only witch doctors wore them, they shook their heads no.

Valerie, Jack and I, with Lisa accompanying us, hiked up to the top of the Heliograph Hill. What a climb! On top of the hill are the remains of a rock wall, apparently the enclosure for the mirrors used by the Germans when they occupied the fort at Ikoma. It has been said that in good weather a message could be sent from Dar es Salaam to Lake Victoria in six hours, and from Dar to Tabora in three hours. It is such a fantastic panoramic view from up here. The hills that the Fort and water tower are on look like anthills. Starting due south and working westward, I photographed the panorama 360°. As we climbed up the hill, we saw a tortoise with part of its shell chewed on, probably by a *fisi*. Under the top layer of the shell are tissue and arteries. Lisa kept up with us pretty well. A couple of times she lagged quite far behind, but always tried her best.

The hike really wiped her out and she slept all afternoon in the Taj. She got a second wind by 6:00 and was very frisky. She would hide from me by crouching in the grass and then she would stalk me very quietly. Now she is in the canna lilies. I keep my eyes down so as not to ruin her game. Ah ha! She leaps across the terrace and is on my leg, wham! A little hug I give her and off she goes.

Raja brought Valerie and me our suede hats that are just like his and I paid him 90 shillings. Now the three of us having matching hats, so natch, we needed a photo. Got a great one of the three of us, with me holding Lisa, on the steps of Dumas Den. He had also brought the mail bag which included photos of our stuffed lion from Costas and the watercolor from Peter Greaves. I had described to Peter the beautiful sunset Skip and I had witnessed and was without a camera. He said that he would paint a watercolor for me. It really captured the memorable moment.

After dinner, Valerie, Jack and I went out to the Taj to record a cassette tape for Shelly Balzac who was Valerie's boss when she worked at Lawry's The Prime Rib. Jack has quite sophisticated recording equipment with which he records animal sounds. We played some of those animal sounds in the background while we recorded a verbal message. We had Daudi add his two bits, too, in Maasai. We also included the recorded radio call about my ticket reservation.

With his Polaroid camera, Cephas took a photo of me holding Lisa. He's making money by charging everyone 15 shillings for a picture. Jack left with Lindblad and Ruth

Ware arrived with a new group. She has two cheetahs at home that she and her husband got from Somalia. She has suggested Dr. Victor Sayer in Kibiti, Tanzania as an excellent cheetah veterinarian. Epidex is the serum for cat distemper and Lisa should have it soon. Before lunch Mcharo and David flew in. We went down to the new bridge and checked it out – *safi sana* (very neat)! They left before lunch.

Big rain storm in the afternoon so I went to the Taj and finished *Serengeti Shall Not Die* by Bernhard and Michael Grzimek. Such a fantastic book about the need for creating the Serengeti National Park to protect the wildlife and great migration that takes place within these borders and to preserve it from the encroachment of human settlements. Their study of the migration patterns determined the park boundaries. Lisa has been really cuddly today. The Taj got soaked during the rainstorm and Lisa cuddled up to me for warmth. Twice today she has grasped my chin in her mouth as a sign of affection. That night in bed, she stretched out along my stomach with her head resting on the pillow, right next to mine.

The army was wandering around so I kept Lisa in the office most of day. I taped some and then sat out by the pool. It unnerved me when I would see these young soldiers with rifles over their shoulders sidle up to the bar window accessible from the terrace and order a soft drink. I thought to myself, "What if one of them goes crazy and starts shooting?" Fortunately, there was never any reason for concern. The soldiers were young and I doubt there were bullets in the rifles. Bwana Cha Cha, a police officer from Mugumu, came. In his high-pitched voice, he brought news that there is a restriction on airplanes landing here, Seronera and the entire area near the border for the next two weeks. Steve Willhite and Mark Habermann arrived about 5:30. Valerie brought them out to Taj where Lisa and I were, just in time to witness a beautiful sunset with the hills so blue and the sky and sun a deep orange. They had stayed with Terry and Veronica in Busegwe last night. Both are American, though Steve has lived in Kenya most of his life. He graduated from medical school in the States in 1967 and now is a doctor working in Tiriki, Kenya. Valerie and I think he looks a lot like our brother Robert. Mark is a fourth-year medical student at NYU and is here for four months on a fellowship. We found them both to be very interesting. They spent the night in the Taj, a free room, and we stayed in room 11.

The Lindblad tour had to drive to Seronera to catch a plane because of the newly instituted flying ban. However, they must have arrived way behind schedule because a plane with only a pilot flew overhead looking for them. This is Africa! I made oatmeal cookies in the afternoon and then wanted to finish the tape to Shelly, but alas it couldn't be found. We had placed it on the bookshelf in Skip's room. Who has the sticky fingers?

Lisa is looking good and eating well. We've been taking care of her for five weeks now. Yesterday she ate all but a thumb-size bit of bone from the neck and back of a *kuku* (chicken). She and I went out to the Taj. The three crested cranes joined us. Lisa had fun chasing them and finally scared them away, causing one to fly from the Taj to the junction of the new road and the driveway to the Fort. One doesn't often see a crested crane fly.

Ian Ross arrived with a Unitours group. Two days before, Valerie had read in the paper about a tour of 46 people who had been turned away at the Tanzania border at Taveta, Kenya because they had South African visas in their passports. Ian said that was Patrice's group. Ian entered Tanzania two days later with no such problems. However, his problem was the flight from Durban, South Africa to Nairobi; the plane never came. So he called up EAA (East African Airways) and got a flight to Dar where he went through Immigration. The Immigration officer looked through his passport, asked how was South Africa, then stamped him in. Then Ian said, "Now I have 30 clients with me." From Dar the next day he got his clients on a plane to Nairobi, but was going to get them to detour the plane to Kilimanjaro airport where he had Patrice send kombies to meet them. I love these guys for how they solve problems. This is Africa! How many times have we used that expression???

We woke up on the first of October to discover that we had no water. Somebody forgot to turn the pump on, then when Mushi did, water still did not come. Stephen was usurping all the water for the swimming pool! It wasn't until 11:00 that we finally had water. I painted the mirror in the Taj bathroom lemon yellow. It looks so cheerful! We measured Lisa. She is 80 cm from tip to tail. That's about 32 inches. Valerie and I took Lisa down to the airstrip about 6:00. She loves chasing the small birds down there.

"Can't educate the public!" Quote from Dad. Kay Bennett was offering her clients personal tours of Lisa without us there. Then Mike Guest's Swann group, which supposedly is made up of Zoological Society people, did precisely what we asked them not to do. They were instructed to keep together in one group and not surround her. I thought she was going to jump off the side of the terrace because the people made a complete semi-circle around her. To hell with them! I scooped her up and took her out to the Taj. I could feel her shaking. These people had made her very nervous, so nervous that she piddled on Valerie's stereo cassette player. The urine seeped right down into the mechanisms, causing the needles to jump spastically when the power was turned on.

An army lorry was here at lunchtime so I left Lisa in the Taj bathroom. She kept me company while I gave the mirror a second coat. Lindblad is flying in and out. Who's paying attention to this flying ban that Arusha and Dar seem to know nothing about?

On the 3rd, Bryan Payne and Tony Wilkes arrived for a conciliatory board meeting. The Workers Committee refers cases to this board if it cannot reach a satisfactory decision with management or if the accused won't accept the decision. Of course, the fellow from Musoma who was supposed to preside over the case never showed, so Tony and Bryan left. Bryan had brought with him an African fellow who asked if Lisa was a tiger, a leopard, oh, a cheetah? Alert! No tigers (or bears) in Africa! It's understandable that people confuse leopards and cheetahs, though once you know the difference it is very easy not to confuse them. The leopard has rosettes and is a more muscular looking animal. Heck, it drags its kill up a tree! The cheetah has solid black dots and the unmistakable black tear-like mark from the inner corner of the eye and down the side of the nose. The tip of a cheetah's tail is white fur, but Lisa's tail was singed in the brush fire when she was but a few weeks old. Therefore, it is very easy to spot our Lisa with her black-tipped tail.

Jack Manuel and his assistant Moez arrived before lunch. They are here to check out the bridge. What a nice surprise. Jack has never been here before. In the afternoon I took Lisa for a walk to the airstrip. As I neared the road separating the Lodge from the airstrip, an army lorry went barreling past. Their camp is on the road past the *taka taka* (garbage) hole. Then I saw three jackals. Thank goodness they are more scared of me so they don't get any ideas about Lisa. After dinner Jack and Moez joined us at the Taj and we uncorked a bottle of Champagne. Jack told us that the government is planning to move the capital from Dar es Salaam to Dodoma, phased over the next 10 years at a cost of 3 trillion, 400 million shillings!

Valerie left with Jack and Moez in the morning for Arusha. I helped her pack and we had a hell of a time because of the new dress code which went into effect October 1st. No bell bottoms, no Levi's, no skirts shorter than knees, no shorts. *Kanzus* and *kangas* are the only things we have which are legal! Viscount Andrew Cole flew in to pick up the Lindblad group. I packed up Valerie's stereo cassette player for him to deliver to Skip who will meet the Trislander in Nairobi and take it to a *fundi* to be fixed, hopefully.

I tried giving Lisa Farex cereal which is like our cream of wheat. She did not mind it too much! Tony and Janice Wilkes, Salim and his wife Azra arrived about 11:00 for another go at this conciliation board meeting. Bryan could not come because President Nyerere is in Seronera. Their meeting started at 12:00 and didn't adjourn until 7:00. Tony's case was about the driver who beat him up on June 29th. Mushi was in the meeting for the FIL case which was about the room stewards who had been fired. I later learned from Mushi that he had not been happy with Juma's work in rooms 1 to 4 so he had transferred him to the *shamba*. Juma never showed up for work after that. Could be that he did take John's money? While the meeting was in session, I entertained Janice, Salim and Azra out at the Taj. We watched Lisa play, then we played the card game spades all afternoon. Since Tony didn't finish until 7:00, they stayed for dinner. They left at 9:30 with 15 people in their mini school bus and they had to drive to Seronera first, drop off Chubie and others, and then drive to Lobo. They won't get home until well after midnight, but President Nyerere might be going to Lobo tomorrow and so they had to get back.

The adult cheetah may be the fastest land animal, but with Lisa not even three months old, I had the advantage right now. At a full run she was catching up to me, but she didn't see a hole and ran right into it. All I saw were her hind legs, up in the air, still running at full speed. Later in the afternoon I walked her down to the airfield. We saw a jackal and then Lisa took after a hare and gave it a good chase, but the full gown hare was too fast for her. I had seen an army truck go by so I took her the long way back to room 11 where I was staying with both Skip and Valerie gone. I had a sore throat and wasn't feeling well, so I went to bed early, slept fitfully for an hour and woke up to find Lisa curled up in my arms. She had piddled in the bed, though, so I moved over to the other one. Lisa kept giving me hugs and kisses. I couldn't sleep though. I thought about my future. What exactly do I want to do? I think I might leave for home after the first of year. I miss my friends. I wonder what they are up to? Why don't they write? I may not be the best correspondent but at least I try to keep up some line of communication.

I wasn't feeling well so I slept in late the next morning. After feeding Lisa her breakfast, we went back to the Taj to the spend the day there. It was a cloudy day, a perfect day for taking a nap, Lisa on my bed and I on Valerie's. What a picture of contentment she is! The way she sleeps all stretched out, her long hind legs extended straight, then bending, then straight, and a stretch of the toes. She sleeps on her side, but with her head positioned so that her nose is pointing straight up in the air and her eyes are closed, oh so tight. Oops, a foot safari just went past. Of course, Lisa had to check everything out so she slipped out of the tent unnoticed by *wageni*. I'm glad they didn't notice her because I don't like the way they ooh and aah over her as if she is here expressly for their pleasure. When she grows out of this cute and cuddly stage, then I hope that they will feel certain trepidation by her size and treat her accordingly, as a wild animal.

I took Lisa for a walk down towards the river. She usually follows me very well, but one time she just stayed where she was while I continued walking a good 100 yards ahead. I called for her, but she didn't come. I couldn't see her anywhere. Now I was getting worried, and then mad. What I discovered is that she stays perfectly still while you are looking for her. This is a survival instinct and she is practicing it on me. When I finally did find her, I picked her up by the scruff of the neck, saying "Come, come!" She was quite obedient after that.

At dinner that evening I joined a young Canadian couple, Harold and Doreen Lissel, who are in the area for a month. Harold has taken over the silo project that Grant had been working on. Mother, Dad and I met Grant our first night at Fort Ikoma. One of the staff came up to me saying a *mgeni* wanted to see me. I got up and followed him to the bar area where I was introduced to Steven Wazera from Musoma. He said he is "in 'Parliant' (Parliament?), and has heard so much about me that he wanted to meet me." He never did tell me from whom he had heard about me. I guess news of two American women living at FIL spreads.

While fixing breakfast for Lisa, head waiter Joseph told me that everyone is going down to the bridge at 10:00

to greet President Nyerere and I am invited...so I went. I was the only *mzungu* there amidst a good 150 staff and villagers. I felt conspicuous wearing Levi's with the dress code in place, but no one said anything. The President's entourage arrived exactly at 10:00 and President Nyerere got out to inspect the bridge. Everyone followed him down the bank as he checked it out. No security that I could see. He's a trim and fit looking man at age 51, and spitting image of his brother Joseph. Apparently, he was cracking jokes in Swahili because everyone was laughing. Then the entourage drove off to Butiama, his home village. I had thought it best not to take my camera so did not get a photo, as much as I would have liked one.

Mr. Robinson flew in at noon to pick up Valerie but I told him she had already gone. He'll be back through Wednesday or Thursday. Ken Sheldrick arrived with an Abercrombie & Kent group and Jerry Rilling arrived in the late afternoon with a Lindblad group. Jerry came out to the Taj to see Lisa bearing gifts. He has brought a goodie bag filled with Skippy's peanut butter, Cadbury chocolate and oregano. What a guy! Jerry stressed that Lisa must have a feline enteritis injection as soon as possible, and a liver virus serum if possible. The symptom is diarrhea and she could be gone in 24 hours if she should get the disease.

Doreen's 23rd birthday is today so I asked John to bake a cake. I instructed the waiter George to bring it to Doreen's table at dessert time, as a surprise. Instead, George goes up to their table and asks if they have ordered a cake! They said "no" and then head waiter Joseph comes out and asks, "Who ordered a cake?" Fortunately, just then George brought the cake out. How to ruin a surprise!

After dinner Ken, Jerry, an English couple and I trooped back to room 11 to see Lisa. I keep her in Skip's room which can be locked.

I took Lisa on a picnic lunch to the base of Heliograph Hill – a chicken sandwich for me, chicken wings for Lisa. I came across a porcupine quill. The quills can be as long as a foot and have a sharp, pointed end. I was told that the way to remove a quill if pierced by one is to cut it in half first. That breaks the vacuum and then it is easier to dislodge the nasty bugger. It started to rain so we headed back to the room. Ken came to play with Lisa. Then the wind started to really blow and the rain came, but only for a short while.

Ruth, Eddie and Freddie arrived in the late afternoon with Dr. Paul and Mrs. Denise DeBie, friends from Brussels, Belgium. Dr. DeBie specializes in cancer treatment and radiology. The two families became acquainted in the Congo when Dr. DeBie treated Leonard's father for cancer. The DeBies were in the Congo for 13 years, until 1961.

Mr. and Mrs. Donald from Redlands had a message from Finn for me, "*Jambo*!" He flew them to Seronera. In conversation with them, I learned that their daughter Cindy is the current Alpha Phi president at the University of Arizona.

Dr. and Mrs. DeBie and Ruth went to Seronera for the day and the two boys stayed with me. We took Lisa for a walk down to the bridge, then up to the water tower. The boys climbed it and Lisa couldn't figure out where they had gone. She kept running around the tower looking for them. We met up with Jerry's walking safari group on the way back. Doreen and Harold joined the boys, Lisa and me for a picnic lunch down at the airstrip in time to see the Trislander land with Ann Morson's group. That meant that we had to say goodby to Jerry and his group. Lisa had lots of exercise today so I let her sleep in the Taj in the afternoon. We went to room 11 early, but Lisa stayed outside. The three crested cranes came walking up from staff quarters, saw Lisa and started to dance around her. She was aware of them, but more or less ignored them.

The next morning I let Lisa play around on the terrace and then she followed me to the office about 11:00. I heard a rumbling on the driveway to the back. It was the Mercedes army truck so I left her in the office. Three soldiers were in the bar, here to have lunch, so I took Lisa to the Taj. Ann came out later and we took Lisa for a walk to the airstrip. Ann became ill in the evening. Her clients were worried that it might be appendicitis. Fortunately, Dr. DeBie was here and he checked her. It was a severe case of indigestion only.

Ruth is very concerned about Larry. He and a friend had planned a motorbike trip through Syria. According to their itinerary they should have entered Syria on October 5th, the day before war broke out between Syria and Israel. We were able to tune into BBC news on a radio and learned that Syria and Israel are still fighting. Larry is someplace in

Syria. They have no idea where he is and have not heard from him.

Ruth also told me that when Leonard was last in Dar es Salaam he stopped by the Russian embassy to check about Yuri. They were fairly rude, but he did get to speak to a Hungarian Doctor who said he feels that Yuri could have made it if he had not been neglected for a critical hour when he arrived in emergency. May Olga never know this. Leonard also learned that Yuri was the only fatality from the accident. The driver was not injured. A very suspicious accident, indeed. The next day the mail bag included a letter from Lyuba acknowledging our letter of sympathy. It was short and offered no information about her father's death, just how very sad she and her mother were. She wrote the letter from Mwanza before they left for Moscow.

I am nervous about leaving Lisa on the terrace so I kept her in the office most of day. Ken Sheldrick arrived with a group at lunchtime. He relayed the message that Skip is retaking his flight test tomorrow. Ken and I went to check out the new bridge in the evening. It's the first time I've driven over it. It looks *safi sana*, but will the buttresses hold with a raging river?

Daudi brought back three *kuku* from Mzumu and is selling them for 4 shillings each. Mr. Robinson flew in to meet up with his family and the DeBies. At his suggestion I bought a *kuku* from Daudi to give to Lisa. This would be her first experience with live prey. Mr. Robinson first tied the legs of the *kuku* and then threw it toward Lisa. How she jumped from fright with the *kuku* flapping its wings! Then he *chinja*-ed it (cut its throat) and I had to go get the still flapping bird to put it within distance of Lisa. She couldn't quite figure it out and decided to climb a tree. Finally, I had to open up the bird, take out the guts, and let her eat from my hand. Then I cut off a leg and she attacked that. After a while she began to work on the bird herself.

Mr. Robinson and the DeBies took off at 10:30 for Kilimanjaro Airport and then Nairobi. I have received word that Valerie is flying into Seronera today. Ruth and the boys are leaving tomorrow. Harold and Doreen have to go to Musoma and will follow them. I took Lisa for a walk to the water tower and we rested for a while. Lisa was about 10 feet from me when something caught my attention. It was a male impala standing about 10 feet from Lisa. He watched us intently and kept snorting. I could wave flies away and remove my sunglasses, but he didn't turn and run until I cleared my throat.

Valerie got back about 6:00 with all sorts of news from Arusha. Shakir is going to the States, but should be back by November 16 for the Roundtable convention in Nairobi. Mcharo had President Nyerere over for dinner when he was in Seronera. The president gave Mcharo the impression that the hunting ban will not be lifted. Bell bottoms are now legal. Valerie also worked on plans for our November safari.

The next day I gave Lisa another *kuku*. This time she was much more interested. She even chased it while its legs were still tied together. Eddie and Freddie *chinja*-ed it. She would jump back when it fluttered, but when it finally stilled, she crawled up to it slowly and started gnawing on the neck until she severed the head. We still had to cut it open, but if we tried to carry the bird away, she would grab it in her mouth and pull with all of her might. Her teeth are too small for her to really tear into it, but she does know it is food now. I had to cut the legs and wings off for Lisa to eat them because she couldn't really tackle the meat with all those feathers. She is so cute with an occasional feather hanging from her chin. I took what she didn't eat to the office and then the boys and I took her for a walk through the Hunters Camp, to the river, and walked down the river a distance, seeing baboons, Vervet monkeys and a reedbuck.

Safaris with the Robinsons

R uth invited me to go to Busegwe for a few days and so I left with Ruth and the boys after lunch. Now that Valerie is back, she will care for Lisa. Harold and Doreen followed us part way. They are off to Buhemba, about a 2½-hour drive. Mr. Robinson flew in about 20 minutes after we had arrived in Busegwe with the news that Skip passed his flight test and would be driving back to Fort Ikoma tomorrow. Yay for Skip! Mr. Robinson brought back all sorts of goodies from Nairobi so we had a tossed salad and strawberry shortcake for dinner.

Ron was back in the States and living in Yucaipa, California near his maternal grandparents. I was sleeping in his bedroom which is in a separate building on the property. It's like a barracks with small bedrooms. Unfortunately, there is no indoor plumbing so if I had to use the *choo* at night, I used the outhouse. There was one bathroom in the house that I could have used, but I didn't want to disturb the family. Luckily for me, their two German Shepherd dogs, Caesar and Major, kept me company.

It was fun to help Ruth with chores around the house, changing the bed sheets, putting away camping gear, and then I baked a carrot cake. Doreen and Harold stopped by on their way back to Fort Ikoma to see a sewing machine that Ruth's friend would be willing to sell to them.

Leonard needed to return to Nairobi and invited me to go along so I went with Ruthie to Musoma the next day to get a visa for Kenya which cost me 22/50 shillings. Her friend Santaben also came with us. Ruthie was the daughter of missionaries and grew up in India. She loves hot, spicy Indian food. Unfortunately, Leonard needs to eat a very bland diet so she can enjoy it only when Leonard isn't at the meal. The three of us savored a delightful selection of Indian food at a little restaurant near the Musoma Hotel and Lake Victoria. Both women are vegetarian. My favorite are the vegetable samosas.

When we returned, Leonard notified Ruthie that a court order had arrived for 'Rerry' Robinson for a car accident in Buhemba that no one knows about. Larry is in Syria and has been gone for a while so this will be an issue that they will have to deal with before he returns. And there is still no news about Larry.

Eddie and Freddie were homeschooled and Ruthie has asked me to help with the lessons. I had no experience teaching, just tutoring in high school. This was a challenge. First of all, the two brothers are just a year and a half apart in age and best friends. Trying to keep their attention on schoolwork was a difficult task. Teaching the "new" math was most confusing. I was good in math as a student, but this method had me seeing cross-eyed. I finally decided to work one-on-one and sent one of the boys outside to play while I worked with the other one. We were doing our reading on the couch when I noticed that Eddie every so often would slap his left upper arm with his right hand, while never taking his eyes off the book. He said nothing, just kept doing it. All of a sudden, I caught Freddie in the act. He was outside the window and when I wasn't looking, he would use his slingshot to hit Eddie in the upper arm with a pebble, then quickly duck down. Eddie sure as heck wasn't going to rat on him.

The next day went a little better with their lessons. Freddie sat at his desk with his slingshot around his neck. He did try to get away with anything and everything! Ruth had to go into Musoma so she stamped us out of Tanzania while there as we would be flying to Nairobi the next day. Freddie's birthday is in two days, on the 19th of October, so we celebrated his birthday today with presents and a cake that I made while Ruthie was in town.

The flight from Busegwe to Nairobi is 1½ hours. We left at 10:10 and arrived at Wilson Airport at 11:40. I stopped in at Bosky's at the airport to see if Finn were there. He wasn't. They said he would be in at 6:30 so I left a note for him. There was a vehicle for Leonard to use and off we went to Kentucky Fried Chicken for lunch. I was blown away that there was a KFC in Nairobi. The Robinsons will eat meat when traveling and we all really enjoyed the crispy fried chicken.

After my "finger lickin' good" lunch, I went off on my own to run some errands in town. First was the Olympic Airlines office to collect the refund on the unused portion of my ticket. Because of devaluation, I made money on the deal! The refund went on the American Express credit card. Then I went looking for Ferdie at the Intertours office. I learned that he had been in Tucson from September 5-12 for a big See America tour operators' convention. He had asked Shakir for Mom and Dad's address and phone number, but Shakir never gave it to him. Thinking that Mom and Dad were still living in San Francisco, he never thought to look in the Tucson phonebook. Darn! Mom and Dad would have so enjoyed seeing him and he them. Ferdie was leaving for a weekend to Dar es Salaam and Mafia Island and invited me to go along. He kept insisting, even though I said that I couldn't. He's having lunch with his good friend Felix Pinto the following Wednesday who will be able to take care of my student charter ticket that I cancelled a few months ago. So convenient having these friends in the tour business. Lastly, he said that Shakir was coming to Nairobi tomorrow, on his way to the States for a business trip.

I stopped in at the Music Corner to buy some records to be taped for Skip and ran into Steve, a tour leader from Club Tours. After that, I went to Woolworth's to do some shopping and ran into Ferdie. In those days, Nairobi really was a small town.

I met back up with Ruthie, Eddie and Freddie at the Thorn Tree restaurant in the New Stanley Hotel at 5:30. Leonard arrived a little later. We had dinner in the coffee shop and then went to Sno Cream for soft ice cream cones. So yummy and delicious. Such a treat given that there is never any ice cream at Fort Ikoma.

We arrived at the Seventh Day Adventist complex at 7:15. It's across from the Starlight Club. I was able to stay in one of the four guest flats. Larry's girlfriend, Cindy, was there. All of us were standing out in the parking lot chatting when an old chap from Room #1 came out to ask if there was a Vicki present, if so there was a call for her. Was I surprised! Who would know where I was? It was a Finn. In my note I only mentioned the Robinsons by name and that they were from Busegwe. He had traced me through a friend connected with the private plane area of the airport who had given him the name of Dr. Mac with the Seventh Day Adventist church. Finn called him, but he wasn't home so he talked to the houseboy who was a ding-a-ling. Finn said that he talked very slowly and had some prize statements: "Well, if Mr. Robinson is in town, then I guess I would know and I don't know." And to Finn's question if there were some guest flats, then could you please go check. His priceless answer, "I can't, I'm locked in." With that, Finn said he slammed down the phone and looked up the guest flats number in the phonebook. What a resourceful guy. Finn invited me out and to wear something pretty; he would be by at 9:30. *Shida kubwa* (big trouble). I didn't bring anything fancy, not even a *kanzu*. All I had to wear were the blue corduroy bell bottoms and a jersey top. We went to the Grill Room at the New Stanley Hotel. They let me in without any problem, but apparently they can be very sticky about dress codes. The cover charge was 30 shillings per person and I in my jeans. There was a floor show with an English comedian who was quite entertaining, and a four-piece band and dancing. Finn had the next day off and wanted the night to last forever, but I had to get back to my guest flat at the SDA complex. It was a lovely evening and the first "date" I have had in a long time. As we parted, Finn had a brilliant idea that if we get five of us to rent a plane, with him as the pilot, of course, we can fly to Lake Rudolf, spend 2½ days and return to Nairobi, for 50 shillings each. That would be fun.

We woke up to a cold and sprinkling morning on October 19th, Freddie's 8th birthday. And yesterday was beautiful. Ruth and Leonard went to the American Consulate to see if there was any news about Larry. There was none. I went to Immigration and got a multiple entry Kenyan visa for 22/50 shillings; now I'm set.

A young man from San Francisco by the name of Steve joined us for the flight to Kilimanjaro. He is the newly hired pilot for the recently purchased Cessna 182 that the church has bought. He will fly for Dr. and Mrs. Thomas who are in Kigombe, Rwanda. We departed from Wilson Airport at 1:05. Leonard says that Wilson is the busiest airport in East Africa. I believe it after having to wait for three planes to land before we could take off. We were headed for the least busy airport in East Africa, Kilimanjaro, landing there at 2:20. It has such a long runway that we could easily do four touch and goes in the small aircraft. The airport was built to handle the jumbo jets bringing tourists from all over the world. One major problem, though. There were not enough hotel rooms to accommodate the passengers upon landing and there was a scarcity of cement so building more hotels was not an option at present. Therefore, it handled only one or two flights a day. We went through Immigration here. The airport is very lovely and modern, kept spotless, but empty. No one hassled me about the Levi's that I was wearing. Steve told me that he had read in the paper that the dress code had been dropped. Apparently, it had been enforced while President Nyerere was out of the country and when he returned, he found out that the young socialists were policing the dress code and then pocketing the fines. Ha ha! That's how socialism works, folks.

After getting stamped back into the country, we departed for Makanya, a 38-minute flight south. We flew over the largest sugar plantation in Tanzania and the man-made lake that supplies Arusha and Moshi with electricity. We landed at an old and seldom used airstrip at an old sisal plantation. It was a very short airstrip and with our heavy load, we used every available inch. We were met by a Land Rover and driver to take us to Suji which is way up in the Pare mountains. Long ago, the Maasai drove the Wapare up and into the mountains. We drove from 3000 to 7000 feet elevation along a handmade twisting road. It took us about 1½ hours. The Suji community is very pretty, offering a majestic view of the steep hills and valley below.

We stayed in the guest house which formerly was the home of the last Europeans who lived up here until 1964. The Germans had been the first Europeans to infiltrate this area in 1903. We had dinner with Pastor Ezekiel Semugeshi. I have met him twice before. He and his wife are Watusi from Rwanda. They are of the Nilotic lineage, tall with long, thin noses. We dined with the Pastor on curry and rice, with cakes for dessert and Indian tea. His wife and children ate in another room.

Saturday is the Sabbath for Seventh Day Adventists. Leonard had to go to another village, but we stayed in Suji and attended the 11:00 service in the old German church. There were 30 pews on either side of the center aisle. The men sat on the right using the first 20 pews. The remaining 40 pews were filled with women and children. All the women were dressed in brightly colored dresses with *kitenge* head-wrappings. The service was in Swahili so I didn't follow it, but loved to hear them singing the hymns. Swahili is such a phonetic and lyrical language. I was fascinated by the small children going out and coming back in during the service and mothers carrying out crying babies. After the hour service, Ruthie and I had an interesting discussion about our different interpretations of religion. It was delightful to sit outside in this refreshing climate and enjoy the beautiful view of the valley below with five young woman singing nearby.

I was up by 7:00 on Sunday morning and was able to see the tip of Kilimanjaro 100 miles away. We were off early for a 1½ hour drive through thick jungle forest to reach the other side of the Pare Mountains for an SDA church dedication. Lots of trees, ferns and wild banana trees. We parked at a Catholic mission and had to hike to the church which was "just over there on the next ridge, about half a mile and a half-hour walk." It turned out to be a 2-mile hike down a ravine and up the other side which took us 45 minutes. We had no water and there was no water at our

309

destination, but we were given fresh sugar cane which hit the spot.

This dedication was a great moment for the people because it had taken forever to build the church. We were honored guests and so we were seated with the other dignitaries in the first pew. The church was filled to overflowing. Children sat on the floor between us and the altar. As more crammed in, there left barely any room for our feet. Pastors Robinson, Semugeshi and Godsan led the service. Then an old codger, about 80 and wearing black framed round glasses, got up to say a few words. He had started the building of the church under the Germans! We were fortunate to have a six-piece band sitting in the pew right behind us. They played every hymn. They didn't sound too bad and had fairly new instruments, except for one coronet which was battered, had rags tied around it to hold it together and no buttons, just the hollow tabs to punch. The funniest moment for me was at the conclusion of the service when everyone was standing for the last prayer. The pastors were behind the altar facing the congregation. Behind them was a big window with no glass. Outside, looking in, was a mother nursing her baby. A mother nursing a baby in public is not an unusual activity to see here in Africa. It was her innocent curiosity, framed by the window, totally oblivious to over 100 pairs of eyes looking her way that I found amusing, and endearing.

The church potluck afterwards was Africa-style. Lots of women were cooking *chakula* (food) in big black kettles on open fires. They were preparing the Wapare dietary staple called Pure (not to be confused with the illegal hooch) which consists of a mixture of overcooked hominy and brown beans, all starch and very bland in taste. Instant heartburn. The other offering was *nyama na ndisi*, the boiled meat and vegetable stew. It had been cooked so much that the ingredients had lost their shape. There were fresh slices of tomato that Leonard warned us were most assuredly instant dysentery. Dessert was bread dough balls deep-fried. Like a large donut hole, but not nearly as good. Needless to say, I didn't eat much. We preferred the sugar cane that Leonard would peel and cut off chunks for us. I drank the hot boiled water and avoided the watery milk *chai* drink with Ovaltine and Indian spices, especially cardamom. In Swahili, cardamom is *iliki* and the plant grows around here. We passed some as we hiked to this village. The plants have green leaves, about 3 feet long. The seed grows in pods at the base of the plant.

At 3:00 we started our long hike back to the Land Rover for the drive back to Suji, arriving at 6:00. Pastor Dave DuBias had arrived from Morogoro with two student missionaries, John Bowman and Jim Lester, from the States. Jim told me that his grandmother Bella was a Vance from Indiana. We could be distantly related! We had been invited up to the Semugeshis for dinner which included meat, lentils, rice, macaroni, cabbage, and gravy with a curry flavor. A simple vanilla cake was for dessert, baked in a square pan and no frosting. Mrs. Semugeshi had baked four loaves of bread for us. Both she and her husband are sweet and thoughtful people, a joy to be around.

The next morning, Mr. Robinson and some others were driving to the other side of the mountain for a graduation ceremony of an agricultural program. Ruth, Eddie and Freddie stayed in Suji. I drove with Dave, Jim and John to Moshi. We got to Makanya just as the Nairobi to Dar es Salaam bus offloaded two missionaries who they knew and were headed to Suji. The drive from Makanya to Moshi is 1½ hours and all tarmac. We drove to the home of Dr. Dick Hart, a Seventh Day Adventist medical doctor at KCMC (Kilimanjaro Christian Medical Center) in charge of public health. He will be giving Jim and John a crash course in public health. Both young men are from the state of Washington and elected to take a year off to be student missionaries before their senior year in college. Jim got married five weeks before coming over here. They will be assisting with the Maasai in the Makanya area who recently have been converted to Christianity. We had lunch with Dr. Hart and his wife Judy in their home – chapatis and beans, and sticky pudding for dessert with real whipped cream! Dr. Hart has climbed Kibo before and a group of SDAs are planning a climb in December. Hmmm? Maybe I could join the group??? We returned to Makanya at 5:00 for the 5:30 rendezvous with Leonard and others, but they didn't get there until 8:00. This is the way things go in Africa. A lot of sitting around and waiting and no way to get word to someone about delays. We finally reached Suji at 9:00 and were obligated to eat dinner at the Semugeshis, as unhungry and tired as we were, and the same fare as last night.

I joined the men for another trip to Makanya and then to the Maasai *boma* of Chief Sikau who converted to Christianity. He gave up all jewelry, his second wife, and supposedly all rituals that would conflict with SDA teachings. His wife and mother are also Christian, but not his father, the old chief. Sikau apparently is very progressive and receptive to new ideas. Leonard would like to see him move his people to a permanent *boma* which would be situated near a hill and bend in the Pangani River. Once here, the plan would be that they would learn health habits such as clean drinking water, latrines and cleanliness, and to start some form of agriculture. Maasai look down upon toilers of the soil, but Sikau is favorable towards the idea. His Christianity has not affected his status as chief either, which was a major concern of Leonard's before he baptized him. Since Jim and John will be working with these people, Leonard wanted to give them an aerial view of the layout. I flew with them and got to sit up front for the very first time. The rest of the men drove.

We flew over Sikau's *boma* where he has lived for three years and saw no one. We landed at the flat airstrip. The land is very flat because it is part of the Maasai Steppes. The Land Rover had just arrived and also Sikau, his wife and about 10 young girls who had come on foot. After we landed, the women immediately sat down under the shade of the airplane wing. The dispenser, Giliad, stayed with the plane and to give the women medical attention. The Maasai suffer from eye disease transmitted by the small flies always flying around their eyes. The women shave their heads or do cornrow braids so that they can easily pick out lice. They will groom each other in the same way the gorillas and chimpanzees do.

I joined the men and Chief Sikau in the Land Rover and we went to check out possible *boma* sites. When we got back to the airstrip area, we met Sikau's mother who had come. She admired my copper bracelet, as did many of the girls, so I gave it to her. Sikau was wearing the watch that a friend of Leonard's had given him previously. An *Mpare* (member of the Pare tribe) who lived close by, insisted on giving us some of his sugar cane so we all trooped down to his plot by the river. He cut a stalk, lopped off the top about two feet long and stuck the top in the ground. That's how you replant sugar cane. We all stood in his field and ate sugar cane. Then we went back to a spot on the river and lunched on boiled corn and the cookie brittle with Nestle's chocolate chips that Dave's wife had made. Yummy!

We went back to the plane and Leonard entertained the women by playing his dental bridge with his tongue. They squealed in alarm at him. I kept my hair in a topknot under my hat. The women were very curious about my hair and so I took off my hat and let down my hair that went past my shoulders. They touched it and shrieked in horror. They had never felt anything like it, so unlike theirs. Actually, they thought it was quite icky. I laughed and then we all laughed. I later learned that for some of the girls, I was the very first white woman they had ever seen. All of them were very friendly and generally fascinated. They didn't mind a camera either and so I was able to get some photos.

We took off about 3:00 and flew back to Makanya. Dave, Jim and John left for Morogoro, a 5-hour drive. We drove back uphill to Suji and supped on soup and sandwiches. George and Roger, the missionaries who we had seen getting off the bus the other day, had returned at 8:00. They had spent the entire day walking to Chome, which is a four-hour walk each way, to visit friends for an hour or two. The walk was uphill and down dale over these mountains! I took a bath in rusty red water. The bathwater is boiled in these big rusty tanks, so rusty water flows through the faucets.

On the 24th of October we departed Suji at 9:00 for Makanya and took off at 10:30 for Arusha. Flying above the clouds afforded us a superb view of Kilimanjaro's snowcapped peak, Kibo. We refueled in Arusha. I saw Tumaini Mcharo's SRI plane so I left him a note. We departed Arusha at 11:30 and flew to Ikoma by way of *Ol Doinyo Lengai* which in Maasai means "home of God" and is the single still active volcano in Tanzania. The wings of the Cessna 206 are above the windows so I was able to get some good photos of both Kibo and Ol Doinyo. Flying over the Serengeti, the plains looked dead and dry. We buzzed Fort Ikoma, landed on the airstrip at 12:45 and were met by one of the staff in a Land Rover.

Valerie was on the terrace with Inez. She's British and Skip's "significant other." I had heard about her and was meeting her for the first time. Skip had gone to be with

Putney over her midterm break. Lisa was out by the pool. She looks so much bigger and her cheetah markings are becoming more distinct. She recognized me immediately, came running over and jumped up into my arms, kissing, nibbling and hugging me. Oh how we have missed each other! We spent the afternoon out by the pool and watched Eddie and Freddie swim. I took a quick shower before departing with the Robinsons at 5:30. Ruthie has asked me to spend a few more days with them.

It's a 25-minute flight to Busegwe and we landed at 6:00 on the airstrip across the road from their house where there is also a hangar for the plane. The Martinsens had us over for dinner with delicious whole wheat rolls. Two telegrams had arrived for Leonard and Ruth. One was from Larry dated October 16. It read, "Complications, detained, alive. Lovlar" The other telegram was from the American Consulate in Dar dated October 20 and was more explicit, saying that Larry had been detained in Asmara by Ethiopian officials and was awaiting word from family as to his plans.

After breakfast the next morning, Leonard and Ruth went to Joseph Nyerere's house to phone the American Consulate in Dar es Salaam that, hopefully, would be able to get in touch with Larry through the American Consulate in Ethiopia. Apparently, and fortunately, he never got as far as Syria, but why was he detained in Ethiopia? They were back at 1:00 after having no luck in getting through. After lunch Leonard flew to Mwanza to call from there.

I walked over and visited the Martinsens in the afternoon. Martha is making placemats for me. She sews and paints on fabric. She gave me a cute baby dress pattern that I cut out and also cut out a dress that I am making for myself out of one of the "keyhole" patterned *kitenges*. I played with the cute little runt of a kitten that they had gotten that day and named Cleo. They invited me to stay for dinner and served waffles with an egg and a cheesy white sauce on top. Yummy!

The next morning Ruth had to go to Musoma and wanted to take the boys with her to keep them out of trouble. Freddie pleaded with her to let them stay with me, saying, "I'll be good. You can even take my slingshot with you." It didn't work, she took them with her. I stayed home and attempted to sew my dress on Ruthie's treadle sewing machine. It was difficult, but I finally started to get the rhythm of rocking the foot peddle and guiding the fabric under the needle. It was actually quite fun and when I finished the dress, I felt very satisfied with my accomplishment.

Leonard returned at noon. he had been able to get through to the American Consulate in Dar, but they didn't know if Larry was still in Asmara and suggested that Leonard contact the SDA mission there and have them advance money to Larry since the American Consulate cannot. Leonard and Ruth decided to have Larry return to Busegwe since he would be more than a month behind in school.

I had made an apple pie for lunch. Leonard does not like spice. After eating a slice, I asked him how it was. His answer, "It was very good except for ¼ teaspoon too much cinnamon." That's exactly how much I had put in the whole pie!

Leonard told us about his trip to Mwanza. When he left the airport at 11:00, the drums were beating and dancers dressed in leopard skins were awaiting President Nyerere's arrival. A big summit meeting was scheduled with the big chiefs from Tanzania, Zambia and Zaire about their poor oppressed brothers in Mozambique and South Africa. All three hotels in Mwanza had been closed to all but presidential parties with the guarantee that "even if rooms go empty, the hotels will be paid for them by the government." Even the Swiss manager at the New Mwanza Hotel had been moved out of his quarters three days before. Leonard was not able to get a room until 7:30 last evening at the Lake Hotel when the manager called the regional commissioner to get special permission since no presidential staff had arrived yet. The conditions were that Leonard had to be out of the room by 8:00 a.m. the next morning. He walked by the New Mwanza Hotel last evening at 7:30 and it was completely dark except for two lights on an upper floor. His departure today was half an hour before the president's scheduled arrival.

Saturday was the Sabbath. While the Robinsons went to church I stayed home and copied recipes. I had been doing some of the cooking while Ruthie homeschooled the boys. Having majored in Consumer Services in Foods at the

UA, I found their vegetarian diet most interesting. A popular source for a meat substitute was gluten. This was made from wheat flour. The flour was dumped into a big bowl. Water was added to make a stiff dough and then left to rest for about an hour for the gluten strands to develop. The dough was then placed into a large bowl of water and the starch was washed away by kneading, stretching and squeezing the dough, leaving just the protein, or the gluten. Gluten is what gives bread the wall structure to trap the air and make it light. Working with the gluten was like working with silly putty. It was actually quite fun. The gluten is then seasoned and formed into patties to make veggie burgers. There were other ways of using the gluten, but since I didn't plan on ever making it once I returned to the States, I simply enjoyed perusing the recipes. [As I write this memoir 50 years later, I am amused by the emphasis on gluten-free diets nowadays. Wasn't aware of anyone back then having dietary problems with gluten.]

After church we walked over to the Martinsens for a potluck. They had some American friends who worked for United Airlines visiting from San Francisco. The Saltzmans were also there. I had come to know the other SDA missionaries who lived within the compound and found them all very charming and welcoming. We had gluten steaks with tomato sauce as our main course which was quite tasty. I had taken over dessert which was the Coconut Steam pudding that I had made the day before. In the evening I played carpet ball with Leonard, Eddie and Freddie. Since the Sabbath is meant to be a day of rest, the food is typically prepared the day before so one isn't in the kitchen doing a lot of preparation. The usual Sabbath dinner for the Robinsons is banana milkshakes and popcorn. Tonight we had homemade ice cream, made yesterday, and served with hot fudge sauce. What a treat!

As if I haven't had enough sweets, I made German pancakes for breakfast. Then I made two cakes for Ruthie to take to an adult supper tonight, to welcome a new pastor to this area. I worked on my dress in the afternoon. Helen and Val Martinsen came over for dinner which was corn bread that all of them ate with milk poured over it and golden syrup or brown sugar to sweeten. Martha Martinsen and Ruth came back from the supper, stuffed. An *mbuzi* (goat) had been roasted. Leonard returned a little later and entertained us with two Super 8 home movies. One was of the Maasai and Chief Sikau's *boma*. Another was of animals in the Serengeti, Ngorongoro and Lake Manyara. We finished off Sunday evening with ice cream floats, just as the lights went out at 10:00. The Robinsons run their generator from 6:30 to 10:00 at night, except for certain days when it is on during the day for cleaning. The refrigerator and stove run on butane gas which is supplied in a tank attached to the appliance. Every so often they have to go into town to exchange an empty tank for a full one.

The next few days I busied myself working on my dress which required some hand stitching, baking desserts, and watching Martha paint characters on the muslin placemats she is making for me. She uses fabric paint and

320

on each of the 12 placemats will be an African animal or bird painted in the lower right corner. One will be a cheetah, of course. The runner will showcase the entrance to Fort Ikoma. It will be a very special souvenir for me and her artwork is very good. Eddie and Freddie got ratted on by the neighbor for aiming at birds with their slingshots. The African kids told them that if they kill a bird and rub blood on the slingshot, it will improve their aim. Mom wasn't too mad, I'm sure she's been through this before with her older sons Ron and Larry. In fact, she's baking the family favorite cake for Freddie because he never got one on the 19th when we were in Nairobi. Raja came by in the afternoon with a note from Valerie. Sending notes with drivers is the way that we communicated. No need for me to hurry back she says, and Ruthie wants me to stay because Leonard is leaving tomorrow on an extended trip.

I prepared lunch while Ruth helped Leonard get ready for his trip. He left after lunch for Nairobi where he will park his plane at Wilson Airport and then fly commercially to Addis Ababa and Beirut. He hopes to see Larry in Addis before continuing on to his SDA summit conference in Beirut. Raja stopped by on his way to FIL and I sent a message to Valerie about what was going on and sent contact lens solution with him. It's Halloween and we have been invited to go over to the Saltzmans for dinner and play games. Eddie, Freddie and I went, but Ruth stayed home. Her friend Santaben was coming over and they were going to cook some hot and spicy Indian food. Ruth only gets to do this when Leonard is away. Mrs. Saltzman made her specialty. I have no recollection of it, good or bad, but this is how it is written in my journal, "fried threaded batter variety with pieces of cheese, soybeans and carrots in a seasoned broth." Am thinking it must be the meat substitute, gluten, which can be prepared in a variety of ways. She also served a cucumber salad and for dessert, the small bananas dipped in coconut with golden syrup drizzled over and cashews and raisins sprinkled around the edge. We played games afterwards: relays; moving mung beans from one dish to another by suctioning through a straw; dropping eucalyptus seed cases into cans; memory (2 minutes to view 15 different objects on table and then see how many you can remember after they are covered up); and a fun game with everyone sitting around the table and blowing a cotton puff to keep it from being blown off their side of the table which counts as a point against. It was a most enjoyable evening.

Ruthie and I have worked out a deal. I'll cook and she can teach the boys. I made three loaves of whole wheat bread, Ideal milk ice cream (Ideal is a brand name for evaporated milk in a can), granola, and mixed fruit milkshakes in the morning. Raja stopped by before lunch and Dolores Nyerere (Joseph's wife) and her older son Milton stopped by after lunch. Santaben came for dinner bringing chapatis, rice flavored with whole cloves and cardamom seeds, and mung bean *daal*. She then cooked up a dish of shredded cabbage and chopped potato to go with the chapatis for the first course. The rice is the second course and the *daal* goes with either or both. The food is served on large round stainless steel trays about 14 inches in diameter with a lip about 1 inch high. The *daal* is served in a small bowl as a side dish. *Daal* is a thick stew most often made from lentils or legumes and is a mainstay of Indian cooking. Indian food is eaten with the right hand only and try to keep the palm clean. We had coffee ice cream for dessert, so refreshing after the delicious, but hot and spicy dinner.

The next day we went into Musoma. I saw a few of the staff from Fort Ikoma and then ran into Mushi who has been in town for a week on business. Dionisia and Judy are with him. They plan to drive back to the Fort today and will stop by the Robinsons in case Valerie has radioed that I should come back soon. We went to Joseph Nyerere's house to buy some eggs. He wasn't there, he would be returning from Kampala, Uganda the next day. They have quite a nice house in Butiama. Back to the Robinsons where I made some more Ideal milk ice cream. Mushi had not come by and it was 6:00 by now. It was starting to rain and Santaben arrived with rolled up elephant ears for dinner. The plant has large leaves that look like elephant ears, thus the name, and clearly edible. A paste is made from garbanzo bean flour (gram flour) and is spread over the leaves, then rolled up and cooked with other seasonings.

On Saturday the Martinsens came over for Sabbath lunch. It started to pour at 12:30, just after they arrived. It rained so hard that we had to forget using the 2-way radio to call Valerie. And since Mushi never arrived yesterday, maybe they were delayed. I made a cheese soufflé for the main course. The Martinsens brought banana bread and brownies for dessert that we served with the ice cream. It rained so hard that we had to use candles for lunch! My soufflé turned out very nice, if I say so myself, considering it was my first attempt and Freddie did slam the oven door after he peeked inside the oven to see what I was making. It was a long, leisurely day. After the Martinsens left, I read. We made banana milkshakes for dinner. Mushi never came by, he must have misunderstood about stopping by before heading back to Fort Ikoma.

Sundays are also days for not doing much. I made up a batch of ginger cookies, Freddie's favorite. The Saltzmans and Martinsens came over for prayer reading week.

On Monday we went into town in the morning. No kerosene and no gas cylinders. The gas cylinders are essential for supplying power to the refrigerator and the stove. We got back in time to get on the radio, but no call from Valerie. I made a pizza for dinner and the Martinsens came over to share it with us. The Saltzmans then joined us for prayer reading week. Meanwhile, Eddie and Freddie kept jumping out of bed in their futile attempts to bother me. Valerie never called.

I made another pizza for lunch on Tuesday. Major had to be tied up all day because an African woman complained that he had chased three of her goats on Saturday and if she couldn't find them, Ruth would have to pay for them. I made ice cream in the afternoon while it rained. Santaben brought over an eggplant dish for dinner. Ruth is in heaven having Indian food every night. Terry and

Veronica Joshua had returned from a month safari. They came over for reading week and I joined the group this evening.

On Wednesday I baked a cake and made some more granola in the morning. Santaben brought over a spinach dish and another dish to eat with the chapatis. The rice dish was called *kichree* and made with split peas and spices.

The next day Ruth took the boys into town. I was invited to the Joshuas for lunch. Veronica is Swedish and Terry has English citizenship, but may be of Indian descent. Veronica prepared a veggie patty with rice, kale and vegetarian cereal. She served them with a white sauce into which hard-boiled eggs had been mixed. I spent the afternoon talking with Veronica. She told me about the railroad that the Chinese were building across the country. The tracks are six inches narrower than the standard European tracks. The train cars will have to come from China. Later in the afternoon, I went over to the Martinsens to supervise a test that Helen needed to take for her homeschooled course. Mrs. Martinsen showed me the placemats she has finished. The birds are very lifelike and the animals all have a whimsical cartoonish style. They have a piano and I practiced some of the pieces I remember from my 3rd grade lessons. Santaben brought dinner again. This time she prepared the kale that the Joshuas had brought back from Nairobi and given to Ruth. She prepared it the same way she made the spinach dish. It is so much fun to watch her cook. I especially love how they season with the spices, choosing which ones to use from a tin with compartments of each one. A pinch of this, a pinch or two of that. Such delicious results. She also made *roti*, a flat bread made from either rice flour or *besan* (garbanzo bean) that has sesame and mustard seeds sprinkled on top, and *siro*, a semolina pudding.

On Friday at 1:00 I talked to Valerie on the radio. This was my first time to speak over the two-way radio; I just have to remember to say "over." She's been planning the safari that she and I are going to take to Kenya. The good news is that we have a Land Rover at our disposal, but we need a driver. Also, we have an invitation to visit George Adamson's camp. Super! I will need to get back to Fort Ikoma soon. I made cheese tostadas out of the leftover chapatis for lunch. Then I made a package angel food cake for tomorrow's Sabbath meal. I had to beat and beat and beat the egg white mix with a rotary beater. Whew! I also made ice cream. It started to rain about 3:00 and continued to rain off and on until midnight.

I went to church with Eddie and Freddie because Uncle Terry was preaching. Ruth is having a bout of malaria so she stayed home. Terry's sermon was translated into Swahili by the African pastor as he went along. He told the story about a dying king who wants to leave his kingdom to the wisest of his three sons. He gives them each 100 shillings and tells them to go out and bring something back that will fill the throne room. The first son brings back sand which fills half the room. The second son brings back grass which fills half the room. The third son has no wagons following him. He marches into the throne room and requests that the doors and windows be closed. He reaches into his vest pocket and brings out a candle, lights it, and announces, "Father, if I am to be the ruler of my people, then let my kingdom be filled with light."

There was a potluck after church. The boys climbed up into the treehouse when we were all ready and wouldn't come down so we started without them. When I went to check on them, I found them in the kitchen making peanut butter and banana sandwiches. Then the rain came. I visited the Martinsens in the afternoon. Mrs. Martinsen had finished my placemats. Six cartoon animals: hippo, elephant, rhino, warthog, giraffe, cheetah. Six birds: crested crane, flamingo, turaco, lilac-breasted roller, sunbird, secretary bird. She is charging me TSh 60/= for the 12 placemats and TSh 10/= for the runner. What a wonderful souvenir. I played Password in the evening with Mrs. Martinsen, Helen and Terry. Planning to leave tomorrow.

On Sunday the 11th we were off to the Fort by 8:55. The Range Rover is far more comfortable over these roads, but we took the Land Rover in case of terrible rains and black cotton mud along the way. Seven of us climbed in: Ruth, Eddie, Freddie, Terry, Veronica, Valerie Martinsen and me. It was a two hour and 15 minute drive to the Fort, and a good road all the way.

Back at the Fort

Lisa has new digs! I was shown to the new run built into the ruins of the 1st officers' quarters on the north side of the courtyard. The wire fencing has thin slats of wood woven through it to provide privacy. She has gotten so big and is much more muscular. And her face is looking more squarish. Oh, how much she has changed in the month that I have been gone! She recognized me right off and was so happy to see me!!! When I picked her up – she's getting so heavy! – she kept kissing me and nibbling on my ear with one paw over my eye!

Lisa needed to be sequestered because Prime Minister Rashidi Kawawa and his entourage were coming for lunch. I never did see the Prime Minister, but did see his car as he was leaving.

The Robinsons and others left after lunch to beat the rains which threatened, but it only sprinkled. Valerie, Skip and I drove down to look at the *shamba* (garden) and ARC 793, the *gari* from Ngorongoro Crater Lodge that we are able to use for our Kenya safari. We won't have a driver; it will be just the two of us. I couldn't sleep that night, kept thinking about our safari.

I made two loaves of bread and rolls, but they were a disappointment compared to the loaves I made at the Robinsons. Not sure why. I also made Ideal milk ice cream and chocolate sauce which we had for dessert after a lunch of moussaka, salad and rolls. That evening we had fried rabbit for dinner. Inez did not come up and so Skip threw his Camus on us.

On the 12th Meshek, Michael, Abasai, and Saulo had to go to court in Seronera because of the 13,000 shillings that have been fiddled from the bar. The next day Cephas was given the sack and Meshek was drunk in the bar, definitely some staff problems.

Meanwhile, I busied myself those two days packing for our safari. I located Putney's tent and the poles that we will use, but could not find the pegs. I dug up the *huevos* (eggs in Spanish). [Have no idea what this refers to 50 years later. I would sometimes use Spanish in my journal. Maybe it was our money buried somewhere for safe keeping?] We are all set for tomorrow. Since there were no *wageni,* we had dinner by candlelight, mashed potatoes with spaghetti sauce and fried onions. Sounds disgusting. Maybe that's why we ate by candlelight?

Kenya Safari

Since it was the slow season, Valerie and I were going to take off on a safari of our own. The staff thought we were crazy, two females going off alone in a Land Rover, especially with no air pump! We had use of a well-used Land Rover, ARC793 from Ngorongoro Crater Lodge, and named her Esmerelda. She showed 9413 on the odometer; obviously, the odometer had been turned over at least once. She was a beaut, a *safi sana gari* (such a neat vehicle)! Well, the hatches leak when it rains, a padiddle (one headlight not working), the gauges don't work and the hand brake is questionable, but she's ours for safari! Minor details! Not issues for a Land Rover that just goes down into Ngorongoro Crater and back up every day.

On November 14th, a Wednesday, we packed up Putney's pup tent, minus the pegs which we couldn't find, some camping supplies, and departed Fort Ikoma at 10:00 a.m. A few minutes later, we met two people on the road who we learned had camped out on the lawn of the Mcharos in Seronera the night before and were passing along their salaams to us. We had to detour around black cotton and, lo and behold, met up with Thomas Joseph who had been the driver for Mom, Dad and me from Nairobi to Seronera. It took us about 40 minutes to reach Ikoma Gate where we picked up a letter to exit at Klein's Gate. It's important to have all the proper documentation when traveling between the two countries. At Banagi I started to drive. We saw topi, *kongoni*, gazelles and giraffe as we made our way to the Lobo turn-off, reaching Klein's Gate at 12:45, a distance of 70 kilometers (or in the popular vernacular, klicks). It was about 17 more klicks to Sand River Gate in Kenya. These are the two northern border gates that made it possible for tour groups to travel a circuit from Nairobi, through Tanzania, and back to Nairobi. (A few years later these gates would be closed due to a squabble between the two countries and it ultimately led to the closure of Fort Ikoma as a game lodge.) We paid our 20 bob fee in Kenya shillings to enter Masai Mara National Reserve and drove a few klicks more to Keekorok Lodge where we saw Jonas, the assistant manager. He gave us a tour of the lodge which is considered the best on the circuit. We fueled up here and discovered that the gas tank cap was missing, so we had to stuff a piece of an old rubber inner tube into the opening. We continued on to Mara Serena and stopped for tea. We really liked the interesting lighting effects with pots hanging from the ceiling to diffuse the light. The workers were very pleasant and welcoming.

About 5:00 we exited through the eastern gate of Maasai Mara and soon pulled into Block 61B, which was near a research center, where we paid KSh 20/= for camping privileges. In one hour we pitched Putney's little pup tent (*piga hema*), made a fire, and dined on toasted peanut butter and jelly sandwiches and canned Bully Beef. Delicious! It was a cozy campsite with no one around, though we could see headlights on cars traveling to the

Research Institute. It was dark by 7:00. We turned in early and were lulled to a peaceful sleep with lions roaring in the distance.

The next morning we awoke a little before 7:00, just after sunrise. Soon, four Maasai wandered into the camp and watched us as we ate our granola for breakfast. We were their morning entertainment.

The night before we had noticed that one front tire was a little low due to a slow leak. Fortunately, it was no lower in the morning. However, we did discover that the gear shift had been spiderwebbed to the dashboard. We broke camp, packed up the tent, made sure that the fire was out and departed at 10:25. In five minutes we were at the gate and reported to the cute attendant that all was well, but that we had a low tire. He directed us to the Maasai Mara Wildlife Research Station to pump up the tire. There we met one of the scientists who told us that it was a new station with three scientists now.

It was sprinkling in Narok when we arrived at 12:50, a distance of about 230 klicks from Fort Ikoma. All of our driving thus far has been on dirt roads and so the average speed is about 50 kph. We filled up the tank and bought samosas and cokes for lunch. Met Bashir, a chap who knows Gideon and said that he was at the Plums Hotel in Nairobi. Bashir also clued us in that Gideon could be reached through Silas at the Game Department. Good information.

Valerie and I took turns driving. We left Narok at 1:35 and it was my turn to drive. The road was terrible, very bumpy and slow driving for 30 km. Had to use 4-WD Hi at times. Finally reached the tarmac an hour and a half later. Valerie's turn to drive. We reached Naivasha at 4:20 and first went to the post office to get Ann Morson's phone number. Discovered that she was in Mombasa so went to the Naivasha Hotel to see about possible camping sites. It was a KSh 12/50 fee at the Marina Club campsite. Lots of monkeys around and litter everywhere. We were the only campers and the monkeys made so much squawking noise as they jumped from tree to tree that we decided to sleep in the car. It was not a restful night. The next morning we bought petrol at the Marina Club jetty which required me to back up a narrow strip of land built up to the tank. Yow! Quite a few boats were docked and the most memorable was named *Sailbad the Sinner*.

Off to Nairobi! Driving up the escarpment was not bad, but city driving is another story. It was my first time to be navigating through a lot of traffic, going clockwise around the 3-lane roundabouts, and finding my way in an unfamiliar metropolis. And mind you, this is with the steering wheel on the right, using the clutch, controlling the stick shift with left hand, and driving in the left lane. The rule of the road is, if your brakes don't work your horn better, and if your horn doesn't work, your brakes better. The other rule of the road is to watch out for the larger vehicles. We had to give the right-of-way to the lorries and the buses. The smaller cars had to watch out for us. Actually, it was quite fun. Our motto was "think left!"

We had lots of people to see and first stopped at the Pan Afric Hotel to look for Shakir who had not arrived yet for the Roundtable convention he was to attend. Ran into quite a few chaps who we knew, including Nick Speath. Working in the travel business, one meets many people. We called Jens Schroeter who had invited us to stay with him and his wife Birke and their 7-year-old daughter Heidi. Jens is the Agfa dealer in Nairobi and they are here from Germany. He met us in the Thorn Tree restaurant at the New Stanley Hotel, took us back to Pan Afric Hotel to pick up Esmerelda and we followed him home. Birke made steak tartare and German potato salad for dinner. It was delicious. That evening we played around with the camera stops and took some really artsy photos. Jens brought us up to date on Coen who had made it to Cape Town, but traveled through Rhodesia instead of the Kalahari Desert. Valerie and I slept in Jens' kombi.

The next day Valerie went to the Lindblad office to see Tony Irwin. Tony was the one who partnered with Lindblad to bring tour groups to East Africa when tourism was in its infancy. He shared the news that the day before seven guests were poisoned by mushrooms and were flown to Nairobi. Not sure where the guests had been staying, but definitely not one of our lodges! We were to meet Bryan Payne (manager of Seronera Wildlife Lodge) and his girlfriend Monica at the Thorn Tree for lunch, but they did not show up. The Thorn Tree is the meeting spot in Nairobi. It is centrally located and when sitting at one of the tables along the sidewalk, one will invariably see almost anyone you know who is in town. [Nairobi's population was around 600,000 in 1973. As I write this 50 years later, the population is now over 5 million.] Valerie thought she caught a glimpse of Ron Johnson. He was the fellow who hired her as the Food and Beverage manager at Fort Ikoma.

After lunch we ran into Bryan and Monica and made plans to meet at the Thorn Tree at 5:00. We also ran into tour guide Patrice DuFar who confirmed that Ron Johnson, indeed, was in town. When we arrived at the Thorn Tree at 5:00, we ran into Ron. I finally met the Ron Johnson who I had heard so much about. After a drink in the bar with Ron, Bryan and Monica, Ron let Valerie drive his lovely Mercedes 200 back to Jens' and I followed in the Land Rover. We made plans to meet Ron at the New Stanley Hotel at 8:00. Valerie and I washed up and dressed for the evening. We discovered that our shoe bag had been stolen from the Land Rover. While we could lock the doors of the Land Rover, we were unable to close all the windows. I had noticed that the mattress and plastic had been tampered with when I got in the *gari* to drive to the house.

Ron caught us up with news about his life in the States now that he and Vikki are married. (Vikki is the Southern Comfort heiress.) He is now in the animal cargo transport business and was in town to fly 48 wild animals to New York for Don Hunt on Monday. He had to leave to pick up a USDA official at the airport so we made plans to meet at the Hilton Hotel at 9:30. We waited around for a while and were greatly amused watching people in the lobby. One very irritated traveler was a hoot. Ron didn't show up so we walked down to the Pan Afric Hotel to wait for him there. He soon showed up and we had a good dinner there. Afterwards, we went to the Starlight for a couple of drinks. What a place! All the call girls!

The next day we headed back to the Pan Afric Hotel to see if Shakir had arrived. He hadn't, so we spent time with Ron, then drove over to visit Jerry Rilling at the Ainsworth Hotel where he lives the week to 10 days a month that he is not leading a safari. That evening we met up with Jens and Birke at the cinema to see *The Day of the Jackal*.

On Monday we went into town to get stamped in by Immigration at the Jogoo House, a government office. We didn't get there on Friday and the office is closed on the weekend. Then off to the Thorn Tree to meet Nick, when who should come in but Jurgen and Gideon. I had an appointment at a travel agency to collect my refund for a departure flight that I had cancelled. I received only 50% of the cost. Had I cancelled 24 hours earlier, I would have received 75%. Bummer! I went back to the Thorn Tree where I met up with Valerie, Nick, Jerry, Jurgen and Gideon for lunch.

After lunch Valerie and I went shopping in the African *duka* section along River Road. We had to buy shoes because we had only those that we were wearing at the time our shoe bag was stolen. We bought Bata "boonie" boots for KSh 33/=, the soft suede laced shoe. The shoe top is high enough to fit under the pant leg hem and is great for walking in vegetated areas where stickers cling to socks.

We then headed to Sanyo to pick up Valerie's cassette player that Skip had dropped off for repair. When Skip took it in for repair, they couldn't quite believe his tale about a cheetah piddling on it so written on the work order was "some urine poured into the machine." They were able to clean it and it was good as new, but written on the receipt was, "Removed urine. Cleaned the whole machine. Please take care next time! If this ever happens again, don't bring it to us!" All the fellows working there had cute senses of humor, but kept stressing, "Don't let it happen again!" When the Asian chap told us we owed KSh 85/=, Valerie and I looked at each other with incredulous expressions. He immediately exclaimed, "Well, it was a lot of work!" We immediately nodded in agreement and had to stifle our laughter because we thought it would have been much more. In American dollars, the repair cost less than $12.

Valerie had to fly to Seronera on Tuesday for a trial about the theft incident at Fort Ikoma. Upon our arrival in Nairobi, one of the people we had met up with was Billy Musset, the pilot who would fly her there and back. I drove her to Wilson Airport that serves small aircraft to meet Bill at 6:45 a.m. It had rained lightly the night before so there was fog cover in the early morning. They waited for the Immigration chap to stamp them out, but when he hadn't arrived, they taxied off at 7:25. I got caught in rush hour traffic on the way back into town. First stop was the Seventh Day Adventist school where I was to meet Mrs. Pottle and pick up two *Missionary Manna* cookbooks. I then met Gideon at the Starlight parking lot and he drove us in the Land Rover to his office, Holiday Hunting & Fishing, Ltd., where he had to meet with Jurgen, Caroline and Daniel. We took Daniel to Zimmerman Taxidermy and then Gideon dropped me off at the Thorn Tree where I was to meet up with Nick and wait while Gideon went to the Game Department. When he returned, we drove the Land Rover to IGS Automobile Engineers run by Gurbax aka "Gearbox" Singh to have work done. It would be ready the next afternoon. I don't recall how we got from IGS to the Junkyard where Gideon had to check something and then to the Hilton Hotel where he took me to lunch at the private Professional Hunters Club.

Afterwards, we went over to his friend Silas' apartment to pick up ARE582, Gideon's Toyota Land Cruiser. We drove out to Wilson at 5:30 to see if Valerie and Bill had returned. The plane was in, but Immigration said they had returned at 3:45. We checked the Aero Club, but they weren't there. Gideon wanted to stop at Dam Busters for a drink, but I nixed the idea because now it was after 6:00 and we were to meet Nick at 7:00. Gideon took me back to the Schroeters. Their German Shepherd, Scout, never barked at Gideon, the first African he had never barked at. Valerie came rolling in about 7:00. Turns out they had returned at 4:45 and were at Dam Busters when we pulled into the parking lot! Valerie described her day to me. She arrived in Seronera at 9:00. Skip got there at 10:00. The three on trial, Meishek, Michael and Abasai, did not get there until 12:30. Court did not convene until 1:30!

Valerie was the first to testify and was on the stand for one hour and 45 minutes. Then she and Bill took off at 4:00.

Valerie, Gideon and I met Nick at 8:00 at the Pan Afric Hotel. We had a few drinks and then drove Nick out to the Nairobi International airport. It was packed! Gideon said that he had not seen it this busy since all the Asians fled Uganda when Idi Amin came into power. Gideon took us back to Schroeters. Exhausting day. Nice to hit the hay in the Schroeters' camper.

Wednesday morning, Gideon picked us up and took us into town. I had to mail a package home filled with mementos from my stay. It would take 3 months by surface mail at a cost of KSh 33/=, less than $5. We picked up gas cylinders for cooking and lanterns. Each gas cylinder lasts 4 hours for cooking and 14 hours for lantern light. Then, off to Shiburam's to pick up the vests we had made for us. It was safer and easier to keep valuables on the body since we never carried a purse. Valerie's was brown and mine was navy blue. They sported four buttoned pockets with flaps, one breast pocket was for the passport and the other for money. A comb and chapstick went into one hip pocket, as well as some folded up toilet paper, just in case. We did not wear makeup and usually wore our hair pulled back into a pony tail or in a topknot so not much was needed. I also bought a Fort Ikoma badge. Gideon had left at 4:30 to drive to Nanyuki so Valerie and I took a taxi out to IGS to pick up Esmerelda. The repair bill came to KSh 150/= and covered one new headlamp, rear lamp (or what we would call a bulb), horn, clutch adjustment and brake adjustment. We should be good to go on our safari. And somewhere along the line, we must have gotten another gas cap.

Thursday was another day of running errands, plans to meet up with people who never show, and bumping into people we know. [Writing this 50 years later, it is important to explain to a younger generation that these were the days before mobile phones, email and the internet.] Delays happen and one has no way to contact the other person who is also out and about. In fact, one of the rules of the bush is that you don't worry about someone's delayed arrival until they are two days late. What's amazing is how "small town" Nairobi was for us and all the people who we did connect with and make plans to do things with, merely by seeing them at the Thorn Tree (the designated meeting spot for ex-pats), the Pan Afric Hotel, the Hilton, or stopping by their office. It was difficult to reach someone by phone, and if plans to meet didn't happen, there would be a very good reason why the other person couldn't make it even though you may never learn why.

I was starting to get a sore throat and went into Dr. Sud's office where for 20 bob he checked my throat and glands and gave me medicine called "The Mixture" and some throat lozenges. "The Mixture" looked like orange Kool-Aid, to be taken four times a day. Maybe it was Kool-Aid, but I did start to feel better after taking it. I still have the corked bottle with its hand-written label.

We've been here a week and still more to do before we depart tomorrow. Went shopping for gifts for Jens, Birke and Heidi. They have been so very hospitable to us. We visited Jens in his office to see the negatives from the photos we had been taking. It was convenient to choose from the contact sheet what photos we wanted printed because it is expensive. After lunch we met up with Gideon and his friend Silas at the Professional Hunters Club. Silas is in the poaching investigation department. Another friend, Keller, is in charge of anti-poaching in Isiolo. Gideon is going to accompany us so we made plans for tomorrow's departure, destination, Marsabit.

More errands to run which included buying extras for the *gari*: 750-16 tire tube, brake fluid, fuses, tire valves, cold patches and glue. We picked up our vests that needed some alteration and our laundry. Back to the Schroeters for dinner and the opportunity to give them the gifts in appreciation for their kind and generous hospitality. Then Jens gave us a tutorial on how to take photos at night without a flash, using the time exposure.

It took us half the morning to get ready and pack up. Plus, I had broken Birke's coffee pot that morning and ran out to buy her another one. I loved how she kept the coffee hot by setting it on an antique iron. She would open the lid and place a votive candle inside the cavity where the hot coal would normally go. I was clumsy when putting the glass coffee carafe back on the iron. Oops!

Heading up to Meru

We picked up Gideon and left Nairobi about 1:00, with Gideon driving. We were headed for Meru, Gideon's home town. At 4:00 we crossed the equator in the town of Nanyuki. Of course, we had to stop and get some photos at the sign. It's fun to have one foot in the northern hemisphere and one in the southern hemisphere. Mt. Kenya looms within view; its snow-covered peaks at the equator. The famous Mt. Kenya Safari Club, founded by American actor William Holden and two others when they bought the existing Mawingo Hotel, is situated at the base of the mountain and is a haven for the rich and famous. It has private membership and a strict dress code is enforced. Men must wear coat and tie for dinner, an unusual requirement in this part of the world.

Two hours later we arrived in Meru and looked for Gideon's friend Silas who wasn't home so went to the Pig & Whistle Hotel. He wasn't there either so we carried on to the Meru Co-op Safari Hotel which is where we would be staying. It's run by Gideon's cousin so we were getting an excellent rate for a double room with private bath. I wasn't feeling well so I crashed. Valerie and Gideon went back to the Pig & Whistle and met Silas and Keller there.

The next morning I woke up with a stye in my right eye. Ugh! All I could do was put a hot compress on it. We left Meru mid-morning and drove to Keller's house which is this side of Isiolo. Best way to find it was to look for the Game Department Anti-Poaching sign. We found the house, only to find out that Keller and Silas were in Isiolo, but were instructed to wait for them. Soon they arrived and we had lunch there. This house has a rich history. It was built for George Adamson when he was the Game Warden in the area. Elsa, the lioness of Born Free fame grew up in this house.

After a nice visit, we left to continue on toward Isiolo. I spotted my first reticulated giraffe. Their markings are very distinct, as if someone used white paint to draw connecting lines to create polygon shapes on a brown canvas. We stopped in Isiolo to buy petrol. There were lots of hawkers and camels near the station. I bought an ostrich eggshell necklace for KSh 6/=, having bargained down from KSh 15/=. The shell had been cut into round disks, like a small washer, and strung on sisal twine. I had never seen a necklace quite like this, found it to be quite unique. A few months later I returned to the States during the height of the heishi shell necklace craze. My necklace didn't look so unique anymore. What a disappointment. But at least I got mine for less than a dollar!

At the Buffalo Springs Gate Post I spotted my first gerenuk. They are also called giraffe gazelle due to their long necks. This was a female, because no horns, and she was standing on her hind legs to reach higher leaves on the tree. The reticulated giraffe, gerenuk and Grevy zebra are indigenous to the Norther Frontier District part of Kenya and only found here.

We wanted to see Samburu Game Lodge, but along the way checked out some self-service *bandas* (huts) as a possible place to stay. At the entrance to Samburu Game Lodge was a family of baboons and a mother with a newborn. The baby was so tiny that it could not yet cling on to its mother so the mother had to carry it in one hand. Another baboon was sitting on a sign post, *karibu*! We met David, a young English chap who is the manager. He used to be at Keekorok. The lodge is situated on the Ewaso Ngiro River which is full of crocodiles. Two were lying on the riverbank just on the other side of a low terrace wall. A sign sits on the wall. On the side facing us it says: "Danger Crocodiles." On the other side it says: "Danger People." Three American women were enjoying cocktails on the patio and we chatted with them for a bit.

We returned to the self-service *bandas* as they were much more affordable. The cost was KSh 30/= per person plus KSh 2/50 for the use of gas, which came to less than $4.00 a person. They were cute *rondavels* with a multi-purpose room with a completely stocked kitchen to one side and a bedroom and indoor plumbing with tub, sink and flush choo. A Tanganyika boiler supplied hot water for bathing. Only drawback, the bugs were horrendous! There was no way to keep the bugs from flying in through the 1-inch wire mesh screen on the windows. We had to sleep under mosquito netting.

Woke up at 6:30, before sunrise, to the sound of Gideon's radio. Found him outside changing the front right tire – puncture! The horribly bald spare tire is what he put on. It wasn't until 9:30 that we left. Next stop, Marsabit to visit Gideon's brother Joe. Four hours later, at the Marsabit Reserve Border, we had another flat tire. This time it was the left rear and the rubber had worn all the way through. That tire had been giving us problems since Nairobi with a slow leak. And now, the starter is kaput! Had to use the crank to manually start the engine. We finally arrived in the town of Marsabit at 2:30 and started looking for Joe. Finally found him at the Lake Paradise Bar.

After a few beers we headed over to Joe's house and unloaded the *gari*. We walked in to a total mess. As Joe described it, "It was a house, but now it is condemned." The place looked like it hadn't been lived in for years! While the men went out to do some grocery shopping, Valerie and I did our best to clean up the place. First, we swept out the living room and arranged our belongings. Then we tackled the kitchen which was a nightmare! There was an old wood-burning stove which hadn't been used for some time. Fortunately, Joe had a gas cooker. The wood stove would have been fun to use, but it would have been a chore to clean before it could be used. What the men brought back for Valerie and me to cook for dinner was, gasp, tongue! Only it wasn't just tongue, it was the whole mouth of the steer, including upper and lower jaws and cartilage. We chunked up the meat as best we could and made a stew.

Joe was a very handsome, friendly fellow who showed us lovely hospitality. He had gone to university at Cal Poly San Luis Obispo and had spent a few years in the United States so he, Valerie and I got along great. He liked Valerie's and my Asahi Pentax cameras and launched into the story of the Honeywell Pentax camera that he had bought in the States and brought back to Kenya. One day he discovered that it was missing. Through interrogation he learned that his houseboy had sold it for the equivalent of $7.00. It was worth far more, of course, but that is all the money that the chap needed. That bugged Joe more than the fact that it had been stolen.

After dinner we went to have a drink at Karatina Tented Camp which used to be owned by professional hunter John Alexander who Gideon knew. I was so tired! But left rear tire completely flat so we had to pump it up before leaving. When we got back to Joe's house we had to park the *gari* on a hill so that we can start it tomorrow by coasting down the hill. Poor Esmerelda, if it's not her shoes (what Valerie calls the tires), it's her starter.

The next morning the ranger of Kenya National Parks who checks on Ahmed every day came by to pick us up so we could go with him on his rounds. Ahmed is an old male elephant with huge tusks. As of 1970 he is protected by Presidential Decree. He's a national treasure. Ahmed is now in the southwest corner of Marsabit National Park and our 20-mile drive took us over barely discernible tracks to a pitched tent belonging to four scouts who continually follow Ahmed. They have three camels which they use to move all their gear when Ahmed's wandering calls for it. From the campsite we walked a couple hundred yards from where Ahmed and one of his escorts were, but we were separated from the elephants by a ravine, approximately 100 yards wide. Ahmed has two younger male elephant escorts, or *askaris,* but one was off by himself. Ahmed is thought to be about 70 and the escorts are about 30 or 40, probably sons or grandsons. Apparently they are quite *kali* (fierce) and will attack if anyone gets too close. However, Ahmed is supposedly very docile and if he is alone, one can get very close. He just seems like an old codger, content with the world, not wanting to hurt anyone. The young ones probably think he is losing his mind at times. It is estimated that his tusks weigh approximately 176 pounds each. They are big, almost touching the ground with his head at the normal level. What a heavy load! I wasn't able to get good pictures because I don't have a telephoto lens, but we did see Ahmed, famous throughout the world. I did get one dark photo which I took through a pair of binoculars that were held up to the camera lens for me. Proof!

The men worked on the car in the afternoon and then brought home liver and some portion of a cow for us to prepare. What a job! Went to the Lake Paradise Bar in the evening. When we came out it was completely dark, no street lights on the main street, the only light coming from gas lamps inside buildings. No moon, just a sky full of stars. It was beautiful!

After last night's clear sky, it was weird to wake up to another cold and foggy morning. We went to the market, not much here though. As a matter of fact, there is not much of anything in this town. We did leave the *gari* at the garage next to Lake Paradise Bar at 11:00 to have the starter fixed. This cranking the car can be lethal! It's a good way to knock out your front teeth or break a jaw. The crank is a steel bar, about 3 feet long, and one end bent with two right angles to form the handle. Should you lose your grip on the handle, it will suddenly spin in reverse. In that case, let go and stand back!

There wasn't anything to do except go into the bar and wait. Boring! Plus, I'm starting to have stomach issues. Must be from all that weird beef we've been eating. The *gari* was ready at 1:30 and we could finally leave. The only other place to go was the Karatina Safari Camp for a few more beers with Gideon. I get so tired just sitting in bars all day long. Neither Valerie nor I are big drinkers, but the men do drink beer! It's like water to them. One good thing came out of it, though. I finally got to hear the song *Malaika* playing on the radio. Miriam Mkeba from South Africa sings it. Gideon wrote down the lyrics for me. *Malaika* means "angel" in Swahili. It is a Tanzanian love song.

We headed back to Joe's at 4:00, rested a little and then went back to Karatina where Valerie and I treated Gideon and Joe to dinner. So glad we didn't have to cook!

I started off the next morning by dropping my trusty Timex watch. It's now kaput! Darn! No rushing this morning, but we did pack up and depart Marsabit by 10:30 after filling up the tank and a 20-liter jerry can at the petrol station. About 30 klicks down the road we almost lost the left rear tire when all but one lug nut came loose. Great way to start this next leg of our trip! We drove very slowly the next 100 klicks to Isiolo, arriving about 3:00. There is a police barrier that we had to drive through, a carryover from *shifta* (highway bandits) days. And, it was time for a beer.

We finally reached Meru at 4:45. Valerie and I stayed at the Pig & Whistle. After we got settled, Gideon met us at the bar where we had a dinner of curry spiced chicken. He saw a few of his friends in the bar so Valerie and I decided to pack it in after making plans to meet Gideon for breakfast the next morning, same place, at 8:00 a.m.

We arrived at 8:00, but no sign of Gideon. We had our breakfast and he finally showed up at 10:00. He and his pals partied until 2:00 a.m. After Gideon had breakfast we took the *gari* to the garage to have the starter repaired, yet again, because it still was giving us trouble. And we had to buy four new lug nuts for the left wheel! Filled the tank and off we went at 1:00, destination Meru National Park about 50 miles away. The drive was very scenic, through agricultural areas similar to the West Kilimanjaro slopes. Coffee and bananas are grown in this region. It started to rain on the red dirt road that wound up and down through the hills. It turned very slippery and dangerous, and our tires are pretty pitiful. *Pole pole!* (Slow)! Meru NP is in the desert valley at the base of the hills. This is where Joy Adamson released the cheetah Pippa to the wild.

Mulika Lodge is 4 miles inside Murera Gate. Gideon got us in as Kenyan residents for KSh 5/= each as opposed to KSh 20/= each for an "overseas" visitor. *Gari* fee was KSh 10/=. We relaxed around Mulika Lodge for an hour or so and Gideon went swimming. Unfortunately, Tony and Phyllis O'Brien, the managers, were on leave. Valerie knew them and had hoped to see them. They used to have a farm in Tanzania, then managed the New Arusha Hotel before moving to Kenya.

Off at 5:30 to look for a campsite at Leopard Rock. The ranger there told us that there was no campsite here, but he needed a ride to Bisanadi Gate and there was a campsite nearby which he could show us, so we drove him the 4 miles. We got to the gate at 6:00. The Gate ranger said the campsite is outside the park and costs KSh 300/=. It is used by big safari companies like Ker, Downey & Selby and Abercrombie & Kent. The public campsite for us was back 11 miles near park headquarters. What a sly ranger. He probably knew this, but wanted the lift. And on top of that, we had a low left rear tire caused by a puncture! Tried to make it the 11 miles on the tire because it was getting late and no driving on roads after 7:00 p.m. This is to protect animals from being poached; animals are mesmerized by headlights. Well, we were in the dark trying to find our campsite. About 4 miles from the campsite we had to stop and pump up the tire. Gideon pumped it up to 40 pounds then we jumped in the *gari* and took off fast as possible to make it to the campsite before it went flat again. Saw a serval cat on the way and some plains game, too. We made it to the campsite just before 7:00. It was dark by this time and there were no lights nor other campers. The tire just about had it, too. With the headlights on, we spotted a water spigot and set up Putney's tent by it. We cooked spaghetti for dinner on the gas cooker because it was too dark to find wood for fire. It took forever for the water to come to a boil on the small flame. After draining the cooked pasta, we threw in tinned tomatoes and dined under a moonless, starry sky. Other than fending off millions of bugs, it was a lovely evening.

About 10:00 the three of us crawled into the tent. We each had a foam mat. Valerie had blankets. I had my trusty sleeping bag from backpacking through Europe and Gideon had a sleeping bag of his own. I heard an animal sound so I asked Gideon, our fearless professional hunter, what it was. He said it was a rhino. I asked if it would be a danger and he answered, "No, that it was probably on the other side of the river." Then the wind kicked up and the tent started to sway. Gideon quipped, "Rhino might charge a moving tent." Thanks Gideon! Just what I need to hear when I'm trying to fall asleep. I tried to settle my nerves as I peered through the pinholes in the roof through which starlight shone.

We were awakened by rain at 11:30. The sky had been full of stars when we crawled into the tent. Where did this rain come from? It turned into a downpour. There was no fly sheet and each of those pinholes became a nuisance with water dripping above each of our heads. A constant drip, drip, drip. It rained with such force that water seeped inside the tent and the foam rubber mattresses soaked up the water like sponges. Everything in the tent was getting wet. Plus, the guy ropes on one side started to give way, causing the tent to partially collapse from the weight of the rain water collecting on the roof. When the rain let up, Gideon went out to redo the ropes and angle the Land Rover so that he could turn the headlights on for us to see what we were doing as we pulled everything out of the tent and squeezed out as much water as we could from the bedding. Valerie and I wrung out the foam pads as best we could, not an easy task. We ended up having to put a sheet of plastic over the mattresses. By this time, Gideon's sleeping bag was completely soaked as well as one of Valerie's blankets. My sleeping bag and the other blankets were only partially damp, fortunately. We reorganized the bedding on top of the plastic and all of us lay down to a reasonably comfortable sleep considering the circumstances. We couldn't move downwards or our feet would end up in a puddle of water at the foot of the mattress. All was well, except for the lion roaring nearby, until we were reawakened about 2:00 by a second rain. This one lasted longer and it was harder than the first, but the guy ropes held and there was already enough water in tent that a little more didn't make much difference. However, the leaks in the roof were most annoying and no way could any of us avoid them. They were right above our heads, too. Try to move and instead of water dripping on the forehead, it would drip in the ear! My sleeping bag became very wet in spots because of the puddles forming on the plastic sheeting underneath my sleeping bag. My entire right shoulder and hair became thoroughly soaked. Gideon was so cute. He would just say, "Now just go to sleep and forget about it." And that I did. I woke up several times hoping it would be morning and eventually woke up to find it was 7:00, daylight. Gideon was the first to exit and I heard him exclaim, "I don't believe it!" I exited next and uttered the same words. Valerie, who can't see far without her glasses, was last to exit, but she could dimly make out what we were exclaiming about. On the other side of our campsite, there stood three unoccupied cabins with porches. We didn't see them when we entered the campsite after dark. We could have had a much drier night had we known about them.

All in all, it must have rained for two hours last night and probably rained a good two inches. In the morning Gideon occupied himself with fixing the puncture, two in fact, the left rear and the spare. At first the car would not start and he thought we might have a dead battery. Finally, through some maneuvering, Gideon got it going. Valerie and I strung twine from three trees forming a triangle and hung everything up to dry. Valerie did a beautiful job cleaning out the tent. Food boxes and such in the *gari* had gotten wet, too, causing the bottoms to fall out and we had to do some reorganizing. In daylight we saw all sorts of goodies that we had not seen the night before, like a pile of firewood, public loos, and the cottages which we could have gone to sleep in after the first rain. We did take advantage of the shower in the ladies' loo. It took us from 7:00 until 2:00 to clean up and let things dry. When we did pull out at 2:00, the mattresses were still rather damp and one blanket was still wet, but we just wanted to get out of there.

Today's destination was to see the white rhinos which were brought up here from South Africa around 1965. Actually, white rhino is a misnomer because they are not white but a grayish black. They differ from black rhino by having a wide lower jaw, or *weit* (wide) in German which gives it the false appellation. The white rhinos are in captivity and only a thin wire fence separated us from them. They were very lethargic.

Then off to look for Pippa's camp which was marked on a map but not on any sign posts. We also visited the site where Kenmare Lodge once stood. Only an empty swimming pool remains. Saw a beautiful red-flowered tree, but cannot remember the name. Did get a photo of it. It was time to head back to Meru. We left Murera Gate at 3:15. The road was not slippery this time and we reached Meru at 5:30. We checked into Gerard's Meru Safari Co-op Hotel and were starving so we just threw our junk into the rooms. At the bar we ordered Cokes and asked Gerard to please make us some sandwiches since we had eaten only a PBJ sandwich at 10:00 in the morning. Then Gideon took us to a 'boomtown" 10 miles down the road. Dimagiri has about two bars and umpteen *dukas* built around an open square of dirt. We had a beer in some joint that had no electricity; the only light was supplied by kerosene lamps. When we left, we had to drive around the square. Although it was well after dark (7:30), all the *dukas* were open and each one had a kerosene lamp sitting on the counter giving a very forlorn effect. We drove back to Meru and went to the Pig & Whistle for drinks and dinner. Back at the Hotel, Gerard tried pouring whiskey down Valerie and me so we toddled off to bed at 10:30.

Both Valerie and I slept until 10:00. That shows how little sleep we had gotten the night before last. Gideon had not awakened either. Later we learned that he and Gerard went to some night club after we went to bed and they

354

didn't get to bed until 5:00 a.m. Valerie and I had a quasi-invite to Harish Wason's at noon. He was someone who Valerie knew. Gideon showed us how to get there and then we dropped him off at the Jubilee bar, though Gideon said he wasn't too keen on beer after last night. We arrived at Harish's only to find out that he had gone to Isiolo. I guess he figured we wouldn't show. We went looking for Gideon at the Jubilee Bar and Highway Bar but he was nowhere to be found. We were hungry so went to the Pig & Whistle for samosas and sandwiches before going back to the hotel. Gideon rolled in right behind us, looking awfully peaked. We all went to our rooms for naps. Fortunately, we could enjoy a lazy Sunday afternoon. We really have been on the move ever since leaving Fort Ikoma almost three weeks ago. We met Gideon in the bar at 7:00. He was starving, and not even drinking, so we went to the Pig & Whistle for dinner. Gideon could barely manage one Dumpy Export before dinner. Got him back to the hotel and to bed before 9:00. Not sure he has ever gone to bed this early.

Nairobi

Monday morning we left Meru at 9:00 for Nairobi. We passed Margot Sheesley driving the opposite way on the road just before we got to a road work area. We honked and stopped but she was too far past. Driving toward Nanyuki we caught a beautiful view of Mt. Kenya. Many times it is shrouded by clouds. I was able to capture a photo of it. We reached Nanyuki at 11:00 and stopped to have tea with John Fairhall. Between Valerie and Gideon, they know plenty of people through the tourist business so it is always fun to stop by and say hi. The hospitality is reciprocated when they stop by Fort Ikoma.

Just outside of Nairobi we heard a funny grating noise coming from the engine and had no idea what it was. Reached Nairobi at 2:30, just as we smelled something burning. Gideon saw smoke coming from engine and said it might be caused by oil spilled on hot metal. Luckily, we made it to Gideon's without blowing up. The burning smell subsided and we had no further problems, for now.

Our first errand was to the market to buy food. We dropped Gideon off in town and spotted Skip's Land Rover at the New Avenue Hotel. He wasn't there so we left him a message. Back to Gideon's where we are staying. Biernard stopped by with loaf of bread tucked under one arm and head of cabbage under the other. He didn't stay long when he saw us. Forty-five minutes later, Michael and some other fellow stopped by with food under their arms. Guess they were planning to use the kitchen here, thinking we might still be gone. How they take advantage of situations! Gideon came back about 7:00 with two friends, Peter and Abraham. We all went over to the Safariland Hotel for a few drinks and met another one of Gideon's friends, Simon.

The next day Valerie and I went shopping in town. We met Skip at the Sunflower Cafeteria for lunch. It's a health food bar. Good food, lots of people. Then the three of us went to visit Tony Irwin who is laid up in bed with flamed-up old knee injuries. Afterwards, we paid a visit to Jens and Birke. They are leaving at the end of the month as Jens' work assignment is up. I called Finn. He is coming over about 9:00. Gideon, Silas and another friend, Henry, returned about 8:00. They had been drinking since 4:00. Valerie made Spaghetti Vongole which was really good, but the men didn't want anything with *wadudu* in it! It's clams, guys, not bugs. Finn arrived about 9:00. Before he even had a chance to sit down Silas and Henry were at him about why no black pilots. Silas' brother is a qualified pilot, trained in U.S. with 2000 hours, blah, blah, blah. Poor Finn. I threw in my two bits about immediately bringing Valerie's and my guest onto the chopping block, yak, yak, yak. Everything became very heated with Silas and Henry. Valerie and I had our senses of humor with us. Gideon just remained quiet the entire time. To break things up, Gideon suggested we all go to Club 1900 for some dancing. So, we did. Things were much better there. Finn left at 1:00 a.m. because he had to fly to Lake Rudolf tomorrow (later today). I pooped out at 2:00 a.m. and Valerie took me back to Gideon's. Then she returned in Gideon's Toyota (ARE185). I crashed. Valerie and Gideon got back about 3:00 a.m. Silas almost got into a fight with some guy at Club 1900 and Gideon said, "It's time to go now." They came in like it was New Year's Eve. Gideon apologized to Valerie about the turn of the conversation at his place. As he said, "Finn is my friend and Silas and Henry are my friends and they're <u>all</u> wrong so what could I do?" He says Silas gets hostile when drinking. I spotted Henry from the get-go as one who likes to antagonize.

Everyone had trouble getting up after a few hours of sleep. Jens and Birke came by to go with Daniel to pick out some skins. Valerie and I had to leave just as Biernard arrived. Valerie and I met Skip at the Thorn Tree at 9:30 and we saw Leonard Robinson. He is here while the 206 has its 100-hour check-up. Also saw Steve Greenfield, Club Tours tour leader. Skip, Valerie and I went shopping for Fort Ikoma. Valerie and I returned to Gideon's at 1:30 to meet Gideon and call Shakir. We waited until 5:30, but Gideon never showed. Skip called at 5:30 and said he would pick us up in 15 minutes for cocktails at Ruth and Bob Ware's home. I know Ruth from the Lindblad tours she brings to Fort Ikoma. Their son David is in the U.S. Army now. We met two other guests who were at the Ware home, Philip Leakey, youngest son of Louis and Mary Leakey, and his girlfriend Valerie. The Wares have two full-grown female cheetahs. Sheba is 9 and completely crippled by rickets. She has to pull herself around by her forelegs and is never able to fully straighten out her back quarters. Also, she is blind. Tanya is 7 years old, sleek and beautiful. They are Somali cheetahs, smaller in size than Lisa will be. Ruth has been very helpful with questions we have had about Lisa. Skip treated Valerie and me to dinner at Bobbe's Bistro. Very good seafood. Skip and Valerie had lobster and I had a seafood Thermidor. Stuffed to the gills! Got back to Gideon's about 11:30 to find Gideon in bed. He said he had been there for a couple of hours. As a matter of fact, we all were beat!

After a good night's sleep, I went with Gideon to check on his car. Then back to the apartment at 1:00 to await Shakir's call. Valerie had called the office earlier that morning and left a message for Shakir to call us at Gideon's. He did and we have plans to meet him at 10:00 tonight. We are eager to hear all about his business trip to the States. Ran some errands in the afternoon. Valerie got her refund from Pan Am and then we went to the 5:15 showing of *Born Free*. Really enjoyed it, especially having just traveled in the area where the Adamsons and lions had lived. Got back by 8:00 to wait for Shakir's call. Gideon got back about 9:00. He and I went out and got some tough roasted chicken to bring back. It's 10:20 and Shakir hasn't called yet. He finally called us at 11:00. He was full of news! He stayed in Los Angeles with our cousin Pamela and had dinner at Lawry's The Prime Rib. Then he was in Tucson for two days and stayed at our house. So glad he got to spend some time with Mom and Dad. He even drove my car! We will meet up tomorrow because the four of us are going to drive to Mombasa.

Mombasa

Valerie ran errands in the morning. Gideon's Saab was not ready and he just discovered that his Toyota had a partially broken mainspring. Tired of all this waiting and indecision. We finally left at 2:00 p.m. for the 309-mile drive to Mombasa in Esmerelda. Encountered some rain on the way and had to pass through two police checks. The second one was after dark and poor Gideon got a KSh 30/= ticket, since he was driving, because we didn't have parking lights in front and were missing one tail light. We reached Mombasa at 9:00 and checked into the Hotel Mermaid on Kilindini. The first thing was to get Gideon a few beers in the bar. Some chick in there was half loco. She would pantomime more than talk. She sat down with us and wove out some tragic story about herself. Such a bore! Valerie's and my hotel room was nice and came with an adjoining bathroom and an electric fan for KSh 45/= + 10% tax. Air conditioning was KSh 10/= extra if we wanted it.

After a good night's sleep, we checked out before 10:00 and wandered down the main drag of Kilindini until we came to the "tusks." These four mammoth aluminum – or as the British say, "aluminium" – tusks arch over Kilindini Road [now called Moi Avenue]. They were constructed in the 1950s to commemorate visits made by the Royal Family and Queen Elizabeth in 1952 when one set arched over the single lane road, and later the present two sets after Kilindini Road was widened to two lanes with a median. The tusks also form the letter "M" to represent the island of Mombasa which has a rich and storied past. The port of Mombasa is very important to the Kenyan economy. We enjoyed ice cream at Wimpey's and wasted time at Mickey's Bar, owned by a friend of Gideon's. We picked up Shakir at the Port Reitz Airport at 2:15. He regaled us with more stories about his trip to the States as we drove to Highways Travel Agency, where he has friends, to arrange accommodations for us. Outside Highways Travel Agency we ran into Ingo Berkenheger of all people! Ingo used to work for Jurgen. He's back and hoping to get a license and will hunt with Franz Lang.

We stayed at the White Sands Hotel on Nyali Beach. It is really nice and we have a view of the ocean and coconut trees from our room. We changed into our suits and went swimming in the Indian Ocean first thing, natch. The water is really warm (80+ degrees Fahrenheit) and although just after high tide, the water is still quite shallow. There are no breakers near the shore, but way off toward the horizon. Great for floating, though. Then we went to the swimming pool and had a dip.

Dinner was at the hotel. Afterwards, we popped into the disco held at the hotel every Saturday night, but it seemed a bummer so we went to Club Florida with live music and shows. There was a fellow doing the limbo. He went under the stick resting on 2 ginger ale bottles. Then there was Mr. Strong Man who carried Gideon around by clenching Gideon's belt with his teeth. Two Zulu dancers were really lively and entertaining. A magician used Shakir as one guinea pig and me as another. With me, he had me hold hands with some fellow. Then he passed water through me and coming out of his "you know where" by the aid of a funnel. The strip tease dancer was cute, but nothing like a Gypsy Rose Lee. We didn't get back to our rooms until 4:00 a.m.

Valerie and I woke up at 11:00 Sunday morning and went to the beach to sunbathe. The men went to the pool. After lunch I stayed in the shade by the pool because I didn't want to get too burned. The sun is more intense this close to the equator. After lunch Gideon said he was going to take a nap. Next thing I hear from Shakir is that Gideon has driven into town. He didn't get back until 8-ish. Before dinner Valerie met Shakir at the bar and I took this opportunity to walk down the beach. A full moon was up and shimmered radiantly on the water. But since there were so many clouds in the sky, the moon was constantly hiding, then reappearing. A beautiful night and a wonderful time for being alone. The sand crabs had invaded the beach and it was so funny to watch them scuttling about and into their holes when I would approach. I was so hot from my sunburn that I went to bed right after dinner, but I was so uncomfortably hot that I slept fitfully.

Everyone took it easy on Monday. We stayed out by the pool and I finished the book I was reading. I had hoped to do something in the evening, but everyone else was lifeless so we called it a day and all turned in early.

Up at 7:00 a.m. and out on the beach before checking out of the hotel at 10:00. I thought it was all arranged that we would stop by Nyali Beach Hotel where Valerie and I could go water skiing since that was all we had wanted to do since we got here. I thought we had passed the entrance so a few miles later I asked Gideon where this Nyali Beach Hotel was. "Oh, we've already passed it." Really!! Change of plans. We will go water skiing in the afternoon after seeing Shakir off at the airport. We went to see Fort Jesus, the 16th century Portuguese fort, and Old Mombasa. Shakir was born here. The architecture reminds me very much of Florence, Italy – yellow buildings with red tile roofs. The streets are very narrow, too narrow for cars so one must walk through the town. It is very charming. We checked into Hotel Mermaid. Shakir and I walked down to Wimpey's for a hamburger. Valerie joined us and Gideon stayed at the bar to drink his beer. He picked us up at 2:00 and we drove out to airport. Big huge squall was brewing, but Shakir's plane was able to take off on schedule.

We made Gideon take us someplace where we could go water skiing, but first stop was the Castle Hotel to see if Ingo wanted to go; he wasn't there. Gideon took us to the Bahari Club and arranged for a boat and driver to rent. Gideon joined Valerie and me in the boat which was a surprise after all his stories about his last terrible boat experience on Lake Victoria. I skied first. I didn't have any trouble getting up but I fell down once because of wide variations of boat speed and a second time because the boatman was going too fast and I couldn't take a hand off the tow rope to motion him to slow down. My frantic yells were of no help. [Note, before skiing we should have reviewed signals. Turns out, whatever I was doing signaled him to go faster instead of slower.] At this point, Valerie got on the skis and I struggled to get in the boat with my terribly cramped hands. Valerie skied to the end of our allotted time. Gideon had gotten us a good rate because he spoke *Kikamba* with the fellow in charge. Instead of KSh 2/50 each for a temporary membership and minimum 30-minute charge for water skiing, he got one membership waived and charged us by the minute for a total of KSh 52/50. And natch, we had to buy a souvenir Bahari Club-Mombasa T-shirt for KSh 15/=. We went back to the hotel. Valerie was not feeling well, a cold, so I went with Gideon to dinner at the Manor Hotel, then to the Oceanic Hotel where we listened to a jazz combo in the bar. We watched fireworks from there at midnight celebrating Kenya's 10 great years of *Uhuru*. I was tired, but Gideon wanted to go to Casablanca so we went. Even a better limbo skit here. The crossbar was on fire at about 15 inches, and then a pole on bottles about 5 feet apart. More entertainment included native dancers from Embu, a gymnast, and a lousy striptease dancer. We left at 2:30, finally!

December 12 – "10 Great Years of Uhuru"

Valerie has a terrible cold. Gideon still in bed at 10:30 when she and I left to walk into town for some food. Everything is closed because of the holiday, even Wimpey's. Mickey's Bar was open, though. We had a really dumb waiter. Valerie ordered a steak hamburger and I ordered fish and chips. Fifteen minutes later he comes back and mumbles something about no meat, no fish, or it's frozen or rotten or something. So we change our order to fried eggs and omelet. Fifteen minutes later he comes back and says no eggs, but omelet already made. Do you want fish or steak burger? Yow! Valerie and I took the *gari* and went to Nyali Beach Hotel looking for "Mr. and Mrs. Franz Lang." We saw Ingo and he directed us to Franz who was without any clothes. His girlfriend had packed everything up and taken all his clothes when he was in the shower and no one has seen her for over half an hour. We went back to the White Sands Hotel and took advantage of their beach. Got back to Hotel Mermaid at 5:30. Gideon had gone somewhere. There was a knock on the door: "Phone call." I zip on down to reception thinking it will be Gideon. "Hello. You don't know me but my name is Dario and I've seen you around. I was wondering if you would like to go out tonight?" "No thanks, we already have plans." Who in the world? How did he get our room number? When Gideon came back, we went out to one of the many little Arab restaurants with a brazier outside on the sidewalk. Yummy.

Nairobi

We drove back to Nairobi on Thursday, leaving at 9:00 and reached Dam Busters at 4:00. Valerie had a cold and went to bed. Gideon and I went looking for an open chemist shop, but everything is closed because of three-day holiday celebrating *Uhuru.*

We were able to run some errands the next day. There may be the chance that I will be able to climb Mount Kilimanjaro with the SDA group so I bought an old wool British army coat at the Kenya Farmers Association for KSh 58/= and with a "spare part" no less! [Don't recall what the "spare part" was, unless it was the part of the coat that had been cut off to make it knee-length.] We picked up Jerry Rilling on our way back to Gideon's where we spent the evening.

We had planned to leave on Saturday, but big doings in Nairobi tonight so will make the trip back to Fort Ikoma in one day instead of two. Valerie and I were charged with the task of buying 50 shower curtains to smuggle back to Fort Ikoma Lodge. This was because no shower curtains were available in Tanzania. Valerie and I stuffed them under the seats of the Land Rover, trying to make them inconspicuous. That evening Gideon took us to Dam Busters for the disco.

We left Nairobi at 10:00 the next morning after being stamped out at Wilson Airport. On the way down the escarpment we stopped to buy some baskets and fresh plums at a roadside stand. Little did we know what lay ahead.

The night I thought we were going to die

Three miles after the turn-off to Narok the generator light came on. We turned around and headed back to the petrol station at the junction. The chaps there weren't much of a help, but they said it was the armature in the generator and that we could make it to Narok. We reached Narok at 2:00. It took three hours for the mechanic and his *mingi* friends to fix it, but they did. We settled on KSh 50/= of which KSh 25/= were for new brushes, and we were finally back on the road at 5:20.

We now are really pressed to make it to the Mara Region Gate by 7:00. Rain clouds are moving in. I'm driving and at 6:45 I say to Valerie, "If Esmerelda and her four shoes can get us to Keekorok tonight, I will love her forever!" No sooner had I said this when, as punctuation to my exclamation, we heard the hissing sound of air escaping from the left rear tire. It is now 7:00 and starting to rain. What choice did we have but to get out and change the tire. While Valerie got the big Tanganyika jack off the back, I undid the lug nuts on the spare tire that was fastened to the hood of the car. We had filled the tire up with air in Narok, but I could see the white webbing through the very thin tread. I lifted the heavy tire and bounced it onto the ground. The spare, too, was flat, but we figured that maybe it had more air than the flat tire so we decided to continue with the plan to change the tire. As we undid the lug nuts, two of the posts broke off the wheel. After a brief assessment, we decided that three lug nuts on posts would have to do. At this point, we are soaked by the rain and so we lowered the vehicle, put the jack away and fastened the flat tire on the hood of the car. The left rear tire is flat and only three lug nuts are holding it on, but we get into the Land Rover and...it will not start. It is raining hard now and we are sopping wet. Lightning is flashing and streaking and the sound of thunder is immediate. It is pitch black except for the lightning directly ahead of us. And, it is marching straight towards us. I thought for sure we would be struck by lightning, it was so close. This was the perfect storm, the tire goes flat just as I made my exclamation, the spare is flat, posts break off the wheel, the car won't start. I was starting to freak out. I told Valerie that I just wanted get out of the car and run away from the lightning. She said, "You can't do that, there are wild animals out there. We have to stay in the car. And don't touch any metal!" She explained that if the *gari* were struck by lightning the rubber tires would ground it and, as long as we weren't touching any metal, we should be safe. She later confessed to me that she was going to have to slap me if I didn't calm down, which I had. She also confessed that if I had been the calm one, she would have been the one freaking out, but she knew that one of us needed to remain calm.

We are in the middle of nowhere. There is no traffic on this road, we are soaking wet, back windows won't slide closed so rain is coming in and getting everything wet. It looks like we are going to have to spend the night in the car, if we don't get fried by lightning first. We figure that we are about 6 miles from the gate, but since no cars are allowed on roads in national parks after 7:00, there will be no traffic going to the park or leaving the park at this time of night. And the lightning keeps marching towards us as if it is on the path to our destruction.

In time, the storm passes us and the rain stops. We have survived the brutal lightning storm but we are shivering in our sopping wet cords, shirts and shoes. I crawl to the back seat to grab a suitcase so that we can at least change our shirts. That feels a little bit better.

Eureka! About 8:30 we see a light on the horizon. We flash our torch. Is it the headlights of a *gari*? Is it a Maasai fire? The light disappears and then it reappears. We pray that it will be a vehicle coming this way. For an hour and a half, we sporadically follow the light. It just seems to oscillate on the horizon. If it's not a *gari* though, it must be a UFO. By 9:45 we definitely hear a lorry. I had imagined an hour ago that I heard the faint sound of a lorry shifting gears. At 10:00 the lorry reaches us. We are parked in the middle of the road so they do have to stop. Three fellows are in the truck, Sgt. Maj. Tombo of the Kenya National Game Reserves, his friend, and the driver. They hear our story of woe and offer to take us to Keekorok Lodge. We decide to leave the *gari* there, take minimum suitcases and go with them. We reach the Lodge at 10:30. Heaven! Fortunately, some people are still up. And, of course, they don't expect guests to arrive after 7:00 so they had to round up someone to get us a room. How glorious it was to see this nice room. We each took a hot shower and then crawled into a warm, dry bed. SO much better than spending the night in the Land Rover. Just as I was nodding off to sleep Valerie said, "We better get back to the car early before the Maasai show up and help themselves to all the stuff in our car." After that, it was a fitful night. I kept getting chills and envisioning the Maasai pulling out the suitcases and tossing out our clothes along the way back to their *boma*. They wouldn't be interested in the contents, just the suitcases, and those were all the clothes we owned between the two of us!

Valerie and I woke up at 6:30 a.m. We checked at the Reception Desk for a Land Rover to take us to our abandoned car and for a spare tire. While waiting for a vehicle, we went into the dining room to have breakfast. We got to chatting with the four men at the table next to us because we could tell that they were American. It was none other than Dizzy Gillespie and the other three musicians in his quartet, Mickey Roker, Earl May and Al Gafa! Dizzy's

Nairobi, Kenya, 1973

*Representing the United States at ceremonies celebrating the tenth anniversary of Kenyan independence, Gillespie composed a song, **Burning Spear**, as a tribute to President Jomo Kenyatta. The musician addressed the audience in Swahili, saying that he considered them his people.*

from Internet

369

quartet had been invited by President Kenyatta to play at the *Uhuru* celebration on December 12th to celebrate the 10th anniversary of Kenya's independence. We had grown up on his music and asked the band members to sign a card for Mom and Dad which they very graciously did.

A UTC lorry driver offered to help us out. As we approached our disabled Land Rover, we saw the first Maasai who were about ten feet away. We literally arrived seconds before them. Whew! Had they arrived before us, they most likely would have helped themselves to anything in the back of the Land Rover because we were unable to lock it. The driver changed the tire for us with the one we had brought and then cranked the car to get it started. We gave the driver a tip, the Mzee Maasai a box of plums, and paid KSh 20/= at the Gate as we wobbled back to the garage at Keekorok with only three lug nuts holding the left rear tire on.

The Mzee mechanic fixed the left rear wheel by welding the posts back on and then was going to work on the starter. In the meantime, we sat out by the pool. David Shores, a pilot for Abercrombie & Kent was in for a day with clients. We also met Mrs. Ringberg, the manager of Keekorok Lodge. The couple who helped us last night, Brian and Deena Vincent, must be some relation to her. We enjoyed a beautiful lunch with David and Pete, a pilot for Bosky who it turns out was one of Skip's flying instructors.

Somehow, I lost 40 bob. Don't know how. I checked everywhere. It must have fallen out of my pocket and maybe a monkey ate it. I checked on the *gari* to see how the repairs were coming along. The rear wheels are fine now, but something is wrong with starter. We will have to start by rolling or will have to crank it.

It was too late in the day to leave so we went back out to pool. Unfortunately, the water was too cold for swimming. I went to the room to get some photos and heard a funny noise. Since no one was around, we had left the top of the double-dutch door open. I turned toward the window and saw a monkey sitting on the dresser and eating our plums. I shouted "Get out, get out, *nenda zako*!" He looked at me as if to say "she means it" and with that he stuffed the plum in his mouth, grabbed three more, jumped down, ran out and leapt up on the low wall outside the door to finish eating the plums he pinched. He sat facing me, but then decided he didn't like me staring at him so he turned sideways and continued eating. Occasionally, though, he looked over his left shoulder to see if I was still staring at him. After closing the door, both top and bottom this time, I headed back to the pool. I turned around once again to see what he was doing. He had gone over to the window, was sitting on the ledge and looking in at the remaining plums. "Paradise lost."

I took a luscious, relaxing bath before dinner. Mrs. Ringberg invited us to eat with her, Bryan and Deena. We had a lovely time.

We left Keekorok at 10:00 the next morning, after having the tube in the spare tire replaced because of a leaky valve. The chaps at the garage pushed us to get us started, but we will have to roll it or crank it if we should stop somewhere. Our only concern would be going through the border gate between Maasai Mara and the Serengeti National Park. I was driving as we approached the gate. Valerie told me to bat my big baby blue eyes in hopes of us not being stopped and searched because we were smuggling in the 50 hidden shower curtains. The obvious question would have been where did we get the Kenyan shillings for them. My answer would have been that I paid for them with American dollars, but that might not have satisfied them. Didn't think it wise to say, "Because no shower curtains are available at the one national supply warehouse in this socialist country and we desperately need them for the game lodge!" Fortunately, we were waved through with no problem, but as luck would have it, the *gari* died just then and I had to crank it right there! I was extremely careful because I didn't want the crank to whip in reverse and knock out my teeth! Success! I got it going and we were on our way.

[Even with all these *gari* problems, to this day, the Land Rover is absolutely my favorite vehicle. However, I don't want to own one in the States. Instead, I want to be driving around in a Defender 110 in Africa. And, having driven in a first-year (1972) Range Rover with the Robinsons, I am delighted that its style hasn't changed much, except now it's a four-door instead of a two-door.]

We drove straight to Fort Ikoma, arriving at 1:00. We lunched with Inez and Putney and got all the news. Skip is still in Dar es Salaam. Dionisia had a baby girl, Frieda, born November 18 at Ngorongoro. She did not make it to Moshi in time. Then the bad news. Someone broke into the Taj, stole the mattresses and jimmied with the locked wardrobe. Whoever the culprit was pried the hasp off and worked the screws out of the wood. Joseph, the night watchman, noticed that the outdoor furniture piled up against the zippered tent opening had been moved. (Since you can't lock a tent, that was our only way of sending the message, "Do not enter.") He investigated and then immediately reported the break-in to Inez and Skip who were at dinner. All of our things were moved into room 29. Fortunately, neither Valerie's camera nor portable record player had been taken. They were the only really valuable things in there. Inez seems to think it was *"shauri ya pombe"* (looking for booze). The only things we noticed missing were two bottles of Scotch, a bottle of brandy and maybe two beers.

President Nyerere with an entourage of 60+ are here for tea this afternoon. Valerie and I had tea with Inez and Putt in room 11. Lisa has grown so big, now five months old. She must be four feet from tip to tip. Her eyes are a beautiful topaz and seem much larger. Her skull is growing and her muscles are really developing.

Not many *wageni*. Before dinner we a had drink with Major Limu, Bwana Shimdolwa and Bwana Adam who are with CID here to investigate bartenders Michael, Meshak and Abasai who are on suspension (do not work but receive half pay). Sherlock has left.

Welcome back!

Christmas at Fort Ikoma

V alerie and I drove into Seronera to get our passports stamped at Immigration. We left Esmerelda at Seronera Wildlife Lodge where she will be picked up by an NCL driver. We will return in a Serengeti National Park Land Rover that the Fort was hiring for Lindblad. While there, we saw Ndosi, Aquila and Bryan. It rained hard while we were at SWL and got back to the Fort at 5:00. I helped Valerie arrange a picnic lunch for Lindblad tomorrow. Bill Hurst is the guide and he has a good group. We went to visit Inez and Putt in room 11, had some wine and chatted. Inez told us that Daudi is very unhappy here. The staff is giving him problems and he is planning to leave when Skip gets back.

The bar cabinet had arrived for the Taj so I spent the majority of the day moving us back in and organizing the Taj. I also figured out that our safari cost 2,980 shillings, or $425.00. I paid for everything as it was my way to thank Valerie for this incredible year. Terrible storm clouds gathered all around us, but it did not rain here, only a light sprinkle. Skip returned from Arusha in the evening. We saw him at dinner and caught him up on our travels since we last saw him in Nairobi.

I spent the next day working on a Christmas present for Inez and Skip. Bill's group has left and Jerry Rilling's group has arrived. He's brought Christmas presents of smoked sailfish, garlic sausage, and maple extract! When they went out for a walking safari they took Lisa along. Ndosi arrived in the taildragger plane that he has been piloting, but I did not see him because he had to check work on the Mugumu Road. In the afternoon I heard a herd of zebra go pounding by the Taj. Daudi came and said they had been frightened away by *simba*. Bill Hurst had seen a pride of eight lion by the Lodge this morning. Lisa has been with me at the Taj all day long, but she didn't sense any danger. She stalked a couple of giraffes that were nearby, but didn't get closer than 100 feet to them. A swift kick from a giraffe would kill her. I measured Lisa. She is 47 inches from tip to tip, her tail constituting 15 inches of that length. Her body length is 32 inches.

Unfortunately, Lisa had to stay in her pen the next day from noon on because of small children and *wageni* around. Skip, Putney, Valerie and I decided to go out and cut down a "spaghetti and meatball" acacia tree to use as a Christmas tree. We drove out past the *taka taka* dump. The marabou stork were having a field day. They remind me of undertakers in poor fitting suits. We found a decent looking small tree and Putney did the honors of sawing the small trunk to cut it down. With all its white needles and brown balls, it was essentially self-decorated. All it needed was some red ribbon for color. We hauled it back to the Fort and carried it into the dining room. As we were hoisting it up, a zillion ants descended from the brown balls. Stomp! Stomp! Stomp! Out it goes until all the ants are gone.

John and June Capon arrived at 6:00 to spend Christmas with us. With them was their 2-year-old daughter, Phillipa, who they affectionately call "Squeak." This cute nickname comes from a favorite English meal "Bubble and Squeak," made with leftovers, potatoes and cabbage. It gets its name from the sounds made when the food is frying in the pan. John is no longer working for TTL (Tanzania Tourist Ltd.) which now is the only concession allowed to take vehicles down into the Crater. He, Skip and Justis are working on buying Ndutu Tented Camp from George Dove. They said they had heard that Gerard got married a week ago to a girl from Iringa (the girl next door). John and June have no earthly idea who she is. It surprised them as much as it did us that he actually got married. Gerard, Terry Irwin and three others are going to start hunting in Ethiopia. Skip was taping Christmas carols in his office. This is the first time it has really struck me that Christmas is almost here. We all had sundowners at the Taj. Jerry joined us – and we all stayed up well past midnight.

It's a gloomy, grumpy day. I brought Lisa out to Taj. She had been in her pen since noon yesterday and she is full of energy today. I finished Valerie's present. Jerry's group left. Azar Chaudry arrived with a family group. Ndosi and Sophia (a girlfriend?) who works in the Parks office in Arusha flew in at lunchtime. I visited with them for a while before Ndosi went to check the Mugumu Road.

John, June and I took Lisa for a walk. By the time we got to the water tower it started to sprinkle so we took refuge in there until it let up. On our way back we were surprised to see about 10 *wageni* sitting outside their tents. Christmas is a very busy tourist season, but we weren't expecting any *wageni* at this time of day. Well, Lisa refused to be obedient from then on out. From 5:00 to 8:00 I tried all sorts of tactics to lure her back to her run, but always at a crucial moment, some *wageni* would appear and Lisa's attention would be diverted. She's too big and too feisty now for me to carry her. I did try, but I only ended up very muddy and dirty. At one point I did get her to the side of the hill facing the water tower. I reprimanded her and she counteracted by hissing and lashing out at me with her paws. I left her alone to cool off, then tried the hide and seek tactic but that failed. Then the three crested cranes, followed by two girlfriends, showed up but even they didn't budge Lisa. She just sat there like Nero looking down into the Colosseum. I decided to get a hunk of meat and entice her into her abode. When I got back from the kitchen, I saw her playing with the *wageni* in tent 48.

The chef had given me a tenderloin. It must have been 12 inches long and about 3 inches in diameter. I stood about 15 feet from Lisa and waved it in front of her. In one leap she was at my feet, grabbing the meat from my hand and gulping it down. She had most of it swallowed when she started to choke. My immediate reaction, without thinking, was to pull it out of her mouth. My concern was, "She's my baby. I'm her mama. I don't want her to choke to death." Well, Lisa was on a different wave length. She didn't want anyone taking food out of her mouth! She chomped down on my fingers with her sharp teeth. Her incisors pierced the pads of two of my fingers to the bone. I let go in a hurry. She proceeded to finish swallowing the log of meat and trotted off. Off I went to Skip's office. The infirmary consisted of hydrogen peroxide and band aids. I poured the hydrogen peroxide over my fingers and bandaged them up. [To this day, I have no sign of a scar on any finger.] Another 1½ hours later, I finally got her into her pen after enlisting the help of Valerie, Skip and finally Inez. Tired, filthy, sore left hand and darn it, another sore throat. My sixth one since September.

We finally got another gas cylinder for the Taj and so I was able to take a hot shower, which I really needed. At dinner, only John, Skip, Valerie and I appeared. Valerie and I admired the Christmas tree that Putney, John and Skip had set up - *safi sana!* A foursome at a nearby table entertained us. The two women must have been drunk. The fat one stood up and started yelling at the other one to drink her drink. "I spent my hard-earned money and now she had better drink her drink. I can't stand her! I have to ride with you in the same minibus for the next nine days." The redhead piped up a couple of times with "OK. I'm going to take the poison." John said they kept it up in the tent the two women were sharing, which was near his, far into the night. Their yelling even kept Valerie awake.

Skip's friend, Chuck, the American Catholic priest missionary has arrived. He's the "queen bee" of the honey production here in Tanzania. I learned that the queen bee is twice the size of the ordinary worker bee and only uses her stinger to sting another queen bee. An ordinary bee dies after stinging because the stinger has a hook on the end which remains in the tissue of what the bee has stung.

Thus, the bee loses his stinger and also part of his tummy when he flies away.

The day before Christmas I went down to see the *dhobi* (Hindi for laundry person) to check on laundry that was sent down the 19th. Hercules hasn't even washed it yet!! All of it was sitting in its original bundle, tucked away somewhere. I'm fed up! Hercules was screaming at me in Swahili. I don't know what he was saying. June thought he was drunk. I am ever mindful that I have to be very careful how I speak to the staff because I am not their boss, but I need these clothes washed. So frustrating! Will have to enlist the help of Skip.

I made a radio call to the Robinsons in Busegwe to confirm the Kibo climb. It is so much fun to use the two-way radio. Mr. Robinson said they are coming tomorrow, Christmas Day, will spend one night, then continue on to Nairobi. It was a rainy afternoon. John, June and Squeak moved into the stone tent, but there is no water hookup yet so we have offered them the shower at the Taj. The stone tent refers to the house being built for Skip and Inez which is situated on the edge of the hill between the front entrance and the tents. It offers a beautiful unobstructed view of the Serengeti plains.

Valerie left at 5:00 to go check on things in the kitchen. By 9:00 she wasn't back so I went up to Lodge. She spent the entire evening in the kitchen helping out. Busy! And who should arrive but Jens and Birke! They had put Heidi on a plane to Germany at 3:00 a.m. this morning and then departed for Ikoma. Heidi will stay with grandparents for the next few weeks while Jens and Birke do some traveling. On their way here they passed Rosie and Claus on the road and discovered that they had turned over in their vehicle the night before while on the way to Molo to spend Christmas with Clarissa and Dennis. Guess all is well that ends well. Life in the bush. Father Chuck was conducting mass at midnight for those interested, but we all turned in before 11:00. Valerie and I brought the Christmas tree back to sit on the table in the Taj. Buckingham Palace (Skip and Inez's residence) had given the Taj Mahal a candle. We arranged all our presents under the tree and lit all the candles that we had. So festive! Jens and Birke parked their kombi beside the Taj and used our bathroom facilities. It's so much fun having them here!

Valerie and I opened our presents upon awakening. Mom and Dad had sent each of us a pretty long dress and lots of little goodies, like brushes, lip gloss, etc. Valerie gave me a safari shirt and 10 candy bars. She bought out the store at Seronera Wildlife Lodge, making Bryan very angry. Ha! I gave Valerie a clay pot filled with Mexican-style paper flowers that I had made using bright colored crepe paper. At breakfast we exchanged presents with everyone else. Skip, Putt and Inez gave me a soapstone bowl made by the people in Kisii, a bar of perfumed soap, talc powder, and a bracelet made from banana fibers with copper ring. Squeak gave us a bottle of wine and from John and June we each got a beaded choker and bracelet. We gave them a *kiko* (pipe) and tobacco. We gave Putt a colorful stool and for Inez and Skip, a big pot with paper flowers. For Jens and

Birke, we gave a bottle of wine in celebration of Christmas and his birthday.

Philip, the FIL scout, had caught a baby mongoose yesterday which was given to Putt. After breakfast we all trotted off to room 11 to meet Riki Tiki Tavi. Tavi for short. He's a cute little thing. Skip and Putt made a cage for it.

The Robinsons arrived in the Range Rover after lunch with news of Larry. Larry and his traveling friend Willy were held up in a port on the Red Sea while waiting for a boat to take them and their *pikipikis* (motorbikes) to Syria. Then war broke out so they had to go back to Asmara. Since they had little money, Larry tried to cash a traveler's check belonging to an Asian friend for an airplane ticket to Beirut and was subsequently arrested. Turns out the traveler's check was counterfeit. Apparently, there is a big ring that Interpol is after and the official thought Larry was connected to it so they took away his passport and detained him for 4 weeks. The counterfeit ring might be operating out of Zambia. Larry got back his passport three hours before Mr. Robinson arrived in Asmara. They flew to Cairo where they had a 24-hour layover and as luck would have it, Cairo was experiencing a partial blackout. They were treated with special courtesy there, however, because of their American passports. In fact, they were given a 24-hour gratis visa for the city. The people there think the world of Henry Kissinger. What a tale to tell!

Jens and Birke collected firewood and made a big fire at Taj fire pit. The Taj is the party place with the Capons and Schroeters using the Taj bathroom. I put on my *maridadi* (pretty) new dress and went up to Lodge. Valerie was supervising in the kitchen until 8:30. I sent her home to put on her *maridadi* new dress. What a group we were – Skip, Inez and Putney; John, June and Squeak; Jens and Birke, Leonard, Ruth, Eddie and Freddie; Father Chuck; Valerie and I – gathered around the large table feasting on a traditional Christmas dinner of turkey with plum pudding and brandied hard sauce for dinner. What a lovely Christmas day with my sister and good friends!

John departed for Nairobi with the Robinsons the next day. Birke and Jens left at 11:30. They leave Kenya the second week of January and will probably head for India. Lisa found a way out of her cage. Valerie spent the day in bed, tired and suffering from a terrible cough and earache. I spent the day getting organized in her office for my big climb up Kilimanjaro. The Joshuas are coming by tomorrow at 10:30 to pick me up. We invited June and Squeak, Skip, Inez and Putney to dinner at the Taj to celebrate the British Boxing Day when, traditionally, staff is given the day off. That doesn't happen at a guest lodge filled with tourists, but any excuse to spend time at the fire pit is good enough for us! I couldn't sleep most of the night because of excitement and nervousness about my upcoming challenge, and also because of a dying warthog's wails.

I was up early and headed for the laundry to stand over the chaps ironing my clothes. They were *pole pole* (slow!) Since there is no electricity, all clothes, bedding, towels, tablecloths and napkins are washed by hand in big tubs and hung on lines to dry. The iron is made from cast metal and hot embers from a tended fire are put into the cavity to heat the iron. As the iron cools, it has to be refilled and so the process is time-consuming. By the time I came back up the hill, Veronica and Terry Joshua and Linden Martinsen had arrived. I was treated to a big farewell at breakfast and Inez gave me a list of helpful hints for the climb as well as a bottle of wine. I decided to leave the wine with Valerie to enjoy upon my return, given that I would be with a group of missionaries who do not imbibe.

At 11:30, the Joshuas, Linden and I departed for Arusha. Just as we reached Banagi in the Serengeti National Park, we suffered a puncture and had to change the left rear tire. We continued on to the SNP garage in Seronera to get a new tube for the tire which is now the spare, and filled up the spare that is now on the left rear wheel. We stopped in at SWL to find Bryan in the midst of a madhouse so we opted for a picnic lunch instead. As we headed for Naabi Hill, the left rear tire blew because of too much air. The tire was cut across completely and the tube was cut in half and landed 20 yards behind the car. Put the spare back on and headed back to SNP garage to buy a new tire. Flat tires are not uncommon given the unpaved roads through lots of brush and I remember one time suffering through about three flats on the way to Arusha. This required jacking up the vehicle, removing the tire, opening the valve to deflate the inner tube, removing the tube, patching it, waiting for the glue to dry, reinserting the tube into the tire, using the pump to refill the tire, replacing the tire on the wheel and securing with the lug nuts, lowering the vehicle, all the while praying that the patch will hold. The whole ordeal would take at least an hour. I always enjoyed seeing some Caterpillar tractor equipment at the SNL garage. Caterpillar's headquarters were in Peoria, Illinois from whence my family came and most likely this equipment was manufactured there.

We finally left at 5:00 and drove straight through to Arusha with no more mishaps. It was beautiful going up the escarpment at dusk, something I had never done before. We saw a rhino, millions of Tommy gazelles, and two lionesses on the rim of Ngorongoro Crater. We also happened to see Jack Manuel as his vehicle passed by ours and he gave a friendly wave. Finally, we reached the New Arusha Hotel at 11:00 p.m. There was a message from Shakir so I called to let him know that I had arrived.

The next morning I went shopping for two photo albums and filled them with pictures from our hunting safari to give to Mario and Costas as Christmas gifts. I had lunch with Shakir at the hotel and then enjoyed a leisurely afternoon. Shakir picked me up at 5:30. With him was John Capon's former boss. We drove out to the Meru Game Sanctuary where there were two baboons, one young male and one old female. Shakir gave her a cigarette to smoke. She spits, too, so watch out! Then she ate what was left of the cigarette, spitting out the filter. Too funny! I am so relieved that Lisa is not here. This could have been her fate had Jurgen had his way. Afterwards, we went to the Tanzanite for a delicious prawn dinner.

After checking out of the hotel the next morning, I loaded up my gear in Shakir's car and he drove me over to see Mario and then out to Tantax to see Costas so that I could give them their photo albums. They both looked really good and were very appreciative of the gifts. Not sure if I will see these men again and am ever so grateful for their friendship and the memorable time we had together on the hunting safari. We drove out to the Seventh Day Adventist Church to confirm plans with the Salzmanns from Busegwe who will give me a lift to Moshi. Shakir took me to Naaz for a delicious curry lunch and then we drove around until 4:00 when it was time for me to rendezvous with the Salzmanns for the drive to Moshi, elevation 3000 feet. It was an easy hour-long drive on tarmac to where my next adventure would begin.

Climbing Mount Kilimanjaro

A desire to climb Mount Kilimanjaro became a reality when the Robinsons arranged for me to join a group of Seventh Day Adventist missionaries who were making the climb over New Year's 1973-74. Fortunately, at a Nairobi surplus store I was able to buy a British army coat for less than $8.00. It had been shortened previously to knee length. Unfortunately, I couldn't find any hiking boots so I borrowed Inez's gardening boots with good tread. As short as Inez was, we had the same size feet. I had packed some clothes for layering in the backpack that I had used throughout Europe and strapped my sleeping bag to the top. Oh yes, I also had the Chianti-shaped plastic bottle with wired cap that I had bought in Italy to use for water. I didn't have a canteen so this would have to suffice.

A group of 40 rendezvoused at the home of a Seventh Day Adventist doctor near the town of Moshi the afternoon of December 29th. I had met Dr. Dick Hart in October while on safari with the Robinsons. From his home we had a beautiful clear view of Kibo Peak. I knew a few of the people, those from Busegwe, and Jim and John, the two college students who were taking a year off to do missionary work. Of the 40, 20 of us were going to attempt the climb. After dinner, Dr. Hart showed us slides from his previous climb and gave us an overview of what to expect. Porters would be carrying our gear. Each porter carries a load of 40 pounds and so we would have to pack together, with at least two people to a porter. Then we all found a spot on the floor, turned out the lights at 11:00, and hoped for a good night's sleep.

We were up at 6:15 and had breakfast. How nice of the Harts to welcome all of us into their home and feed us, too! Our first stop was the Kilimanjaro Guide Association to rent mittens (TSh 7/=) and to buy a walking stick (TSh 10/=). Next stop was the Kibo Hotel at 5000 feet to meet up with the porters and guides. All of our belongings were packed into duffel bags. I combined my stuff with that of Terry Joshua and another couple. I was bringing a sleeping bag, more clothes to layer, army coat, and snacks of a mango and trail mix. Our group needed 12 porters plus two more to carry the porters' supplies. We also had one guide and two assistant guides who would carry light loads, 20 pounds versus 40 pounds. And all this would be carried on their heads! Dr. Hart then shuttled the porters and luggage to a starting point 3 miles in the opposite direction of where we would start. This required multiple trips. The porters had a 20-mile hike to the second hut where we would meet up with them that evening.

Our group was shuttled 5 miles past the Catholic mission at 6000 feet to the park entrance where we would begin the climb. I wore a hat and carried my camera and my one-liter plastic Chianti bottle filled with water. We started up a road which turned out to be the wrong way, so turned around and ate our sack lunches while waiting for the drivers who were parking their cars and then hiking to our location. They hadn't arrived by 1:15 p.m. so we started up the right trail and soon they caught up with us.

Several families were only planning a day hike through the rain forest and then returning to Moshi. Other members of the group would continue the climb. I quickly realized that, essentially, I was on my own. I did not want to intrude because others had their own hiking companions. Everyone hiked at his or her own pace. The children would run ahead, then stop to wait for their mother and father. Jim and John who were closer to my age were fast hikers and I wasn't able to keep up with them.

The first few hours of the climb was through the dense rain forest. The ground was muddy and slick. The plants were so tall that it was impossible to see the sky or feel the sun. It was dark, but not difficult to see the beauty of the foliage that has adapted itself to live in these conditions. Suddenly, the rain forest ended and the high tundra began. We had started climbing at about 6,000 feet elevation and now were at 8,000 feet. Clumped grass replaced the slippery floor of the rain forest and Joshua-like plants dotted the landscape. We continued on for another few hours until we reached Horombo Hut, elevation 12,335 feet, at 7:15, after dark. The last 300 yards to the hut were steep and it was cold. It had taken us six hours. Many hikers start at 3000 feet and overnight at Mandara Hut, elevation 8000 feet. We opted to start higher and bypass the first of three huts along the Marangu Route.

Since I had joined an already scheduled climb, I did not have any idea how arrangements were made. I soon learned that four outfits organize climbs and each outfit books the hut to capacity. Thus, four times as many hikers as beds descend on the hut and it is first come first serve. Our group had reserved 15 beds, but all the beds had been spoken for by the time we arrived. The "beds" are really bunk bed shelves, with no mattresses, along the walls of a rather large hut and sleeps 60 people. Each hiker provides his own sleeping bag. In the center are tables for eating and there is a fireplace in the corner should you want to boil water or cook a hot meal. Some people came well-prepared. No one had told me that I needed to provide my own food on this expedition so, needless to say, I was surprised to not find a hot meal waiting for me. I ate my mango for dinner. At this altitude, though, I didn't have much of an appetite. The porters arrived at 9:00 with our belongings. They had departed from Marangu Hotel, elevation 3000 feet. In 11 hours they had hiked 20 miles and ascended a mile in elevation, all the while carrying 40 pounds on their heads. We were told that these men who do this day in and day out have enlarged hearts which shorten their lifespan. I was able to secure a spot on a shelf with two other people, strangers to be exact. We slept in our own sleeping bags, head to toe. Those not so lucky to find a shelf or floor space had to sleep outside. Some had tents and others simply threw their sleeping bags on the cold ground. A stream ran nearby and icicles formed along the waters' edge during the night. The hut housed an international group of adventurers. Many languages were spoken that evening. Since this hut houses hikers both ascending and descending, we had the chance to hear from those who had already reached the top. The oft repeated comment was, "You need to reach Gilman's Point (at 18,655 feet elevation) in time to see the sunrise and before the clouds roll in."

People started to wake up at 6:00, an hour before it is light, in order to be outside to see the sun rise through the blanket of clouds – a spectacular view. I was able to capture a photo just as the sun peeked through. It's not often that one is standing far above the clouds and ascending sun. I had some tea for breakfast, I am not very hungry at this altitude. We departed at 8:15 and reached the "last watering hole" at 9:30 where everyone replenished their canteens, and I, my Italian Chianti bottle. It would be 24 hours before returning to this site and filling up again. I had a quart of water to last me that long. Now, as we continued our hike, we could see Mawenzi Peak to our right and Kibo Peak to our left. Two peaks, on the tallest free-standing mountain range in the world, as different as night and day. Mawenzi, with its majestic, jagged spires and loose lava rock, is not considered safe to climb. Kibo is the caldera of a dormant volcano that is a steep climb, but no special equipment is required. We reached the saddle between the two peaks at noon. It looks like a moon landscape with no vegetation, just big lava boulders strewn about against a backdrop of blue sky. At sea level, one could run to the boulders and back in about 15 minutes. At this altitude, it would take 45 minutes to reach the boulders. Off in the distance toward Kibo, the metal hut glimmered like a small jewel in the sun. I finally reached it at 4:00 in the afternoon after an agonizingly steep climb the last few hundred yards.

As predicted, Kibo Hut, elevation 15,520 feet, which slept about 30, was already claimed by the first arrivals. The rest of us would have to sleep outside in tents. The Johnson family of four invited me to share their tent, for which I was very grateful. My dinner meal consisted of some trail mix. I really wasn't very hungry. We all went to bed about 5:00. I was in my sleeping bag with a child to one side and about 2 inches of space between me and the tent wall. The wind picked up and blew cold air into the tent. I was freezing and had a difficult time sleeping between the chill and the noise of the wind. I kept thinking, "I can't get air." Not as bad as last night, though, when I woke up thinking someone had stepped on my chest and broken my ribs. This two-day ascent does not allow the body enough time to acclimate to the high altitude.

At midnight we were awakened by the guides and porters banging on the tin hut and yelling "Happy New Year!" The racket continued for about 15 minutes with the Germans and Italians joining in. I may have had no alcohol, but at 15,520 feet above sea level, I was higher than any of my friends on New Year's Eve. Not sure if some climbers started the final trek at midnight, but my journal records that our group didn't head out until 2:15 a.m. We must have fallen back to sleep after ringing in the new year. I crawled out of my sleeping bag and donned the few remaining clothes I had brought. My layering included the following: a nylon jersey, cotton jersey, two pullover sweaters, windbreaker, two pairs of cords, two pairs of socks, Inez's gardening boots, wool army coat, two pairs of mittens, and a crochet cap under the windbreaker hood.

All but two of our group headed out under the starry sky. Rae Lee and Kathy decided to stay at the Hut. Fifty yards out, two more turned back including 12-year-old Waid Johnson, bringing our group down to 16. The glow of flashlights were the only indication that a parade of hikers were on their final ascent. At first I had been walking in front of Tita because she paced me well and she also had a torch (what the Brit's call a flashlight). But when we stopped for some of the group to catch up, her husband Carl wanted to go in front so I moved behind her. Soon, hikers were passing me by. Now Terry Joshua, Chuck and John Stafford, the assistant guide Christopher and I were trailing the rest of our group. Chuck led us and seemed quite fit for the climb. Terry kept wanting to pause and I began to feel that we were holding Chuck back. At this high altitude it's a slow journey and even slower for some of us. Now some of the German and Italian hikers ahead of us had turned back and passed us on their way down. Hard to believe, but none of us had taken any water with us and so we were asking them for water, to no avail. At one point I went over to a small patch of snow next to the trail, broke some off with my hiking stick and sucked on that. About 4:30 a.m., Carl and Dr. Hart passed us on their way down. Carl couldn't make it and Dr. Hart accompanied him rather than let him walk alone. John returned with them.

The trail was getting steeper, about a 45-degree incline, and starting to zigzag, but we have not yet reached the cave or the 20 switchbacks. Scree, the loose stones, was prevalent, too, so it was one foot in front of the other and many times a backward slide. Two steps forward, one slide back, two steps forward, one slide back. On it went. In the starry night I did see three falling stars. I was getting very tired. All I wanted to do was lay down by the side of the trail and sleep. This is a sign of altitude sickness, and if one does this, one may not wake up. The lights of other groups were getting farther and farther ahead. At one point our guide Christopher offered to carry me piggyback. I thanked him, but declined his offer. That was not the way I would reach the top.

I haven't reached Meyers Cave yet and they say it is about halfway distance-wise, and a quarter of the way time-wise. This would mean another five hours at least to reach Gilman's Point, getting there at 10:00. A light was coming down the trail at 5:00 a.m. It was Fritz Martinsen and I decided to turn back with him. After it being stressed by other hikers that the summit should be reached in time to see the sunrise, I didn't see the point of continuing this arduous trek, only to reach the top when it would be enveloped in clouds, obscuring any view. We were at 17,000 feet, eyes even with the top of Mawenzi. I couldn't bear the thought of the steep climb ahead, especially the last 200 yards which is a 55-degree slope of loose scree. And I was dehydrated and thirsty!

Going down was tough. I hadn't realized how steep it was in the dark and that I had climbed as far as I did. They say it is a 7-mile climb to Gilman's Point. I must have climbed 3 miles in three hours. The sun was not up yet, but across the saddle, Mawenzi, silhouetted against the eastern sky with a horizontal orange streak just above the horizon on either side of the peak, was food for the soul. It took less than an hour for Fritz and I to reach Kibo Hut and I crawled back into my sleeping bag and slept until 9:00.

I decided to leave for Horombo Hut with John Stafford. Just before we left at 11:00 a.m., Dave Dobias and Corky Johnson returned. They had made it to Gilman's Point and signed their names in the book. On their way back down, they passed Chuck and Terry who were persevering. John and I took it nice and easy walking back to Horombo and stopping at the "Last Water Hole" to fill up our bottles and quench our thirst. Oh how good the mountain spring water tasted! Dave caught up with us and we reached Horombo Hut at 3:00. A bunch of crazy Italians were there and we also met three Americans who were on their way up. The father-in-law in the group has climbed over 300 mountains. His son-in-law and friend are frogmen in the Navy and based at Coronado Island, California.

Everyone from our group gathered at 6:00 to share stories. We congratulated the four who made it to Uhuru at 19,340 feet elevation, Linden Martinsen, Lyle Johnson, Chuck Jensen and Jim Lester. Those who made it to Gilman's Point at 18,665 feet elevation were Corky, Dave, Tita, Dennis Casper, John Bowman, Chuck Stafford and

Terry Joshua. Nine out of the 20 did not make it to the top. They were Fritz, Dick, Carl, John, Waid, Ruth, Rae Lee, Kathy and I. The group that made it to Uhuru told us about a Japanese ski champion who took his skis with him and skied on the glacier for about 15 minutes. Then four porters had to go get him and carry him down the mountain.

Dinner was some trail mix, as it was all the food I had. Once again the hut was overbooked. This time I slept on a cot under one of the tables. So glad that I didn't have to sleep outside!

I arose at 6:00 the next morning, having slept almost 11 hours. It is still dark outside, but difficult to sleep as the other hikers start to stir. Those heading up the mountain are eager to get going. We were off by 7:45 as we weren't in a rush. My bottom lip was blistered very badly and I had a bad blister on my left foot. Descending the mountain is actually harder on the body. I was sore and took it slow and easy. I walked most of the way with Chuck Jensen, collecting straw flowers along the way. Rae Lee and Jim Lester caught up with us in the rainforest. The nature lovers picked about 17 different kinds of ferns. Mary Sue would have loved seeing all these beautiful rain forest plants. We were the last to reach the waiting car at 2:00, yet the first to leave the hut. We were driven to the Kibo Hotel to collect our gear. Here, porters presented wreathes of everlasting flowers to those who made it to the summit. Those of us who attempted the final ascent, but didn't make it, received small bouquets of everlasting flowers.

We were driven back to the Harts' home where a spaghetti dinner was awaiting us. The men went off to play volleyball at 5:00. I collapsed on the sofa. My turn in the bathroom was at 6:30. The shower felt so good after 4 days in the same clothes. I weighed myself and disappointingly discovered that I had lost only two pounds on this three-day trek with minimal food whereas Jim and John had lost 14-15 pounds each. Such is my sluggish metabolism due to hypothyroidism. My left foot started to really hurt, causing me to limp. I don't recall spraining it. It must be from the constant pounding the feet took hiking down the mountain. By bedtime an isolated spot on the inside arch was causing me agony. No doubt, the borrowed gardening boots contributed to the cause of the pain as well. We all were spread out on the floor throughout the house in our sleeping bags. I woke up in the middle of the night in excruciating pain. I thought my foot might be broken. I had to scoot over to a door jamb and use it to pull myself up to a standing position. I was in so much pain that I limped my way to Dr. and Mrs. Hart's bedroom, knocked on the door and woke him up. I was crying, I was in so much pain. He gave me some aspirin and said he would look at it in the morning.

After Dr. Hart examined it in the morning light, he said that there was a very slim chance that I had broken any bones in the foot, particularly if I couldn't remember ever injuring it and there was no bruise. He wrapped it in an ace bandage and I walked around like Mama Mzee. Good thing I had my trusty walking stick! I left with the Martinsens at

9:00 who were giving me a lift to Fort Ikoma on their way back home to Busegwe. Our first stop was in Arusha to take care of some errands. I happened to see Shakir and Beryl and told them all about my climb. We stopped for lunch at the Lake Manyara Hotel. It was 7:00 by the time we reached Fort Ikoma. I could barely get out of the car, my feet hurt so much. They were very swollen from sitting in a car for the last four hours when, ideally, they should have been elevated. It was as if I were crippled. I should have played volleyball with the guys last night. Maybe that would have loosened up the tight muscles.

It was anything but a hero's welcome when I returned. The Lodge had been overbooked by 19 people and it was a madhouse with everyone running around. Also, I was notified that I had offended Hercules and he refuses to do my laundry. I went to bed tired, achy, miserable in more respects than one. Oh yes, "And don't create waves with Sylvester, the new room steward." Don't understand why the warning, I have always been very courteous to our room stewards. Hercules, on the other hand...

Back at the Fort

I was awakened early in the morning by hyenas and jackals very close to the tent and actually heard a hyena laugh which is a real treat. I spent the entire day at the Taj resting my feet. Both were very swollen, especially the left. Since Hercules has refused to do my laundry, I did my own washing. June came out to see me. I so enjoy chatting with her. She is very good company. Later that evening, June, John and Squeak came out to the Taj and we enjoyed sitting around the fire.

The next day I talked to Skip about Hercules. Skip advised me that I would need to apologize to Hercules about offending him. Hercules was in the courtyard and so I made my apology for being rude, with Saulo as my interpreter. About 20 Africans were witnesses and now everything is okey-dokey between the two of us. It is important to be heard by the witnesses. It is impolite to whisper in front of Africans because they will think you are saying something negative about them. I learned this the hard way when I was reprimanded by Valerie after an incident that had occurred a few months ago when Lyuba and I were sitting in the bar. She leaned over to whisper in my ear that she loved Russia, the land of her forefathers, but she did not like the USSR. Certainly, this was something that she could not announce aloud. The next morning Valerie called me into her office and said that some of the staff wanted me deported. I was incredulous and asked why. She said it was because I was whispering in the bar. I thought back to that incident and relayed it to Valerie, telling her that I had not whispered, only Lyuba had. She was satisfied and said that she would clear it up for me, which she did.

As to this incident with Hercules, I must tread carefully. I am not management and am not related to the manager. I do not recall treating staff in a condescending way and actually got along with most of the staff very well, but there were troublemakers among them. Some had real attitudes. I never felt that I was giving an order, but as I was not their boss, even a request could be interpreted as an order. Also, in this culture men do not like taking orders from a woman. Valerie issued orders as their boss so it was tolerated. Skip was a man and the manager and expected to issue orders. Essentially, I am a guest in this country and must act accordingly. It was never my intention to be rude to any of the staff as I was ever grateful for being here.

Beryl's friend Jock had arrived by lorry the day before. He was on holiday from England and Shakir had arranged a ride for him to Fort Ikoma. Skip, Putt, June, John, Jock, Valerie and I went on a picnic out in the bush. It was delightful! We set up a table and covered it with a beautiful *kitenge*. The kitchen crew had prepared quite a spread for us to enjoy. With this crowd it was hard to get a word in edgewise or be one-upped when you did. We saw lots of game. It was most relaxing and everyone was in good spirits. We got back at 5:00. Poor Lisa had been cooped up in her "apartment" most of the day. I spent time with her and took lots of pictures of her playing with my leather hat. I hate to think of it as a cage, but now there is a lock on it because *wageni* were walking in there by themselves. She is almost six months old now. Mrs. Geichi has arrived from Mwanza with Erika and they joined us for dinner. After dinner Skip, Putt, John, June, and Jock came out to Taj to sit with us around the fire. Jock played his guitar and sang. A lovely way to end the day.

Mrs. Geichi has approached the Capons about managing the Kibo Hotel in Moshi. The next morning John, June and Squeak left for Moshi with Mrs. Geichi and Erika. I let Lisa run around the Taj before lunch. It rained in the early afternoon and we took refuge in the Taj. It cleared up in the later afternoon and I went swimming with Putt on her last day. Mario arrived.

Today marks the one-year anniversary of my arrival in Nairobi. I would never have anticipated then that my stay would extend beyond the six weeks I had initially scheduled. How lucky for me! Jock and I took Lisa out for a long walk toward the airstrip. We encountered a herd of 14 *twiga*, two impala rams having it out, and the ever-present Thomson's gazelle. We also startled a family of warthogs. How funny it is to watch them run off, always with their tails in the air, like flagpoles. After lunch Jock and I spent the afternoon with Inez pouring over her beautiful Ethiopian jewelry. It rained mid-afternoon. After dinner I recorded cassette tapes of records in the office and didn't get to bed until midnight. Soon after, Valerie alerted me to a giraffe not 10 feet away from her side of the tent. Then the big bull giraffe moseyed over to the fireplace, and straddling the hot embers, nonchalantly browsed on our terrace tree. Lions started to roar in the distance, probably near Heliograph Hill, and the *twiga* took off. That enormous male easily stood 18 feet tall. We woke up to find our giraffe friend reclining a few feet from Valerie's side of the tent, what a treat for us.

All the *wageni* left after breakfast so I took Lisa out by the pool. She refuses to let me have more than five minutes peace. I left her playing with all the chaise lounge mattresses piled up under the bar window. A few minutes later she pounced on me, going for a headshot, naturally. I never heard her approach. Undoubtedly, she stalked me all the way, and, man, how quietly she can move! Mrs. Geichi returned before lunch. She's optimistic about John and June being installed at Kibo Hotel. Only problem is, the present manager (German), who allegedly is horrible and has really ruined the hotel in the eight months he has been there, refuses to leave even though he's been given the sack. Jock left with Mrs. Geichi for Mwanza. I spent the afternoon taping. Ndosi dropped by.

Mario gave Valerie a lift to Seronera in Carolina II the next day. Ndosi will fly Valerie to Arusha to get her broken molar fixed. That is from when she broke the cusp off trying to pop the cap off a coke bottle on our hunting safari. I took Lisa out by the Taj where she lolled around like royalty. I enjoyed watching her from my perch in a canvas chair on the terrace. She then jumped into my lap and lay there for 15 minutes, purring in her magnanimous manner. She kept trying to hug me and lick me as if to say, "I love you." Such a sweetie! I took her for a walk to the airstrip and noticed that we have a new windsock, finally. The old one has been in tatters since I got here. I spent the afternoon in the Taj thoroughly absorbed in Herman Wouk's, *The Winds of War*. The hotline was not on so I couldn't tape. Inez and I dined together. Daudi was in a strange mood.

I didn't awaken until 9:15. It's the latest and best sleep I have had in months. I took Lisa out to the Taj. Joseph, the night watchman, brought a couple out to see Lisa. I could have killed him. Word spread and about six others came out, but I told them that Lisa was not on display. They cussed me out in German, but left. I had a hell of a time enticing Lisa back into her apartment. Aquilla, Roni and Kiko Mcharo arrived before lunch and are planning to spend the night here. The Mcharo children's names are Nimiwindie (Roni) 13, Kiwota (Vikki) 10, Vida (Lisa) 7, Lukiko (Kiko) Tumaini 3. Aquilla and I talked all afternoon. I really do dig her. Aquilla loves coming up here whenever possible and being around some other Americans. It's been difficult for her to adjust to raising a family in Tanzania. Aquilla is college educated and Tanzania does not require girls to go to school beyond 6th grade. She is the mother of three daughters. I have found it interesting that any American Blacks coming through the Fort make a beeline for Skip, Valerie and me. They have far more in common with us Americans than they do with their African "brothers." I dined with the Mcharos that evening. Skip had returned and he and Inez enjoyed a dinner for two, sautéed prawns.

I slept in until 10:00. Yow! The Mcharos had already left by the time I got up to the main area, as well as Skip and Inez who had gone to Seronera for the day. Finally, the hotline was turned on during the day. I was all set to tape and what do I find... Skip had taken his cassette player. A whole wonderful day for taping was wasted. The night sky was fairly clear and about 8:00 I was lucky enough to spot the Kohoutek Comet in the western sky with my naked eye!

Valerie returned by car from Seronera on Sunday with the news that Ndosi won't fly anyone unless you sleep with him! She wasn't having any of that. Meshak and Michael stopped by for a visit. We could smell them a mile away. Three *wageni* hitchhikers from Mugumu arrived in the evening. They had met Meshak the day before in Mugumu and told them their plans. He said he would help them get a ride to Ikoma and locked up their backpacks in his room. When a ride had not been found, they had to pitch a tent in the Mugumu Police Compound. They were abruptly awakened in the morning to find that recovered poached cattle had been turned loose in the compound. The cattle knocked down their tent with them still in it. They finally retrieved their luggage after 30 hours and eventually arrived here. There was a heavy rain in the afternoon. I was able to tape. Too cloudy to see the comet.

Lisa is six months old now. She is 32 inches from the tip of her nose to the base of her tail, and 49 inches from the tip of her nose to the end of her tail. Skip and Inez left for Arusha. I taped all afternoon and evening.

It was a year ago today, January 15th, that Mother, Dad and I met up with Valerie at Seronera. Rose Marie's Lindblad group took Lisa out on a morning foot safari. One of her clients is Pat Cunningham of Paradise Valley, Arizona. He has agreed to take an 8 x 10 photo of Lisa to mail to Mom and Dad. It's the photo of Lisa by the Zanzibar chest in Skip's room that Dr. DeBie kindly sent me. I was addressing the envelope on the courtyard tree well when Lisa, back from her morning stroll, took a flying leap and landed on top of my head, getting mud all over me and the envelope. Earlier, as Lisa was jumping up on the tree well, she hit her legs and did a somersault. She does amuse us. Lisa went out again with Philip's walking safari. The group got back at 5:15, but Lisa remained at the cement waterhole past the Taj. I decided to let her be since no guests were in the tents. I got back to the office just as the heavens opened up. Man, did it rain! The office roof is like a sieve. Valerie's office upstairs was completely flooded, with water splashing down from the ceiling and through the floor to Skip's office below. Rainwater leaked right into the safe in Skip's office and soaked all the money. The rain lasted about half an hour. I wonder how Lisa survived her first big rain out in the open? I went looking for her when the rain let up. She jumped on me by tent 37. She was drenched. She followed me up to the parking lot, but would not go any farther so I left her there. Later, Lisa found Valerie at the Taj and followed Valerie back to the courtyard. I picked her up and got her inside her pen, where dinner was awaiting her, with no trouble at all. She was tired, hungry and wet. Valerie and I dined with Adrian Luckhurst and his small group of Americans.

After yesterday's exploits, Lisa had no vim and vigor in the morning. I brushed her coat beautifully, and then she up and rolled herself in the mud! We went out to the Taj. She stayed out there until 3:00 when I went out and bodily carried her all the way back to her pen. Whew! She is big, heavy and feisty. People were booked in the tents and I had no choice but to get her sequestered. A swim felt good after that. It rained at 7:00. Valerie decided to tape and not go to dinner so I dined with Adrian and two of his clients. We got into a giant discussion (argument?) about this generation. I returned to the Taj at 12:30 a.m. Joseph, the night watchman, called me out a few minutes later. Three *simba* were not more than 100 feet from the Taj. One male, two female, six yellow eyes looking at us. I have heard the roar of lions ever since I first came here, yet this is the first time I have ever seen any Ikoma lions!

In the morning I let Lisa play around the Lodge after the *wageni* had departed for the day. I had to carry her back to her pen, though, when a clamor arose that she might pull a tablecloth off one of the tables. I moved the stereo into the Taj. It's a beautiful day and now I have music. Skip and Inez returned. Bill Hurst is here with a Lindblad tour. It is a clear night and we all saw the Kohoutek Comet. Skip and Bill came out to the Taj to sit around the fire and enjoy the wonderful sounds of being in the bush at night. In the wee hours of the morning, hyena chewed on two of the canvas chairs, leaving all sorts of teeth marks.

Mail from the States took a long time to reach us. On the 18th of January I received a letter from Carol that she and Hobey were getting married February 17th and she would like me to be a bridesmaid. Wow! I need to get back to the States for that! I had set up my cousin Hobey Vance with Carol Altorfer when she transferred to the University of Arizona for her junior year. Our fathers were childhood friends, having grown up in Peoria together. It was a perfect match. Hobey had completed his F4 flight school for the Air Force in December and proposed to her after the graduation ceremony. He was to be deployed soon. The wedding was planned without delay so that Carol could go with him to Hahn Air Force Base in Germany. I immediately wrote Carol back to say that I would be there for the wedding. Wouldn't miss it for the world! And I knew that the time had come for me to return to the States. I have been so very fortunate to spend a year here in this splendid place, but the party can't go on forever. To cap off this wonderful day, Lisa, who had spent the entire day at the Taj, obediently followed us back to the courtyard and into her pen when we went up for dinner.

Lisa wasn't able to roam around the next day because Bwana Kitia arrived with 60 game scouts. Then we had great excitement in the afternoon, a Tanzania *Polisi* helicopter landed at the Fort. On board were Stuart Whitehead, a pilot instructor, two engineers, the wife of one, and a woman guide with Abercrombie & Kent. The men are aiding the Tanzania Police Force with its helicopter program. They stopped for tea and a look-around, then flew back to Lobo. Joseph Nyerere arrived with eggs. A good thing because we have had no eggs for two days.

When the coast is clear, we can take Lisa to the Taj to spend the day. She must get bored, though, because she comes back to the swimming pool where I am sunbathing and reading. She is quite social, given that cheetah are solitary animals by nature .

The Monday mailbag included the Saturday edition of the Tanzanian newspaper bearing the sad news that Ahmed is dead. He must have died the 17th. How fortunate we were to have seen him just a month ago, in the nick of time. The cause of death was reported as old age, estimating it to be 65. It is planned that he will be stuffed and displayed in the National Museum in Nairobi. The taxidermy will take 3 to 4 months at an estimated cost of 6000 pounds sterling. His tusks measured 9 feet and 10 ½ feet, each weighing 150 to 160 pounds, and 18.75 inches in diameter. Ten bags of salt were required for drying the hide. Rest in Peace, Mzee.

Photo of Ahmed from Internet

Four police helicopters made a grand appearance this morning. The crew will be staying here while the Tanzanian pilots train in anti-poaching procedures. Lisa is very interested by these big birds. She is proving to be a nuisance out by the swimming pool. Ndosi came for a meeting with Stuart. Baked brownies in the afternoon.

Caught rays in the morning and chatted with the five *wazungu* here with Police Air Wing Command. Colin and Stuart are instructors, Sammy and Dietmar are engineers. Don't recall what Gunnar does. There are six African pilots in the program. The Tanzanian pilots went to Sweden in 1971 for a six-week training program, then the pilots returned to Tanzania on one airplane while the four helicopters (two Bell 206 Jet Rangers and two Bell G47) returned by air cargo. The cargo plane developed problems and had to force land in Kampala, Uganda. Idi Amin confiscated the helicopters because, previously, Tanzania had confiscated 11 million shillings worth of ammunition that belonged to Uganda. It took a year to settle that one. Then the Swedish instructors backed out of the deal so Tanzania had to find new instructors. The five here presently came on the scene in February 1973. Then there were contract problems and so the instructors and engineers went on strike in May. The contract terms were settled in September 1973 and the program finally resumed. Had a nice chat with Stuart and Colin after dinner. Finished *King Solomon Mines*.

Caught rays. Read *Mash*. Stuart flew to Nairobi in one of the Jet Rangers after lunch. Colin took Skip, Inez, Valerie and me up in the other Jet Ranger for a 20-minute spin. What a fantastic sensation to fly in one, especially to hover. And what a fabulous way to observe game. We saw giraffe, buffalo, zebra, impala, warthogs, eland and *kongoni*. All the vegetation is so green! I got some great photographs of the Fort through the open window. One was later used in a publicity brochure for Fort Ikoma Lodge. The 20-minute ride used 40 liters of petrol which actually is kerosene. The Jet Ranger has a turbine engine. Another nice chat with Colin and Dietmar after dinner. I was awakened by a noise and saw a strange animal from my tent window about 1:00 a.m. It might have been a white-tailed mongoose.

We bid goodbye to the air wing the next morning. It's been so much fun having the group here these last few days. They figure it will be a 3½ hour flight to Dar es Salaam in the Jet Ranger with an average speed of 120 mph. I left Lisa down by the airstrip. She is quite independent now and we want her to become accustomed to being on her own in the wild. I napped in the afternoon. I have been very tired these last few days. Mrs. Geichi came with two friends from Switzerland. She brought a beautiful bouquet of roses from her own garden for my birthday and also brought us homemade butter and cream cheese. They were the only guests that evening. We dined on baked potatoes smothered with butter.

Today is my 24th birthday and the second one I have been fortunate to celebrate here in the Serengeti. Valerie gave me a tray with Lisa's picture on it. Well, it's a cheetah at any rate. By the way, Lisa stayed out all night. A jackal barking close by woke me up. It was barking at Lisa as she nonchalantly made her way back to the Taj. She was wet with dew and seemed to have achieved a new maturity with her adventure. At breakfast I opened up a gift from

Valerie and Shakir. It's a purse made from zebra hide. Skip and Inez gave me a beautiful red, white and blue *kitenge*. Then Skip had Lisa and me pose for photos by the swimming pool for the brochure he is working on. I caught some rays afterwards. Hans Krug and Fiord, two scientists at SRI, stopped by after lunch. A lorry arrived later in the day with a mailbag. In it were the pictures from Skip's negatives. I sorted through them, fantastic! I finished *Hotel*. I have read a lot of books these last few weeks. There always seems to be a traveling library of books. Guests leave one they have read and pick up one they haven't. I got all dolled up in my Christmas dress for a fabulous candlelight dinner, with Mrs. Geichi's beautiful roses to grace the table. Skip tossed his signature spaghetti with garlic and oil at table side. Salad with an oil and wine vinaigrette, hot bread and wine rounded out the meal. Dessert was strawberries and cream. Yum yum! What a birthday party!

Lisa and I lazed out by the Taj most of the next day. I decided to forgo dinner and read *Captains and the Kings* instead. When I get home, I am going to have to buy Skip's recommendation, *Don't Stop the Carnival* by Herman Wouk. It's about two New Yorkers who decide to buy a resort on a Caribbean island and all the problems they encounter. Skip said that he doesn't need to keep a journal anymore. For instance, he can just write on his calendar the page number of the calamity in the book that happens to correspond with whatever he's facing that day.

Now that I am planning to leave, I had hoped to find a ride to Musoma, but no such luck. But Ally's bus came this evening and it will return to Musoma tomorrow. Skip came out, guitar in hand, to watch the sunset. The sun was dipping over the western hills just at 7:00. Dusk lasts until about 7:30 and then it is pitch black. When there is a new moon, it is perfect for stargazing. I always look for the Southern Cross with its four bright stars. Valerie has always had an interest in astronomy and has a book of the constellations. Since we are in the southern hemisphere, I have been introduced to a whole new world of stars not visible from "up north." Inez didn't come up for dinner, but Cathy Potter is here with Lindblad and she joined us.

To Musoma...by Bus

I was up bright and early to take Ally's bus to Musoma, leaving FIL at 7:15 Monday morning. It cost me TSh 9/=. The bus was not crowded, but I still had to share a seat with two others at times. It wreaked of B.O. And then there were the chickens in a rickety crate that one of the passengers had. I was the only *mzungu* on the trip. Quite an interesting experience. The bathroom break consisted of the bus pulling off to the side of the road. The men went to one side and the women to the other. The women wear *kitenges* and, obviously, no underwear because they stand, spread their legs and pee. I was self-conscious, having worn jeans, and went to find a tree. We reached Musoma a little after 11:00.

I spotted the Robinsons' Range Rover in front of Raju Patel's auto parts shop and found Ruth inside having a refreshment while she waited for work to be done on the vehicle. She then took me to find Raja to see if he would be driving to Fort Ikoma soon. He said he was leaving tomorrow and I asked if he could delay a day and go on Wednesday. In his nonchalant way, he agreed. I had come to town to buy gifts for the staff. Unfortunately, all the *dukas* were closed today because of the death of an Ismaili Muslim shop owner. The Asians had closed their businesses out of respect because the funeral was this evening. Eddie and Freddie had gotten new Chinese bikes and were riding them around town. Ruthie took me to the Customs office because I needed to get an export license for the zebra purse I had received for my birthday. When we drove up, the two customs officers were sitting outside on the steps doing nothing. I explained my purpose and the officer asked when I was leaving. I told him next week. He said to come back then. I told him that I couldn't so he begrudgingly got up, filled out the proper forms which didn't take long, and off I went. This is so typical of how they operate. A mañana attitude. I also made reservations for Valerie and me on an East African Airways DC3 flight from Musoma to Nairobi for next Monday, a week from today. The tickets are TSh 250/= each, plus airport tax that costs TSh 20/=. We went back to the Robinsons. Leonard was out of town again and so Santaben came over for dinner. Another delicious Indian meal! Veronica joined us, too, because Terry was out of town.

Very early the next morning we took Santaben to Musoma because she had to meet with a judge before 8:00 about her deceased husband's frozen bank account. And for the seventh time, he told her to come back. He's waiting for a bribe. It is so frustrating to witness persons in authority wielding power over the innocent who are just trying to get things done. Women do not have many rights in this country. They are considered property of their husbands. When the husband dies, it puts the widow in a difficult situation, especially if she doesn't have any children. I was able to get my shopping done. I bought a lot of pens, colored pencils and a drawing pad, mirrors, lots of hankies and a shirt. There was no electricity in Busegwe that evening so we made pancakes out of the waffle batter.

After breakfast the next morning we visited the Martinsens who had returned the night before. It was so good to see them and thank them again for their kindness to me on the Kilimanjaro climb. Raja arrived at 10:30 and we left for Fort Ikoma soon after. Five miles from the Fort we had a puncture. I sat on the side of the road while Raja changed the tire. I have lost count as to how many times I have been riding in a vehicle when a puncture has occurred. It seems to be the norm. In fact, I'm always grateful when we make it to a destination without a puncture. On one of my many safaris I caught a photo of a parked petrol truck with "Danger Petroleum *Hatari*" written in three lines on the back. A closer look revealed totally bald tires on the left and good tires on the right. I wouldn't want to be around that truck when it had a flat.

I was thrilled to see that Mohamed Ismail had arrived with a Lindblad group. He presented Valerie and me with four Cadbury candy bars. What a sweetie! An American couple joined us for dinner. They happen to live in Rome, Italy where they have a pottery shop. Skip was in his usual rare form, making Spaghetti Carbonara for us at table side. He warned our "Italian" guests not to drink the last of the wine. "Save some for the gods!" was his mantra. The wine was served from a glass decanter. If you should empty the decanter, you were guaranteed of getting the dregs.

Kwaheri

Poor Lisa is inflicted with fleas. She stayed out by the Taj all day. Ann Morson had arrived with a Lindblad group and she arranged for a walking safari with Philip. As Philip was pointing out giraffe, topi, gnu, etc., all of a sudden he said "cheetah," seeing Lisa. Then Lisa started to approach the group, scaring one of the women considerably. Just as Lisa reached the people, Philip explained that she lives at the Fort. It's always fun when the mailbag arrives and this one was full of birthday cards for me. The Lodge's mail address is a PO Box in Arusha. The office sends it along with a supplier coming our way. This time Peter Joseph brought it along with a load of vegetables and fruit for the kitchen. I also received a notice that the flight from Musoma to Nairobi has been changed to the 6th. And darn it, I feel another sore throat coming on.

Lisa stayed out by the Taj all the next day as well and watched Makuru as he planted a euphorbia hedge to give the Taj some privacy for when guests are staying in the tents. Meanwhile, I caught some rays by the pool and finished *Captains and the Kings*, which I enjoyed thoroughly. I have had quite a bit of time to read lately. I also need to work on my tan since it will be winter in the States when I return.

Nostalgic emotions surfaced as I packed my backpack. There wasn't much to pack because most of the clothes will remain with Valerie. I just need enough to get me to Peoria and then plan to go shopping. Peoria weddings, and the honor to be a bridesmaid in each, will be the bookends of my time spent abroad. I left the States a year and a half ago, right after cousin Tina's wedding and will return for cousin Hobey and Carol's wedding. At least I don't have to worry about shopping for a dress to wear. I've had an incredible opportunity to see the sights, taste the food and meet the people in 18 European countries. And what a bonus to add on a six-week visit with Valerie in Tanzania that has turned into an unbelievable 13 months in East Africa. I was the third person to balloon over the Serengeti; I've gone on a hunting safari; helped raise an orphaned baby cheetah; climbed Mount Kilimanjaro; flown in small aircraft and a helicopter; been in the presence of the president, vice president and prime minister of Tanzania on their visits to Fort Ikoma; not to mention all the daily joys of life in the bush and the people I've met, both African and *wazungu*. And people ask if we get bored living in the bush! What a gift it has been to spend this year with my sister who is six years older than I and went off to college when I was 11. I shall cherish this time we have had together and the memories we have made forever.

Tanzania has granted me a visitor's visa for a year. Being in the country for three weeks with an expired visa actually worked to my benefit. And today, the first of February, technically marks the 14th month, if you count two Januarys and two Februarys. Should I desire to stay longer, I would need to leave the country for a month and then reapply. But the time has come for me to get on with my life, sad as it is to leave. My original plan after graduation and four months in Europe was to move to Boston and live with two classmates from my freshman and sophomore years at DePauw. However, after extending my time abroad, they have established themselves and are not interested in a third roommate. I can certainly understand. I think I will move to Los Angeles. Cousin Pamela is still in Valerie's charming apartment on Sunset Boulevard in Brentwood and would love for me to come be a roommate. The three of us lived together the summer of 1971 when I worked at two Lawry's restaurants to earn money for Europe and we got along famously. With my degree in Consumer Services in Foods, I will apply for a job at Lawry's Foods, Inc. in their Consumer Services Department. This is a plan that I can get excited about.

To celebrate my positive thoughts, I opened up the cupboard where we stashed our treasured Cadbury chocolate candy bars that Mohamed had recently brought us. We just break off a square at a time to prolong the enjoyment. Who knows when more will come? And as sometimes happens, the teeny-tiny *sisimizi* have found it. Well, I'm not going to let these sugar ants keep me from my small candy bar so I flick them off and pop a square into my mouth. I've heard that in some parts of the world people eat chocolate covered ants. Here we have the opposite situation. I thought to myself, if I ever write a book about my time in Africa, *Ant Covered Chocolates* would be a great title. We do have to put up with a lot of inconveniences, but the rewards are superb!

Lisa came moseying up to the Taj at dusk. She stood as if she were our *askari*. All of a sudden, she took off and a few seconds later we could hear a jackal barking, getting farther and farther away. The jackal must have been only 50 feet away or so. I shone the torch in their direction. Staring back at me were the jackal's yellow eyes and Lisa's green eyes.

I woke up the next morning with a worsening sore throat. Ugh! I went to get Lisa out of her pen because the flea situation is terrible. The loose stuff will be raked up and burned and then the pen will be heavily sprayed in hopes of killing off all the rest. She came out of the pen and rubbed herself against the rock tree well in the courtyard, itching from the fleas. I then took her down to the airstrip and left her there for the day. Awhile later, Ruth Ware arrived with a Lindblad group. She suggested that we use Malomite on Lisa to get rid of the fleas and ease her discomfort. Not sure what that is or where to get it, but Ruth has two domesticated cheetahs and she would know.

Carol Perkins, wife of Marlin Perkins of *Mutual of Omaha's Wild Kingdom* TV show was here with a group handled by Bateleur Tours and led by Peter Davey. I had met both of them last July when he and Mrs. Perkins brought another group of her friends. Of course, they were fascinated by Lisa who had not been here the last time. This group was very respectful of her. The last thing I want is for her to be approached by strangers. It has always astounded me how some strangers would walk right up to Lisa and start petting her. I would never do that to an unfamiliar dog, let alone a wild animal. Fortunately, Lisa never became aggressive, perhaps because one of us was around and she didn't sense danger.

I had been making enchiladas for our dinner when Augustino turned up in the kitchen 1½ hours late and drunk. Valerie was none too happy. Daudi is going to take on the whole staff with his *mkuki* (spear) and *panga*. He's a little "fonny" these days. There are definitely some staff issues going on. Probably it is a good time to be leaving.

We did have our cocktail party in Duma's Den as planned, when to our great surprise and delight, the Robinsons arrived at 7:15. They couldn't bear the thought of Valerie and me taking the bus to Musoma tomorrow morning. How dear they are. We all had dinner together. Even Leonard didn't think the enchiladas were too hot, although he chose to have a dinner off the menu.

Leonard regaled us with a story about Spotty, the leopard his mother took care of for a year. Leonard was the son of Seventh Day Adventist missionaries and had grown up in Rhodesia. The family was going on a yearlong furlough so Spotty was put in the zoo. When they returned, his mother learned from the zookeeper that Spotty had no spirit and was degenerating. She asked to see Spotty. She called to Spotty who perked up at the familiar voice and leaped over to where she was and hugged Mrs. Robinson through the bars. Mrs. Robinson visited Spotty every month or so in her cage, but when the Robinsons were transferred and Mrs. Robinson couldn't visit Spotty once a month, she learned that Spotty died a few months later.

Leonard's Greek friend had a chimp, Alfred, who he taught to drive his Ford pickup. Alfred joined his master for an alcoholic sundowner every evening and had a place at the dining room table. His Greek friend was fixing a gate and asked Alfred (in the French language they spoke) for a screwdriver which he nonchalantly handed to him.

Valerie and I returned to the Taj just before midnight. Joseph, the night watchman, had built a fire for us. What a lovely way to spend the last night at the Taj Mahal. Joseph gave me a 5x7 picture of himself and a thoughtful, accompanying letter. Earlier, John Wangere paid me a high compliment by saying that Africa needs people like me who understand Africa and its standards.

Departure day has dawned. Patty, an American gal about my age who had arrived the night before, really got on my nerves at breakfast. She's been in West Africa for about three years and was currently traveling through East Africa with an Asian "professional photographer" from Mwanza or Dar. What angered me was that she considered herself on special terms with Lisa.

I took Lisa out to the Taj so that she could roam around and I could cool off. Lisa could sense my irritation and something else. I knew that this was the last time that she and I would have "alone" time together. I sat on one of the canvas chairs on the front stoop of the tent and watched her as she sniffed around for about 15 minutes. All of a sudden Lisa came over to me, jumped in my lap, and stretched her long body across it. Then she started purring. It was a deep rumbling sound. I scratched her behind the ears and stroked her. It was as if she was telling me that she also knew that this was our last day together. It was magical.

The Mcharos came for the day with some friends from Nairobi, Be'at and Elena Jenny. Be'at is Swiss and Elena is a black Panamanian. A super couple and both pilots. I was so happy to see the Mcharos one last time before I left. I have met so many wonderful people over the course of this past year and whom I will dearly miss.

After lunch I handed out gifts to the staff and said my goodbyes. For Mushi, the assistant manager, I gave him a shirt and for his wife Dionisia, a nightgown. For Isaac the tailor, a seam ripper, and Saulo who worked at the reception desk, a pen and bottle of ink. For Philip, who will care for Lisa, a drawing pad and colored pencils. For Paul and Fidelis, who worked in the front office, I gave them each a mirror. For Valerie's staff which numbered 20, I gave them each a nice pen. For Mushi's staff which numbered 24, I gave them each a handkerchief. I have come to know the *watu* over the course of the year and wanted to show my appreciation to them for their friendship and service this past year.

My final goodbye to Lisa was in her pen where Mr. Robinson took photos of Lisa and me. I had taken her some meat and she let me brush her and stroke her as she chowed down. Just before I exited, I knelt down to give her a hug. She gave me a hug of her own as she nibbled at my scalp, giving me love bites. This is the photo that graces the cover of this memoir and truly captures the very special bond we had. What a privilege it has been. I am profoundly grateful and will cherish it forever.

Skip and Inez walked out with me for a final farewell. My gift to them was a copy of the Seventh Day Adventist cookbook. Eddie and Freddie loaded my backpack into the Range Rover. After a tearful goodbye, I climbed in along with Valerie and we departed Fort Ikoma at 3:00 for the two-hour drive to Busegwe. As we drove away, I took in one last look at this exquisite place I have called "home" for the last year, wanting to remember every detail.

After a scrumptious dinner and chocolate cake for dessert, Mr. Robinson set up the movie projector and showed some recently arrived Super 8 movies. Best of all was the one Larry took of Lisa, and then he gave it to me.

Monday morning, February 4th, Grandma Strehlow's 80th birthday. The Robinsons took me around Busegwe to say goodbye to all their friends, who had become my friends, before we headed to Musoma. I have come to know this little town on Lake Victoria. It's not large like Arusha or Mwanza. The roads are dirt and it is easy to walk around the few blocks that are the center of town. The tailors are busy sewing on their treadle sewing machines set up outside their little stores. The children run through the streets, full of joy, with their homemade toys like a car made out of wire, or a pull toy made out of a matchbook box with bottle caps for wheels. Men play checkers on a painted board using bottle caps with ridges up for one player and down for the other. Then there are the amusing signs posted in the *dukas* like "In God we trust, all others pay cash." Or, "God gave us two ends, one to sit on and one to think with. Heads we win, tails we lose."

The DC3 landed just as we arrived at the airport, but it will fly to Mwanza and return before Valerie and I board. I had bought the tickets a week ago from a fellow in the East African Airways office in town. Now this same fellow took the tickets at the airport and then reported to pilot of the plane. I had hoped to get a picture of the DC3 and got the pilot's permission, but a worker in coveralls stopped me. He forbade me to take a photo and said that since the pilot was not Tanzanian, the pilot did not have the final say. The flight was scheduled to leave at 12:35 but we left at 12:15 because all ticketed passengers had boarded. There were 22 seats on the plane, four rows on the left and seven rows on the right. Behind the fourth row on the left was a cargo pen where our luggage went. My backpack weighed 34 pounds and the Carly bag weighed 12 pounds. It was a comfortable flight. We landed in Nairobi at 1:45. I got a cholera shot and then we took a bus into town where we offloaded at the Hilton and walked to Brunners Hotel where we were staying at a much more affordable rate. I went to Trans Globe to buy my ticket. The agent said it would be KSh 1400/=. "What?!" I had been quoted KSh 1200/=. I got it for KSh 1200/= although the price has gone up. We ran some errands and I bought an elephant hair bracelet for Ron Robinson for KSh 45/=. We checked out the movie times but were too late to see the early showing so went back to the Hilton where we ran into Ann Morson. Her Lindblad group was in Nairobi for one day. After dinner in a coffee shop, Valerie and I headed back to Brunners and turned in early.

I made a reservation on Pan Am from London to New York. I still have this nagging sore throat and therefore have no desire to stay in London. I am looking for a cheap fare back to the U.S. At this point I just want to get back and it is worth the extra money. We visited Adrian Luckhurst at Root Leakey where we met his wife Vicki who is from Minneapolis, then stopped in at Intertours to say hello to Ferdie. Valerie and I lunched with Aghar Chaudhry, a tour leader for Lindblad, and his girlfriend at the Thorn Tree. Valerie was not feeling well so she spent the afternoon in bed while I went shopping. I bought her a black with white stitching Indian blouse. As a wedding gift for Carol and Hobey, I bought a sisal lamp shade, something unique from Africa. Back at the hotel I gave Valerie her gift. She loved it. We were waiting for Shakir but he had not arrived yet. The telephone was giving me problems and I couldn't get in touch with anyone, but was able to leave a message for Finn with Bosky. I was bored so went out again to walk the streets. I stopped in to see Ferdie and asked if he had heard from Shakir. Ferdie said Shakir was to arrive about 6:30 or 7:00. Back to the Hilton I went and passed by the Professional Hunters Club. I glimpsed through the open doorway and saw Gerard Ambrose sitting there. What a surprise! I went in to say hello. He introduced me to his partner Terry Irwin. They were the only two in the club and invited me to sit down and chat. They are off to Sudan tomorrow for a month of hunting. I mentioned to Gerard that I had heard from June Capon that he had gotten married and congratulated him.

Good news, both Shakir and Finn had called and were coming over. Finn arrived first. I showed him the slides he had taken of Lisa with my camera. Shakir arrived a little later. His cousin Mamudt was visiting for a while so we went over to Shakir's room at the Hilton Hotel to meet him. Finn kept trying to find excuses to bow out because he wasn't dressed properly, but we rigged up one of Shakir's coats for him to wear. Ferdie came and we all went to a Mandarin restaurant for dinner where we drank hot sake and enjoyed a delicious meal. Afterwards, we went to the Milimani Hotel for dancing in the Malaika Lounge, but not much action there. Everyone was tired but me. My last night in Nairobi to party and they all are tired! All are asking me why I was leaving. We stayed at the lounge until midnight and then Finn drove us back to the hotel. He kept saying how tired he was so we let him go after his halfhearted promise about coming out to the airport tomorrow night.

I awoke at 9:00 and went out to do some errands. I needed to mail the slides and hatband home, and the wedding present to Carol and Hobey. I then stopped in at the Pan Am office because Vicki Luckhurst had suggested that I look into a Pan Am flight from London to Detroit. Valerie and I checked out of Brunners and went over to Shakir's room, getting him out of bed at 11:15. We moved our stuff into Shakir's room and then the three of us went to Sunflower for lunch. Afterwards, Valerie and I went out shopping for her and got back to the hotel at 5:00. Shakir got back about 6:00. We ordered up room service for dinner. Ferdie called to say he couldn't take us to the airport because of a family emergency. Finn never called, though he had promised. The three of us took a taxi out to Embakasi, Nairobi's international airport. I checked in at 9:00 and went through Customs which was painless. Valerie and Shakir stayed with me until boarding time at 10:15. I hate goodbyes and this one was painful. So many memories welling up in me. I was already missing Valerie and Shakir, even before I made it through Immigration. I turned around for one last look as I walked across the tarmac to the plane and saw them staring out the window. One last wave. I think the two of them will miss me, too. The British Caledonia flight took off at 11:00 p.m. *Kwaheri* East Africa. I hope to return one day. How true the adage is: You may leave Africa, but Africa never leaves you.

This charter flight that I was on had a scheduled refueling stop in Benina, Libya at 3:30 a.m. local time (4:30 a.m. Nairobi time). As we descended, I could see scattered circles of fires outside, the only thing visible in the pitch black night. They must have been where oil drilling was occurring. Only runway lights were visible at the airport. The terminal itself was completely dark. It was very eerie to be in this remote area in the middle of the night. There were no other planes around, just us as we sat on our plane, packed in like sardines, looking out into total darkness. I was so relieved when the fasten your seatbelts announcement was made and the plane lifted off and away from this desolate place at 5:45 a.m., a full hour and 15 minutes later.

We landed at the London Gatwick airport at 6:30 a.m. London time, a three-hour time change from Nairobi. The actual flight was nine hours plus the one and a half hour stop in Libya. It was not a bad flight, but lots of people of many different nationalities and most don't use deodorant. Now I had to board a bus for a two-hour drive through heavy traffic from Gatwick to Heathrow. Pan Am was in Terminal 3. At the ticket counter I was able to change my flight for New York to Detroit via Boston without any difficulty. I had changed a $5 bill for 2.05 sterling at the rate of 2.32. I spent 60 pence on the bus ride and the rest on a cable to Mom to tell her about my arrival in Detroit. Then I went to look for the loo. Just inside the door sat a little old lady directing traffic. As I walked past her she started to say that this was the women's bathroom and then when her eyes met mine, she abruptly stopped. I couldn't blame her. She had been looking down and first saw my boonie boots and walking stick, then my Levi's, then my oversized British Army coat, then my floppy suede leather hat that hid my hair which was in a topknot underneath. Once she looked at my face she realized I wasn't a man. I had no idea that a coin needed to be inserted in the stall door. The dear lady provided me with one.

The Pan Am flight, destination Detroit with a stopover in Boston, left at 11:45 a.m. after a 25-minute delay. The stewardesses in my section were so nice and it was fun to chat with them when they weren't busy. Christel was

German. She had been to Fort Ikoma Lodge with her American husband in July 1972. I was able to watch a movie, *The Tall Blond Man with One Black Shoe,* on the flight after paying $2.50 for a headset rental. This was my first experience to see a movie on an airplane. Too bad it was so hard to hear. After a seven-hour flight, and five time zones, our expected arrival at 3:00 p.m. local time in Boston was delayed due to smoke on one of the runways. So far I have added eight hours to February 7th. We finally landed at 3:45. I left Nairobi 24 hours ago and have had only catnaps, but I am back in the States after a sojourn of 18 months abroad. There was snow on the runway and a very low ceiling over the city that gave the day a very dreary look. That first impression convinced me of never wanting to move to the cold East. We had an hour layover. Those of us who were continuing on to Detroit could deplane, but not leave the transit lounge. I called Grandma and Pop. It was so good to hear their voices. They said Mom was at the Altorfers and so I called over there. Carol was in the midst of having her wedding portrait taken. I told Mom that I had asked a Pan Am agent in Boston to make reservations from Detroit to Peoria for me and would be home sometime tonight. I boarded the plane and departed Boston at 5:00, arriving in Detroit at 6:45. Before landing, one of the stewardesses asked over the intercom for Miss Vicki Vance to please identify herself by pressing the call button. A cute stewardess came running up – she instantly reminded me of cousin Tina – and said word had come over that I was to be met by an agent when we landed. Indeed I was. Pan Am had waitlisted me on three flights to Chicago and confirmed me on the Ozark 9:05 flight to Peoria. Vicki Luckhurst had told me that Customs in Detroit doesn't take an eternity like it would in Boston, Chicago or New York where there is much more international traffic. She was right. I breezed right through Customs. They did question my zebra purse for a minute, though, but then a superior gave his OK. For my $300+ imports, I had to pay only $10.11 duty. My walking stick didn't make it off with me so I had to run up to the Pan Am desk to leave information. On the three flights I have taken with it, it was put in a coat closet at the front of plane. I had forgotten to ask for it. Then I rushed over to the American Airlines counter to see if I could make their 7:35 flight. (It was now 7:30). They said yes because it was delayed 10 minutes. Just then, a Pan Am agent came up to tell me that my walking stick has been found. He ran down to get it while I dragged my backpack and Carly bag to the check-in counter. I am all reunited and away at 7:45. What luck! Everyone has been so nice and helpful. I really do attribute it to the way I am dressed. The flight was full of businessmen in their dark suits. We landed in Chicago at 8:00, another time change. I had an hour layover before catching the Ozark flight so I called Mom to tell her "I'll be home!" I arrived in Peoria, Illinois at 10:00 p.m. local time, 1½ years after departing from this same airport for New York City to meet up with Mary Sue and board our Icelandic Airlines flight to Reykjavik, Iceland, first stop on our European backpacking adventure.

As the people deplane, I gather my stuff, and remember to ask for my walking stick. Unfortunately, Ozark has misplaced it. I go down the stairs of the plane to the tarmac and walk toward the terminal gate. A sea of people are in there, all those waiting for arriving passengers and those who have just deplaned. I walk inside and don't see any familiar faces. I can't believe this! My big homecoming and no one is here to greet me? As the gate area starts to clear out, I soon spot four women against the far wall, doubled over with laughter. It is Mother, Harriett Altorfer, Carol and Tina. As they point at me, unable to speak, I soon realize that the way I am dressed has caused their hysterical laughter. I was a little taken aback. Except for the British Army coat, I've dressed like this for the entire past year. For that matter, so has Valerie. We didn't think we looked strange at all. Soon enough we were all hugging and Carol realized that I hadn't freaked out. It is good to be back and warmly welcomed. As I was filling out the lost report for my walking stick, an Ozark agent brought it to the desk. On this flight it had been stowed in the cockpit. Now I was complete once again. This walking stick has been up Kilimanjaro with me.

February 7, 1974 has been a very long day. By the time I had landed in Peoria, 32 hours after leaving Nairobi, and nine time zones later, I calculated that Valerie will soon get up after two nights of sleep. It was now time for me to hit the sack and then get on with the rest of my life.

Oh, but what adventures I have had!

Epilogue

The scout Philip took over Lisa's daily care after I left. Jack Wolf, or as we called him, Bwana Jack, visited Fort Ikoma again in September 1974. He arranged to stay in a tent set up away from the main compound so that he could record animal sounds with his sophisticated sound equipment. Lisa would come and spend the afternoon with him. Jack gave me photos of Lisa and a 45-minute cassette of animal sounds, including a minute of Lisa's purring and him saying, "Nice Lisa."

In March 1975, our hopes and dreams were answered. Lisa was released to the wild in the Serengeti National Park by George Frame, a scientist at the Serengeti Research Institute. George and his wife Lory later wrote a book, *Swift & Enduring*, about their work at SRI and several chapters are devoted to Lisa's release. While writing the book, George corresponded with me about questions he had when Lisa was in our care at Fort Ikoma. Skip and Putney, Valerie and I are acknowledged as her caregivers. On her release, Lisa wore a tracking collar. Eventually, the battery died and her whereabouts were unknown. So the story goes, about six months after her release she wandered into Mary Leakey's camp at Olduvai Gorge and proceeded to jump on her table and eat her omelet. Mary saw the collar and no doubt had heard about Lisa so she didn't freak out. She noticed a thorn in Lisa's eye and notified her son Jonathan in Kenya who had a rehabilitation center for injured wild animals. He came to get her. While on his annual safari, Jack Wolf made a special trip to Jonathan's refuge and took photos of Lisa in September 1975 while she was in Jonathan's care. Lisa became a political football between the two countries and Tanzania demanded that she be returned. Though it is not cheetah territory, Lisa was released in Ngorongoro Crater because Olduvai Gorge is in that conservation area and that is where she had last been. In the Summer 1977 issue of Kappa Alpha Theta magazine is an article by Susan Ward who was a tour guide with Abercrombie & Kent. She wrote about her encounter with Lisa in Ngorongoro Crater and there is a photo of the two. In 2006, Valerie received an email from Bill Hurst with a photo of him and Lisa in Ngorongoro Crater. He doesn't remember the year it was taken, probably 1976 or 1977, when he was still leading Lindblad Wing Safari tours. He said that she was the only cheetah in the Crater at the time and he really astounded his clients when he got out to greet her. He knew that she remembered him from Fort Ikoma days. Apparently, one day she just disappeared out of the Crater. I would hope that she mated and added to the cheetah population. When I took the family on safari in 2002, we saw only two cheetahs. One was in Ngorongoro Crater and the other was in Olduvai Gorge. Could they be her descendants? I can only hope.

I had recalled the article about Lisa in the Theta magazine, but didn't have a copy. In 2006, prompted by the email Bill sent to Valerie, I wrote Theta headquarters and inquired. They were so intrigued by the request that they wrote an article for the magazine titled, *Three Thetas and...a Cheetah* for the Winter 2006-2007 issue.

My UA Theta roommate, Lory Bradbury, went on safari in 1976. At the Lake Manyara Gift Shop she found the poster of Fort Ikoma with the photo of Lisa and me and brought it back to me. It is framed and hangs in our zebra-themed bathroom.

The border gate between Serengeti National Park and Maasai Mara was closed by Kenya in late 1975 or early 1976, negatively impacting Fort Ikoma Lodge on the tour circuit. It transitioned into a vacation home for President Nyerere, and later an army base. It now serves as the headquarters for the Serengeti National Park.

After Fort Ikoma closed, Valerie managed Momella Lodge outside Arusha National Park. The movie *Hatari* featuring John Wayne was filmed at this location. The German actor Hardy Krueger bought the property and built Momella Lodge. Valerie returned to the States in mid-1976 for an extended vacation. It was her first time home since she left in 1972. She stayed through Allen's and my wedding and then returned to Kenya in early 1978 to work for Abercrombie & Kent. Valerie moved back to the States in May 1980. She settled in Tucson and completed her college education, earning a degree in Cultural Anthropology from the University of Arizona. Valerie volunteered as a docent at the UA Flandrau Planetarium where she met her future husband, Bob Goff. He was a master optician who had made the lens for the telescope that was available to the public. He would come down from Kitt Peak, where he was superintendent of the 4-meter telescope, one night a week to volunteer at the telescope. Bob passed away in 2001.

I've been fortunate to keep in touch with many of the people whom I befriended that year. When I moved to Los Angeles in May 1974, I immediately got in touch with Ron Robinson who was living in Yucaipa and with Jack Wolf who lived in Marina del Rey. I was going through severe culture shock and these two men were my lifeline. We three would get together at least once a month and named our gathering the *Wajinga wa Taj*. Translated, that means the "fools of the Taj." What are we doing here in California when we should be sitting by the fire at the Taj? Over the years, the group grew by invitation to friends and acquaintances who also had been to Africa.

After Leonard Robinson retired, he and Ruth moved to Loma Linda and we kept in touch. We would see Larry, Eddie and Freddie when they would be in the area. The Robinsons had been our "American Family" in Tanzania.

Shakir Moledina passed through Los Angeles in 1979 and visited Allen and me in our home in Glendale. He later married and moved to England. We kept up a Christmas card exchange until he passed away at too young an age.

Lyuba Vishnyakova and I kept up a correspondence after she and her mother moved back to Moscow in 1973. After the Soviet Union collapsed in 1989, Olga was able to access Yuri's UNESCO bank account in Paris, France. She then made three trips to the United States and stayed with us each time. Lyuba had married Krzyzstof (Chris) Pawlik

434

from Poland who was studying at a university in Moscow and Olga was his Russian tutor. By 1986, they were living in Poland with their three children, Richard, Karolina and Mariola, and Olga as well. In August 1992, on a trip to Switzerland, Valerie, Bob, Mother and my family met in Grenoble, France for a 24-hour reunion with Olga and Lyuba, and met Chris and their three children. In 1996 and 1998, Lyuba, Chris and children came to visit us during the time they were living in Shanghai, China. Chris had earned a PhD in Mandarin and sold coal-mining equipment to China. Allen and I visited the family in Chorzów, Poland in 2006. Lyuba, Chris, Allen and I have taken two cruises together, one to Alaska and the other to Norway.

Skip and Putney Leavitt eventually settled in Southern California. I saw them in Dana Point in 1993. Later, they each visited us in Tucson. Skip passed away in 2008. I am indebted to Skip for enabling me to stay for as long as I did and to Leonard Robinson for getting my visa extended several times. Putney and I still keep in touch.

In the 1990s, David Babu was Minister of National Parks in Tanzania. He was on a group tour to visit the ten best zoos in the world. The Arizona-Sonora Desert Museum was on that list and Valerie invited him to her home where we had a wonderful visit. We keep in contact through his son Julius on WhatsApp.

In April 2000, Ruth Robinson was living in Big Bear, California. Leonard had passed away in 1982. Her four sons were coming to visit – Ron and his wife from Idaho, Larry from Tanzania, Eddie from Kenya, and Freddie from

Rwanda. Olga happened to be visiting us in Tucson and so we planned a reunion in Big Bear. Putney and her daughter Tiffany joined us. Unfortunately, Skip was on a cruise and unable to be with us. He was missed! I talked to Larry about taking my family on safari and he said that he would arrange it and be our guide.

In May 2002 that dream became a reality when I took Allen, Robert, Greg and Charlie to Tanzania. I connected with David Babu and Isaack Mushi whom the family was able to meet when we were in Arusha. Sadly, Dionisia had passed away. Judy, their daughter, was married and we met her husband who worked at Ngorongoro Wildlife Lodge when we spent a night there.

I wanted to show my husband and sons Fort Ikoma where I spent this serendipitous year. It was then and still is the headquarters for the Serengeti National Park. It had become a village with many more buildings to the west of the property. I was shocked to see the disrepair it was in, a far cry from the glory days as one of the finest lodges on the tour circuit. The big picture windows in the dining room were gone and the openings bricked up with some small windows. The kitchen that once held state-of-the-art stainless steel equipment was now bare, but evidence of small fires to cook food were seen. The swimming pool was empty. Every *rondavel* had a port-a-potty outside. I saw one African woman in the doorway of her *rondavel* washing clothes in a plastic tub. Apparently, the bathrooms did not have running water. Valerie wanted me to scatter some of her husband Bob's ashes at the fire pit at the Taj, and I did.

A house now stood on the plinth where our tent, the Taj Mahal, had been. Charlie took video of our visit to Fort Ikoma. Somehow the memory card of that segment of our trip got lost. Divine intervention, I think. It would have broken Valerie's heart to see the state it was in. However, it was an excellent idea to move the headquarters out of the Park because the number of workers and family members has swelled over the years.

Jerry Rilling moved back to the States and we kept up a correspondence until he passed away in 2020.

Mohamed Ismail lives in Mombasa, Kenya. He came to the States in 2009 to visit his son Naheed who was working in Minneapolis. Naheed's twin sister Naheeda came from Turkey to join them. Mohamed contacted Valerie and the two of them arranged for Valerie, Mother and me to meet up with the three of them in Sedona and go to the Grand Canyon. We had a super time. Later, Naheed moved to Phoenix and we saw Mohamed and Naheed quite often when Mohamed would come for visits. On several of these occasions, Mohamed gave us some of the fabulous artwork he has painted of African animals which we proudly display in our home. Naheed has returned to Kenya and leads safaris now. He sends me wonderful photos. Naheeda is a psychiatrist and lives in Turkey with her husband and three children. Mohamed sends me daily emails of photos he has taken and paintings he has done of the animals he has photographed over the many years he was one of the premier tour guides in Kenya and Tanzania.

In 2014, Lyuba, Chris, Allen and I went on a cruise to Alaska together. We rented a car for part of the trip. On the long drive from Fairbanks to Anchorage, I asked Lyuba if she would be willing to share with me what happened after they received the news about her father. She talked for two hours. I wish I had a tape recorder. Here is a brief recap: They were met at the Dar es Salaam airport by their Pakistani friend Ibrahim, from whom they learned the fate of Yuri. He drove them to the Russian embassy where they were informed that they would have to fly back to Moscow on the next flight out of Dar es Salaam, in a day or two. (Only a few flights a week.) Olga refused. She said that she had to go back to her home and pack her personal belongings and the manuscript she was writing. With that, a big KGB brute grabbed Lyuba's arm. Olga grabbed Lyuba's other arm. Lyuba had just turned 15 on August 28. Three weeks later she learned that her father, who she adored, has been killed in car accident (a very suspicious one since he was not the driver), and now she feels that she is going to be split in half. With that, Olga, who always had lovely nails, clawed the KGB brute's exposed arm. He released Lyuba and they dashed to Ibrahim's car. He sped them to the Tanzanian government offices where Olga found the Vice President. (I am assuming it was Aboud Jumbe who had been at Fort Ikoma in May.) Yuri and he had formed a nice friendship. Olga explained what happened. He offered protection and immediately called the Mwanza police department to send officers to guard their house. They later learned that the police arrived moments before two

KGB brutes who wanted to enter the house, but the police refused them entry. Olga and Lyuba returned to Mwanza to pack up their belongings. Lyuba said that the two brutes stayed the whole time. She said that they weren't particularly bright and would play cards in the living room. Within two weeks they were back in Moscow and life as she knew it was over. Lyuba has never wanted to return to Tanzania because of what happened to her father, even though up until his untimely death, the five years in Tanzania had been the happiest days of her life.

Larry Robinson and his family visited us in Tucson in 2015. Larry pitched the idea of a road trip through southern Africa to Allen and me and we did just that in June and July of 2016. We visited Freddie and his wife Andrea in Namibia. In August 2016, Allen and I spent a month with Susan Hall at her home outside Nanyuki, Kenya. Susan and Valerie became friends when Valerie dated her brother Andrew after Valerie returned to Kenya in 1978. We met Susan when she came to Tucson to visit Valerie. She came a second time in 2006 and invited us to come visit her, extending the invitation every year in her Christmas card to us. We met Andrew in 1981 when he came to the States. Sadly, he passed away of cancer in 1991. Susan published her memoir, *My Vanishing African Dreams*, in 2016.

It has taken me two years to write this memoir. So many times I have wished that I could call Valerie to ask her a question or simply share a laugh together over a funny incident. Alas, that is why I created the *Serendipity in the Serengeti* photo album, because there was only me who could tell the story about the magical year we spent together, sharing a tent in the African savanna, having one incredible experience after another. Valerie passed away from lymphoma in 2011. I shudder to think of us casually spraying Black Flag over our bodies to repel the tsetse flies, saying, "If we ever get cancer, we will know why." When Valerie was diagnosed with cancer, her wish was to pitch a tent in the Serengeti and live out the rest of her life. Though that did not happen, her wish to have some of her ashes scattered in the Serengeti has been fulfilled. In Valerie's absence, I have relied on dear friends for help. I would like to acknowledge and thank Putney Leavitt Kemp for Fort Ikoma and Lisa memories; Coen Eckhardt for the first few days of Lisa's care; Eddie and Freddie Robinson about their dad's plane and life in Busegwe. Mohamed Ismail has been an invaluable resource with his vast knowledge, having graduated with highest honors from the College of Wildlife Management in Mweka, Tanzania. He served as a game warden, senior instructor for Lindblad Travel, professional hunter, and is an accomplished photographer and artist. An author himself, having written *The Lost Wilderness* about his days as a game warden, he has very kindly reviewed this manuscript for accuracy. And last but not least, a very special thank you to Linda Holt, Valerie's Theta sorority sister who called her one morning in 1971 and asked, "Chickie, how would you like to go to Africa?"

You can leave Africa, but Africa never leaves you.

Maps

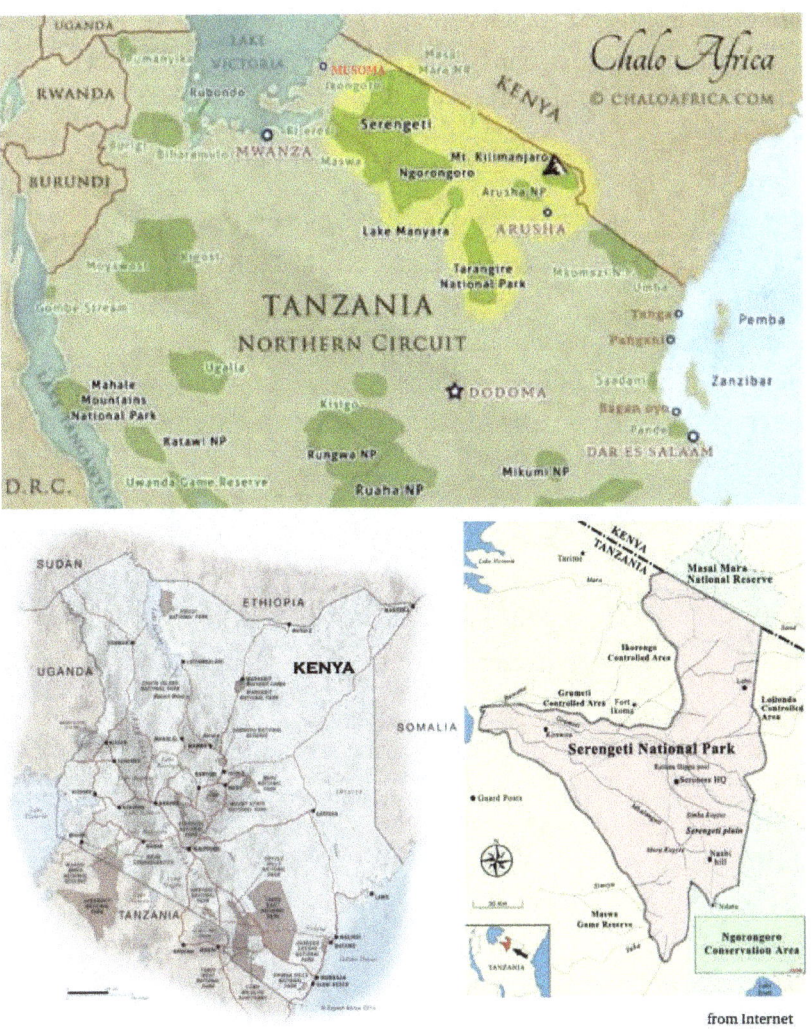

*If you hold your right hand in front of you with fingers pointing up and thumb
extended, think of your hand as the Serengeti National Park
and the fingernails of the three middle fingers as the Maasai Mara.*

Glossary

asante; asante sana	thank you; thank you very much
askari	guard, scout, usually armed
ayah	nanny
banda	hut
barabara	road, highway
bob	British slang for a shilling
boma	livestock enclosure (Maasai)
bunduki	gun, rifle
bwana	master, owner, term of respect
chakula	food, meal
choo	toilet
chui	leopard
dawa	medicine
dhobi	person washing clothes (Hindi)
duka	little store
duma	cheetah
fisi	hyena
fundi	expert
gari	vehicle
habari yako	how are you?
habari gani	what is the news?
haraka sana	quickly
hodi, hodi, hodi	hello, anyone home? May I enter?
iliki	cardamom
jambo	hello
kabisa	completely
kali	fierce; angry
kanga	guinea fowl
kanga	colorful rectangular cloth, 1 meter x 1.5 meters
kanzu	Arabic-style ankle-length robe worn by men
karibu	welcome
kifaru	rhinoceros (rhino)
kikapu	basket

kiko	pipe
kikoi	woven cloth, worn as a wrap-around
kelele	noise
kitambaa	piece of fabric
kitenge	colorful, patterned cloth worn for clothing
kombi	Volkswagen multi-purpose minibus (German)
kondoo na viazi	boiled meat (usually lamb) and vegetables
kongoni	hartebeest
Konyagi	Tanzanian liquor, similar to gin
kopje	rock outcropping
korongo	gully
kubwa sana	very big
kuku	chicken
kuni	firewood
kwaheri	goodby
kwisha	finished, no good
loo	British term for toilet
lorry	British term for truck
maji	water
malaika	angel
mama	woman, mother, term of respect
maridadi	pretty, neat
mashua	boat
matata	problem
maziwa	milk
mbuzi	goat
mbweha	jackal
mdudu; wadudu (pl)	bug, insect
mgeni; wageni (pl)	guest; guests
mingi	many
mkate	bread
mkuki	spear
morani	young male warrior, post circumcision (Maasai)
mpishi	cook

mtego	trap for an animal
mti wa mswaki	twig used to brush teeth
mtoto; watoto (pl)	small child; children
mtu; watu (pl)	man; people, staff
murram	a fine red gravel used to surface dirt roads
mwalimu	teacher
mwenge	torch
mzee	old man, term of respect
mzungu, wazungu (pl)	European, white person
mzuri	good
ndege	bird
ngiri	warthog
njema	good, very well
nyama na ndizi	meat stew made with green bananas
panga	machete
piga hema	pitch a tent
pole pole	slow
pole sana	so sorry
pombe	beer, booze
porini	the bush
punda	donkey
pundamilia	zebra
pure	homemade distilled liquor, illegal, but cheap
rafiki	friends
recce	British term for reconnaissance mission
risasi	bullets
rondavel	round African hut with thatched roof
safari	trip
safari njema	wishing you a good trip
safi sana	very great
salaam	peace (Arabic)
sana	very
sarara	boneless roast, tenderloin
shamba	garden plot
shifta	highway bandits
siafu	safari ants

sijui	I don't know
sikoliu	just circumcised young male Maasai prior to *morani* stage (Maasai)
simba	lion
sisimizi	harmless little black ants, sugar ants
sufuria	large metal bowl
taka taka	garbage
tembo	elephant
topi	nyamera; antelope with blue haunches
twiga	giraffe
ugali or posho	cornmeal porridge made from white maize
ugero	snuff
uhuru	freedom
ujamaa	brotherhood, collective
weka maji	bring water
wezi	thieves

CID	Criminal Investigation Division
GWH	Great White Hunter
FIL	Fort Ikoma Lodge
KSh	Kenya Shilling (100 centi = 1 shilling) KSh 7/= to $1.00 in 1973
NCL	Ngorongoro Crater Lodge
NUTA	National Union of Tanganyika Workers
PPL	Private Pilot's License
SDA	Seventh Day Adventist
SNP	Serengeti National Park
SRI	Serengeti Research Institute
STSC	Seronera Tented Safari Camp
SWL	Seronera Wildlife Lodge
TANU	Tanganyika African National Union
TSh	Tanzania Shilling (100 centi = 1 shilling) TSh 7/= to $1.00 in 1973
UA	University of Arizona
UNESCO	United Nations Educational, Scientific and Cultural Organization
UTC	United Touring Company

Acknowledgments

It has been my desire for over 30 years to record my memories into a readable format. Today's technology has been of great assistance. Composing and editing on my Mac computer and its Apple Pages program were a breeze. A dictation app transcribed my journal as I read it, though time-consuming and hilarious as I had to go back and make corrections every few sentences. For example, *Fort Ikoma* transcribed as *40,* (forty comma). The Internet was a valuable resource. With my iPhone and computer, I could call, email, text and use WhatsApp to consult with friends acknowledged in the Epilogue. Those include Linda Holt, Putney Leavitt Kemp, Coen Eckhardt, Ed and Fred Robinson. Mohamed Ismail graciously proofed the manuscript for general accuracy and Swahili. I would send him a few chapters at a time by email halfway around the world to Mombasa, Kenya. In a day or two he would send back the edited copy. *Asante sana* to all of you!

Now, how to get this manuscript published into book form? I thank Lyn Keller for the initial proofreading and her constructive criticism. I thank Susan Cummins Miller, an author, for recommending Ghost River Images. Mike and Tama White have been a pleasure to work with in my attempt to get this book published in time for Christmas so that I can surprise my family with it when we will all be together. Other than the *rafiki* mentioned above, only my husband Allen has known about this project that has consumed much of my time these last four years. I thank him for keeping the secret and sharing the laughs.

About the Author

Vicki Vance Stanton grew up in Tucson, Arizona. After graduation from the University of Arizona, she backpacked through Europe and spent a year in Tanzania. Upon her return to the States, she moved to Los Angeles and worked for Lawry's Foods, Inc. where she later met her husband Allen Stanton. They moved to Tucson in 1986. They have three sons, Robert, Greg and Charlie. Vicki took the family on safari in 2002 and was able to show them Fort Ikoma. She hopes that one day her sons will take their families on safari to roam among the animals in a Land Rover, sleep in a tent and experience the glorious wonder of the Serengeti.